LOREENA McKENNITT

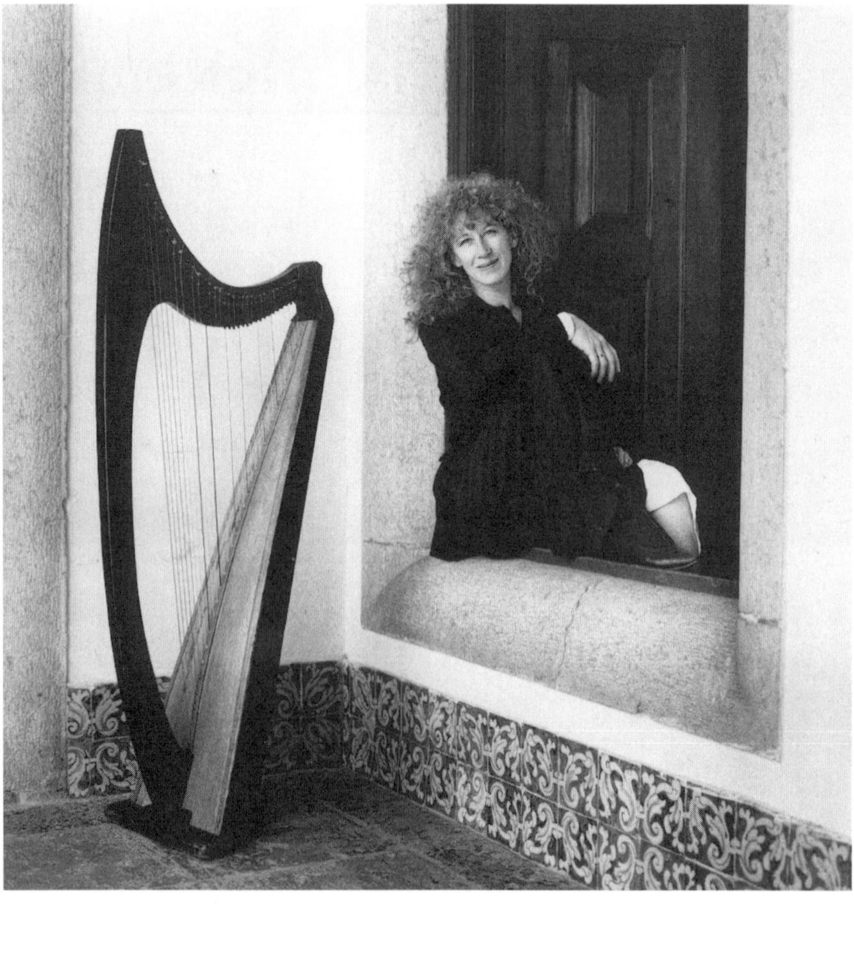

LOREENA McKENNITT

Celtic Quest

Geoff Hancock

QUARRY MUSIC BOOKS

Copyright © Geoff Hancock and Quarry Press Inc, 2001.
All rights reserved.

The publisher gratefully acknowledges the support of the Book Publishing Industry Development Program of the Department of Canadian Heritage.

Loreena McKennitt: Celtic Quest is a serious biographical and critical study of the career and art of Loreena McKennitt. The quotation of lyrics from songs composed by Loreena McKennitt and commentary published by Loreena McKennitt about her life and music is intended to illustrate the biographical information and criticism presented by the author and thus constitutes fair use under existing copyright conventions.

All lyrics by Loreena McKennitt copyright by Quinlan Road Music Ltd. (SOCAN/BMI) for the world, excluding Europe, South America, and Southeast Asia, where copyright by Quinlan Road Music Ltd./BMG Publishing International.

ISBN 1-55082-254-3

Editorial development, design, type, and imaging by Quarry Press Inc., Kingston, Ontario, Canada. Printed and bound by Vicks Lithograph and Printing Corporation, Utica, New York.

Distributors:

General Distribution Services, 325 Humber College Blvd,
Etobicoke, Ontario M9W 7C3 Canada.

Music Sales Corporation, 257 Park Ave S, New York, NY 10010 USA.

Music Sales Limited, 8/9 Frith St, London W1D 3JB England.

Music Sales Pty. Limited, 120 Rothschild St,
Rosebery, Sydney, NSW 2018, Australia.

Published by Quarry Press Inc., PO Box 1061,
Kingston, Ontario K7L 4Y5 Canada, www.quarrypress.com.

contents

PRAIRIE MADONNA

1. Sunrise over Southern Manitoba — 9
2. Under the Sign of Aquarius — 13
3. Mapping Morden — 16
4. Parables of Trees — 21
5. Winter in Manitoba — 28
6. Buffalo Ghost Dance — 35
7. Multiculturalism — 47
8. Frostbitten Folk — 51

CELTIC CROSSROADS

1. The Calling of the Harp — 61
2. The Bards — 73
3. Elemental Celtic — 80
4. The Books of the Celts — 90
5. Colonization — 93
6. The Great Hunger — 96

QUINLAN ROAD

1. Stratford — 113
2. The Festival, the Theatre, and the Dance — 118
3. Dead Poets — 124
4. Indie Artist — 136
5. Epiphanies — 147

PILGRIM'S PROGRESS

1. No Journey's End — 155
2. The Road to Santiago — 159
3. Mystics and Sufis — 165
4. Night Rides — 172
5. Real World Music — 180
6. Biography — 187

Discography — 193
Bibliography — 199
Acknowledgments & Credits — 205

If one begins with the big questions of "Who am I?" and "Why am I here?" the understanding of the roads back in history seem as important as the ones forward, whether or not it pertains to the individual or collective ...

(LOREENA MCKENNITT)

To take some of the pieces that seem at first glance to beckon a more conventional treatment and then take them elsewhere in a cultural or an ethnic sense — that's been at the foundation of my quest ...

(LOREENA MCKENNITT)

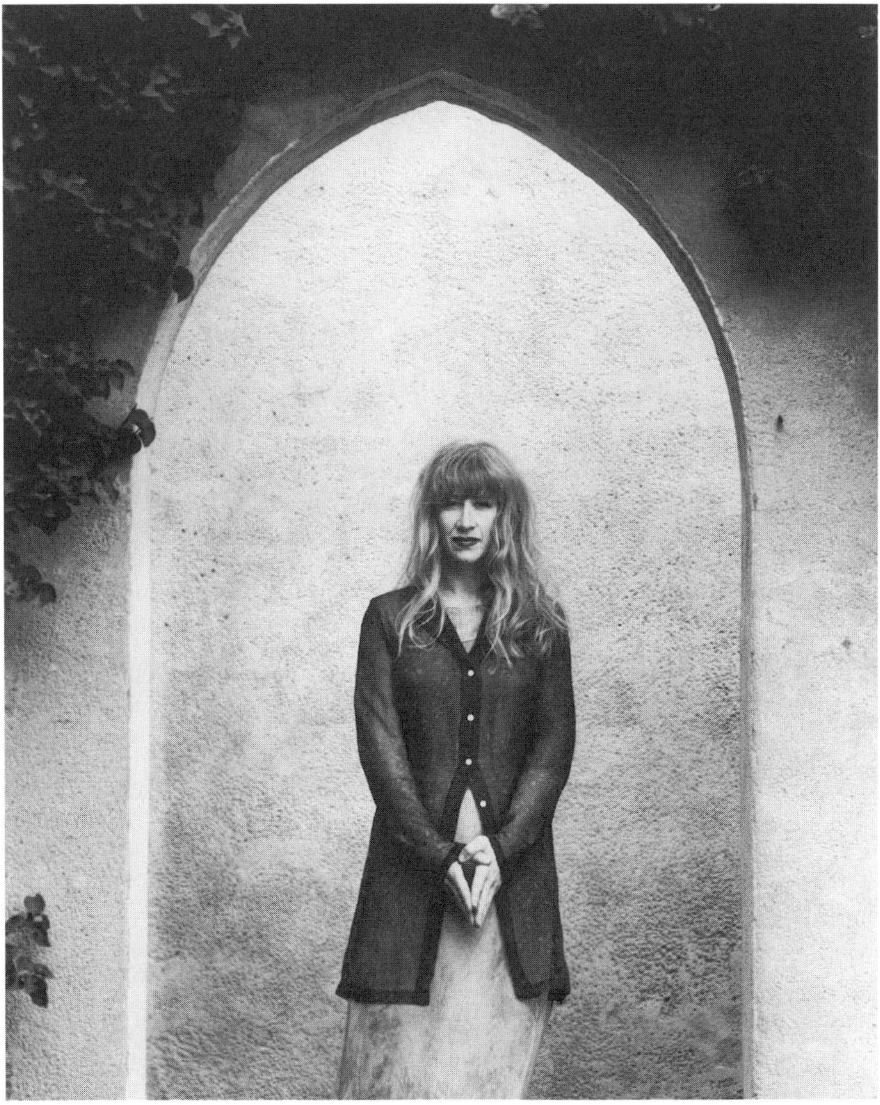

PRAIRIE MADONNA

1
SUNRISE OVER SOUTHERN MANITOBA

The morning light splits heaven from earth. Ten-foot high sunflowers catch the slant of the rising light pulling across the horizon. Gold threads catch the leaves, flash across the fields, glow in the transparency of stones, the edges of coulees, flash and burn, illuminating the plains, spilling and sparkling over southern Manitoba, Canada, birthplace of Loreena McKennitt. In the distance, from the corner of my eye, across the prairie fields, a summer lightning storm someplace in the Dakotas, on the other side of the border. In front of me, the map, a flash in the car mirror. I'm on the path of indirection, the miles of blank pages shimmering with mirages. So that's where I start, the impact of place, looking at Loreena McKennitt as a singer, a musician, a poet from Morden, Manitoba, Canada.

I was going to Altona, a small Mennonite community with one of the largest printing presses in the Western Canada to confer with a printer about the latest issue of the magazine I then owned and edited, *Canadian Fiction Magazine*. The little town, with its tidy buildings white under the sun of August, is named after a fertile German plain but has picked up the nickname the 'sunflower capital of Canada' for its miles of sunflowers, thick as a forest, yielding gallons of sunflower oil, packages of sunflower seeds. Why are these little towns — Altona, Winkler, Miami, Morden — here on this flat plain?

PRAIRIE MADONNA

What was here before that? Buffalo grass, animals without number, as far as the eye can see carrying the rush of light across the horizon. Spend some time in prairie Canada, and soon enough you'll find medicine wheels. Stand in the midst of one and feel yourself in the mirror of life. Connected equally to the wind, breathing as if alive, swaying the trees, forming the clouds. Then you know of *spiritus*, the spirit, the breath, the atmosphere (from *atman*, the breath), the circulating creative awareness, the long gone bison, the dinosaurs, the field mouse, the red-tailed hawk, and that farmer on the distant horizon in his combine.

Over there, a road sign emblazoned with a bison, the symbol of Manitoba. Yesterday in a Winnipeg museum, I looked back at a diorama of a buffalo hunt from another world, a dirt road, wagons with big wheels, the still mirror of a little river. I get a quick glimmer, a flash, of the wild road in the buffalo grass and sagebrush before I'm back in the world of highway engineers and auto designers who have imposed their shapes and forms, added mileage signs, billboards, asphalt, gas stations.

A car travels at right angles over this land, but is that any way to know a place? What forces go into the shaping of a person's character? What was unnoticed, undiscovered, unwritten or expressed creatively on this brilliant sunflashed mirror with immeasurable space in all directions? Loreena McKennitt was born here, just over the slow moving horizon on the top layer of a prairie history that literary critics and maybe archeologists would call a palimpsest. What chain of origins moors her to this place? Does it matter that her soul chose to begin this life here, to search for hidden things, to wander under stars, and to look back at other worlds?

Canadians at the edge of the North American west inhabit a different mythology than Americans in North Dakota ten miles away. Canadian artists are preoccupied with borders, boundaries, thresholds, unassigned frequencies, cross over. In the American West, the frontier was the tense point of individual freedom confronting a hostile wilderness, vast land in conflict with the civilizing desire to impose order. In the 19th century, Canada did not have a manifest 'westward ho' destiny. By the time settlers arrived, the prairies had been surveyed by land speculators and railway companies. Important characters in prairie Canada became the farmer, the priest, the Mountie, and the schoolteacher — the secular, sacred, social, and cultural forces that passed for social order.

Because the prairie provinces began only loosely tied to Canadian Confederation, the West developed as a set of colonies belonging to central Canada. The plains were seen only as a source of raw materials, furs, and food, not a vigorous frontier of a great, growing nation. The imperial values of the dominant British minority, a situation that curiously mirrors the history of the Irish in the same years, created the weird sensation of being simultaneously active both in one's own culture and at the same time outside culture. Canadian-born, American author Wallace Stegner, in *Wolf Willow*, his novel about growing up in southern Saskatchewan, thought history and geography ended at the Great Lakes. As self-assertion against the 'East', the prairie mind is disposed politically to oppose eastern imperialism. Through the Grain Growers' Association, and in such diverse radical political parties as the CCF, Social Credit, Reform, and Canadian Alliance, the edge challenges the center. This doubleness created a pressure, a 'duplicity' poet Eli Mandel called it, as Canadian artists struggled for cultural identification. A duplicity at the heart of prairie history.

Where the winds met no resistance, Europeans saw only the empty land flattened by the Ice Age and the long ago Colorado Sea. This sea-floor prairie is strange as the flat beaches, menhirs and dolmen, and friendly skies in a Tanguy print or the False Mirror of Magritte, the Belgian painter who claimed the world is a dream. A landscape has no symbols and meaning until we have faith they are there. In empty space lie the beginnings of possibilities. The incongruities and elusiveness of prairie artists suggest metaphors of a long lost golden age, scattered images as contrary as Metis, bison, Mennonites, railworkers, the great elephant ears of the drooping sunflowers, great highways, and large cities. One hears about the edges of things: fairy rings, buffalo wallows dug into boggy areas, rolled in mud. Puffballs shoot out clouds of powder called the dusty stars by the Blackfoot. The dusty stars are meteors, stars that change their places in the sky. On the prairies we fall easily under the influence of shimmering connections that compares puffballs and meteors and the starry fields known in Spain as the Compostella de Santiago.

Because the empty prairie creates an optical illusion, artists have to imagine a new space. Jump from detail — the grain of wheat in hand — to macrocosm, the big sky. Prairie scale. Under that big prairie sky, the constant motion of earth, air, sun, water, the compelling qualities of light, gilt, and shadow. You don't have to be in training as a shaman-poet or philosopher to see every element is part of the dynamic. Here the horizon line is over-determined, with no real vanishing point. The extremes are easy, but the middle is a puzzle. Prairie art is open, no confines. The vision pierces distance and gives an impression of great depth. But it's hard to determine distance, except by how long it takes to drive to town. Illusions are due to light and absence of large forms making relationships among things. Measure comes in the bigger patterns, the large cycles of seasons: spring planting, summer crops, fall harvest, winter fallow.

Make a simple shift in focus. Boundaries fade and blend. Dualities fade. What we thought as opposite is seen to be single. In southern Manitoba, empty spaces, distant horizons, unreal perspectives, the stillness of a nostalgic mood all brought together. The blank space of the deep blue sky is azure as seawater. Look into the deepest part of the blue to find the palimpsest of all the versions of the truth. Squint — is that a small blue flower, a many petalled cloud, or the complex shape of a star?

Simple and giant forms like the prairies affect the imagination. Some withdraw from this pancake flat windswept part of Manitoba in terror of spiritual annihilation. The prairie is an Old Testament experience, with cosmic beginnings, fierce climate, and apocalyptic endings — a land that attracts God fearing fundamentalists like the Mennonites. Others approach the prairie in the spirit of our 19th-century writers, as a garden of the world awaiting cultivation, an Edenic glimpse of first creation. All art from the West begins with the impact of the landscape on the mind. For the prairie artist, the problem of being born here seems simple. If one sees a landscape without boundaries, then one's art will expand into tomorrow where the sun rises on a river of song with no banks. The prairies are an intense state of mind, a land of extremes: flat expanse, big sky, intense heat, bitter cold, grass fires, spring floods, drought, blizzards, tornadoes. The land is a harsh fact, a mirror of the first settlers' psyche, old bones buried, the hidden edges and ends of things bared. Older worlds and deeper music. History is seen as continuous, circular, often contradictory, never linear. An artistic awareness of the prairie is an exploration of the fluid memory of ancestral time, the mix of dream and legend, creation and apocalypse. For a prairie artist, meditation and mysticism come naturally.

So this is my starting point. No desire to cultivate the cult of celebrity. Not to write a biography. Begin with a sense of place and a feeling for history, seeking for the individual and the collective answers to "Who am I?" and "Why am I here?" Taking some pieces that seem at first glance to beckon a more conventional treatment and teasing out their cultural and spiritual sense. That's the foundation of this quest to glean the context of Loreena McKennitt's music and follow the course of her career, enriching our appreciation of her artistic achievement by the way.

2
UNDER THE SIGN OF AQUARIUS

Loreena McKennitt was born at 7 p.m., February 7, 1957, under the sign of Aquarius. An air sign, Aquarius has the associated images of pouring water, atmosphere, rainstorms, or thunder. Aquarius in her heavenly aspect sits atop the clouds above mountaintops connecting the electromagnetic currents surrounding the earth, a symbol of the elements of lightning as fire and rain as water stretching from the heavens to the earth. In Homer's *Iliad*, women born on this day are compared to Athena. Statues show brilliant eyes and golden rays emanating from the head, which some say inspired the Christian halo, St Elmo's fire, and the body's aura. Rebellious when young, an Aquarius has sympathy for outsiders and works for the civic good. In Egyptology, Aquarius is connected to the goddess Isis who pours the water used in many rituals and ceremonies to inspire life or consciousness. Aquarius is the sign of baptism. Images of running water, rain, seashore, waterfalls, thermal springs, morning showers, and rivers that have electrically charged particles or negative ions. In the Chinese horoscope, Loreena McKennitt is a Fire Rooster.

An astrologer would suggest this date and time makes her thoughtful reserved, intense, and strong willed, destined to become a social reformer, writer, and innovator. She may be attracted to electromagnetic energies, physics, optics, ceramics, or NASA style computers, but she would be anti-industrial, pollution conscious, like clean or intermediate technology, and, being somewhat mystical, she would use technology within a holistic and peaceful framework. Independent minded, she would be sensitive to interference, like to be alone, and hesitate to ask for help.

"We were quite excited when Loreena was born," her mother Irene told *Saturday Night* magazine. "Warren, our son, is three years older and then along came a girl, with red hair just like her father's. We had family in California who told us of a little girl named Loreena. And it just seemed to go with McKennitt."

Irene was a career nurse at the time who coordinated home-care service in the local district and raised Loreena and her two brothers. She has since moved to Saltspring Island, British Columbia. Her late husband, Jack, was a drover who ran a thriving livestock business with an auction barn just west of Morden that sent him to district farms as well as the Winnipeg stockyards. "My father built his business up from scratch," Loreena commented in

Saturday Night, "and he worked very hard. He would be up at five, six in the morning, and he'd be gone until ten. To serve as a self-employed person you have to do those kinds of hours and there is a cost. My father always felt badly that he didn't spend time fishing or whatever ... but I understood. Often we'd just talk. They could be very ethical kinds of conversations. My father would talk about 'the little guy', explain that you have to give him just as much attention as the big guy. Not for better business, but because it was a good thing to do." Jack McKennitt died of cancer in 1992, the week before Loreena McKennitt won her first Juno Award, Canada's version of a Grammy. Loreena's brother, Warren, took over the family business.

Young Loreena developed into the most vigorous Highland dancer in town before going to school, doing such old warrior dances as the highland fling, once performed by victorious chieftains on a small spiked shield, and the sword dance, in remembrance of a chieftain who defeated a rival in battle and danced in exultation over his and the opponent's sword. But during a Sunday drive when she was five, the family car collided with another. She was in hospital for several days with two broken legs. Her grandmother sent over the family piano to ease her recovery — and Loreena's talent "just seemed to fall out of the sky," her mother recalls. Loreena studied classical piano up to Grade Nine, then voice for five years. She sang in the choir, played piano for school concerts and Chamber of Commerce receptions, as well as organ in the local United Church, though she claimed she lacked the discipline and dedication for a career in classical music. Preoccupied with music, "she never seemed to matter very much about having a lot of boyfriends and all that," her mother remarks.

The McKennitt family "was not a typical Irish family," full of traditional Celtic music and song, Loreena told *Folk Harp Journal*, but her home was not bereft of music. When her grandmother came by to babysit, they had what Irene McKennitt calls "little concerts at home." And Loreena fondly recalls her music teacher, Olga Frien, a mother of three who directed the Morden children's choir, painted, cooked, put on musicals. "She had tremendous flights of fancy ... she was not your regular music teacher," McKennitt told Lauren Foster-MacLeod of *Folk Ways Journal*. "She and the man who came to be my Grade-Ten English teacher co-wrote an operetta and they brought in someone from the Royal Winnipeg Ballet to choreograph a bunch of us kids. She would forever be producing this thing or that thing with a children's choir, which certainly was one of the best in Manitoba and in Canada (in competition). It always came very close to the Winnipeg Mennonite Children's Choir."

The family attended the United Church, founded in the merger of several Methodist and Presbyterian denominations in the early 20th century, a plain church, almost as strict in conduct as Mennonite sects. The schools in Morden were no less staid. "I went to school with students who weren't allowed to have television in their house or wear makeup or dance," Loreena told *Chatelaine* magazine. An honors student, McKennitt was often absent from class because she was playing music or sports. "I was playing sports and I was playing music in my kind of creative and wilful way," Loreena's remarks as she recalls her adolescence. "But I was different, you know? I wasn't a real social creature like a lot of other girls my age. And because I felt older and different from many of my school chums, I spent time with my phys-ed teachers," she told Peter Feniak at *Saturday Night*. Which, not surprisingly in a small town, led to false rumors about her relationship with her Grade Seven teacher. "But there developed the sense that this was unusual," Loreena explains, "that there were lesbian kinds of overtones to the whole friendship when in fact there was not a hint of that." Her teacher was dismissed from her job, as was Loreena's next phys ed teacher, this time, a man. "Similar kind of thing.... This man liked to talk philosophy, he played pieces on the piano, we'd just hang our after school and talk, just on the edge of the gymnasium. There was great concern that this was 'unnatural', and he was dismissed."

By the time Loreena graduated from Grade Eleven she was ready to dismiss the school and the town. Apparently perceived by the community as a rebel, Loreena was implicated in a round-up of so-called delinquent kids. With the support of her parents, she left town to enroll at Balmoral Hall School for Girls in Winnipeg. "We never told anyone at the old school ... I just never showed up for Grade Twelve," Loreena told *Saturday Night*. From there she attended the University of Manitoba to study veterinarian medicine and worked in her father's Winnipeg office, but she soon found herself hanging out at folk clubs like the Hollow Mug, listening to the Celtic music of Planxty, Pentangle, Steeleye Span, the Bothy Band, and Alan Stivell, the celebrated Breton harp player whose instrument would steal Loreena away from her agricultural studies and prairie community. Stivell's music "enthralled me so," Loreena recalls, "I put it on a reel-to-reel tape so I could go to bed listening and wouldn't have to get up to turn the record over." As she explained in *Dirty Linen*, "It existed in an instinctive kind of way in that I didn't seek out Celtic music — I maintain that it really chose me. There's something about the music that I was just instinctively drawn to."

3
MAPPING MORDEN

Canada's writers have created a subgenre called small town literature. Margaret Laurence writes of Neepawa a.k.a. Manawaka (Manitoba), Robertson Davies of Deptford (Ontario), Sinclair Ross of Horizon (Saskatchewan), Stephen Leacock of Mariposa a.k.a Orillia (Ontario). Small literary towns like Mariposa, Crocus, Jubilee, Salterton portray a matrix of social growth, a point of departure from which authors vow never to return. Yet towns have a power of influence on the people who live in them. The isolation of small groups of people in a vast landscape contributes to one's personality and, oddly enough, creates the atmosphere for great art.

"When I was eighteen, I couldn't wait to get out of town and away from the prairies," celebrated novelist Margaret Laurence wrote about her home town of Neepawa, about 100 kilometers north-west of Morden. "I did not even think that I would carry the land and town all my life within my skull.... The gist is this: no matter where I go or what I would do for me this is the backdrop of my work.... This is where my world began. A world which included the ancestors — both my own and other people's ancestors who came to be mine. A world which formed me, and continues to do so, even while I fought it or some of its agents. A world which gave me my own life work to do. Because of this I learned the sight of my own particular eyes." Perhaps not coincidentally, when Margaret Laurence's most celebrated novel *The Diviners* was made into a television movie directed by Anne Wheeler, Loreena McKennitt was asked to sing 'Pique's Song', which Laurence had composed for the novel. The main character in the novel, Morag Gunn, a Scottish descendant living in southern Manitoba, has a troubled daughter, Picque, whose father is Metis. Pique struggles to come to terms with her 'mixed-blood' (Celtic, Native, French) ancestry while growing up on the prairie.

Pique's Song

There's a valley holds my name, now I know
In the tales they used to tell it seemed so low
There's a valley way down there
I used to dream it like a prayer
And my fathers, they lived there long ago.

*There's a mountain holds my name, close to the sky
And those stories made that mountain seem so high
There's a mountain way up there
I used to dream I'd breathe its air
And hear the voices that in me would never die.*

*I came to taste the dust out on the prairie road
My childhood thoughts were heavy on me like a load
But I left behind my fear
When I found those ghosts were near
Leadin' me back to that home I never knowed . . .*

About her home town of Morden, McKennitt has said on her website (quinlanroad.com), "it was a very robust community. People came from immigrant stock. Survival was the order of the day and in some ways broad cultural experience was limited. Although my family's ancestors for the most part came from Ireland, there was very little overt 'Celticness' in my upbringing in the sense of music or story telling."

Culturally narrow, in small-town Canada the social system is based on thrift, hard work, pressure to conform, to be respectable, to have financial success. A social map is drawn dividing the right from the wrong side of the tracks. The old standards remain. Land is cheaper near the tracks. Godliness and business intermingle. Individuals are expected, by commitment and need, to give evidence of their partnership in community ideals by hard work. To fall short, or to resist the rigid control, means personal loss and social peril. In these communities one is assigned a role and individuals are seen in relation to those roles. The tension between how we are perceived and our private calling is the source of much great Canadian art.

The township grid which overlays rural Canada appropriated native settlements, animal migration corridors, determined the right to European settlement. Townships, concessions, lots, laid down the grid across the sacred hoop. The grid included and excluded, marked off civilization from 'wilderness', the known from the 'unknown'. A mapped civilization was under control; unmapped native lands were out of control, savage. I have a map of Perth County, Ontario, dated 1837, and the area north of Stratford is called 'Indian lands'. Georgian Bay was called Iroquois Bay. What is not mapped was savage and barbaric, which gave Europeans the right to seize it by culture, history, and civilization.

Morden is located near the surveying site that established the 49th parallel of latitude drawn between Canada and the United States. In the winter of 1869, General George Syder received an order to establish an army post and make a survey of the border. In May 1870, he staked out a line 4,600 feet north of the previously accepted boundary. This placed the principal Canadian presence in what is now southern Manitoba, the Hudson Bay fort at Fort Pembina, in North Dakota. In May 1872, Congress passed legislation approving $50,000 and assigned regular officers of the army. Fort Pembina became US headquarters of the Boundary Commission. As a result of this survey, the British North American government agreed to make a survey of the 49th parallel from Lake of the Woods in Ontario to the Rocky Mountains. Some 45 sites are designated as historical along the boundary route in southern Manitoba.

Mapping and boundaries are part of how we see ourselves as a nation and as a people. Because Canada is a new country, Canadians have almost perfect records of their origins. And because of this youth, argues novelist Aritha van Herk, Canadians continue to participate in their mapping. Mapping strategies in Canadian culture emphasize colonizing and decolonizing the landscape. Maps mark out the cartography of exile, cartography of difference. Maps are like books: instruments of power and knowledge. Such mapping is specific. It places, organizes, and creates a mental state. Such issues seem neutral, but they are not in creating borders and fixing limits, constraints to what we know and what we don't, including the limits of a certain kind of freedom. What does a creative person do in a place with boundaries? Try to understand and interpret new areas? Explore new tendencies of the mind? Artists address themselves to the uninvented world. Creativity and exploration go together. Loreena McKennitt grew up on the path of the explorers. One dominating question in Canadian art is, 'Who am I?', as McKennitt herself recognizes. Celebrated Canadian critic Northrop Frye added the next question: 'Where is here?'

When Loreena McKennitt was a child, Morden had a population of 3,500. The vista — an expanse of grain, grasses, and poplar bluffs — hasn't changed. The flatness ends at a small crescent of hills on the south side of town. By 1996, the population had not quite doubled to 5,900. Morden is 122 kilometers (a 90 minute drive) southwest of Winnipeg, the self-styled Chicago of the north. The population growth of Morden, with its echoes of Mordor, Mordred, Middle Earth, and King Arthur, came from migration to its dynamic industrial sector and an appealing business district with a mile of specialty stores and warm brick sidewalks lined with potted trees, shrubs, and flowers.

The prehistoric world is important to Morden. In 1971 the Morden District Museum was established in the lower levels of the Morden Recreation

Center to collect, preserve, and display examples of the area's natural history. The museum now houses the largest collection of marine reptile fossils in North America. Giant marine reptiles, fossils of fearsome alligators, mosasaurs, pleisosaurs, sharks, and turtles, from that long ago Colorado Sea of 80 million years ago were all collected locally. But in Morden, modern history is sold as quaint. "Enjoy the charms of the past today," states the billboard with images of older buildings and a cartoon Victorian family on the Morden city limits. Morden is famous for its unique fieldstone mansions and heritage buildings. The Morden Historical Society offers local tours. A self-guide to the Morden Mansion, by foot, bike, or car, suggests an architectural historical tour of highlighted public buildings and private homes dating from the 1800s to about the 1930s. Not surprisingly, Loreena grew up with a sense of heritage and maintains both a sense of social history and cultural continuity. In her new home community of Stratford, Loreena would become active in the Stratford Heritage Trust.

The little river that runs through town is 'Mort Cheval' Dead Horse Creek, named by the French fur traders. At nearby Fort Pinanicwaywinning is an historic cairn. The name means 'going over the ford' in Red River carts with their seven-foot high wheels. The fort was built in 1802 under the orders of Alexander Henry the Younger, a partner in the North West Company where trade was developed with the Cree and the Assiniboine tribes.

But Morden depended on the steam locomotive. Canada as a postmodern nation is among the pioneers in the physical connection of uniting long distances and large-scale communication technologies. When the railroads ran through town, east and west, a lovelorn poet saw goals of hope and escape. Even the sound of Canada has vastness and space. The train whistles of Canada, in E flat minor, as Canadian composer Murray Shafer observes, are deep and haunting, not the high pitched piping of European trains. To be Canadian means to be disoriented in space, even lost in space and time. Or make the choice to stay in a final despair.

Railway stations were determined by the locomotive's need for water and coal and by the distance a farm family could travel with a team and wagon. Towns built almost identically were no more than 20 miles apart. The railway station and grain elevator anchored one end of main street, with a general store, hardware merchant, blacksmith, hotel, newspaper, and one branch bank allowed the pick of the main street as an outpost of world capitalism. So the Canadian Pacific Railway arrived in Southern Manitoba, slowed, chuffed, and bellowed clouds of steam, in the winter of 1882, and set up a temporary station two miles east of the current town. The station was named Stephen, after CPR President George Stephen. To ensure a water supply for the engines, the rail company soon abandoned Stephen and moved to present day Morden. The town was named after Avy Morden who came from Walkerton, Ontario.

In 1885, the town was close to its beginnings. Board sidewalks, oil lamps, and a few successful businesses. A cemetery, an undertaker, and churches: Presbyterian, Methodist, Baptist, Congregationalists, and Mennonites. All other sects who established their churches in the small towns of Canada carried with them religions that leaned more towards fear than love. Pioneer service required hard service before rejoicing. The land demanded battle, said the settlers, and the land does not love. Like the God of the Old Testament, life in Morden was in a climate of extremes.

Painted by the Pembina Hills Art Group, the Morden Murals are based on the earliest known photograph of Morden. They depict the supply train for her Majesty's British North America Boundary commission at Dead Horse Creek. The North West Mounted Police, with 274 mounted officers and other personnel, 73 wagons, 114 oxcarts, horses, and cattle gathered around midday, July 13, 1874. The scene is on the east side of the Olympic Sports Center built in 1995. Prime Minister John A. MacDonald came by on July 15, 1886, with passengers knocking cinders off their shoulders. The mural is on the side of a drugstore.

These paintings, with their wild vitality and original strength, are in a spirit of romance. A visual record of specific historical moments that have disappeared. A single focused image, not a lengthy memoir. Why paint such a scene? Why reinvent the past? It's a contact with the first hand of feeling, an appreciation for the lives of the forefathers, the pioneers, the values of a society that this small community inherited. This strange and free art comes from experience. We sabotage ourselves if we move too fast into other eras. The murals are not exactly realistic, but experientially realistic.

Some artists dream of the homeland and paint pictures symbolic of the pains endured as a settler. Such art is rooted in authenticity, intensity, and integrity not always found in the high arts. Folk art is an expression of one's life, not one's culture. The past and the present co-exist. Local artists have an instinct for creation. In a place without tradition, they make art that does not look like art. Let's call it community spirit, it's sensitive and open-minded. Human-centered. Making a home out of existence. Canadian artists have a preoccupation with place, time, landscape, memory, and the hierarchy of human figures in the localized environment of memory. A folk artist takes pride in bringing back memories, recreating scenes of the past. Art is dreams and treasures in the flow of life. Such an artist is a kind of historian, re-living good or bad, beautiful when expressed in art, even if on the side of a building in downtown Morden.

4
PARABLES OF TREES

In one corner of Morden's Confederation Park is the largest tree in Manitoba, the Van Gort Cottonwood. The cottonwood was the 'rustling' tree of the Plains Indians that played such an important part in the Ghost Dances. Air circulates around a tree; oxygen and carbon dioxide are transformed and returned as part of our well being. McKennitt sings frequently of trees (*Two Trees, Ancient Pines, Bonny Portmore, The Mummer's Dance*) and uses a pomegranate tree image as her web page logo.

Because of Morden's long growing season and number of frost-free days, the federal Department of Agriculture established a Research Station in 1915 to test crops, including fruit trees. Trees have long held a special place in mythology. On my business card is a green man with a face of oak leaves coming from mouth and third eye. The Celts saw him as Esus, god of spring, or Cerunnos, god of the ancient forest and the underworld. The figure is often found high on columns of 11th- and 12th-century European churches. In the Sufi tradition, the Verdant One is like the Green Man, a green khadir, with the gold light shining through the green robes. The god connects the creativity of nature with our own creative expressions to protect the earth. I have a prairie friend who can pick up a handful of wheat, rub the grains, smell them, then he tells me the ph factor of the soil, the yield per acre, and the gross revenue. He can tell stories about the daily and seasonal rituals. He can hear the names of the ancestors echoing across the fields, calling him out. Other such parables of trees have been told over the years.

Fragments of the Parable of the Bountiful Tree appear in the Gnostic Library of Dead Sea Scrolls:

Please consider this, you who are wise: If a man has a fine tree, which grows high, all the way to heaven (. . .) (. . .) of the soil, and it produces succulent fruit every year with the autumn rains
and the spring rains, (. . .) and in thirst, will he not (. . .) and guard it (. . .) to multiply the boughs (?) of (. . .) from its shoot, to increase (. . .) and its mass of branches (. . .)

The Tree of Life, a cross-cultural symbol, is a poetic system older than the Tree of Knowledge in the Garden of Eden ("And he placed at the east of the Garden of Eden Cherubim, and a flaming sword, which turned every way, to keep the way of the tree of life." *Genesis* 3, 24.), in traditions as varied as Jewish mysticism (the Qaballah), most North American shamanic systems, and the Celtic bardic teachings. No matter what the tradition, the remarkably harmonious form of a tree is seen as an axis mundi, connecting all three realms of the cosmos — the roots of the underworld, the trunk of here and now, the crown of spirit. The tree has a connection with Celtic maypoles. On this tree are many life forms, or god forms, either as nature spirits, ancestral beings, fairies, power animals, divine messengers, solar deities, the gods of the planets, and images of the astrological zodiac. On the shaman journey, the drummer takes the traveler down into the roots or up the trunk and into the branches. The New Testament says, "And he looked up and said, I see men as trees, walking" (*Mark* 8. 24.) The tree is fenced for protection from those who would cut her down. The Breath of Life, Holy Spirit, Soul, Spirit, and Air surrounds the tree. Spirit is seen as a gentle air and mighty wind linking the matter of earth, a tree, with heaven.

In Jewish mysticism, the book of wisdom, the Qabalah, means The Tree of Life, a focus for spiritual seekers for thousands of years. A concentrated book of theology, alchemy, and symbolism, the Qabalah connects the physical world with ethereal beings in the universe. In the realm beyond the five senses is the sixth sense, source of highest joy and healing. Typically portrayed as a pomegranate, the tree of life, with its ten centers and twenty-two pathways, was said to be a map of the psyche. Likewise, in Zoroasterianism the pomegranate is referred to as Urvaram, 'the tree of knowledge'. When benedictions are recited upon a child during its investiture with the sacred shirt and thread, grains of pomegranate mixed with grains of rice and raisins are sprinkled as symbol of creation, fecundity, prosperity, and immortality. The pomegranate is an evergreen plant considered an emblem of immortality of the soul and a sign of prosperity from the fact that it contains numbers of grains within itself. Significantly, William Butler Yeats, whose poem *Stolen Child* was Loreena McKennitt's first Celtic composition, was a member of Qabalah 'Order of the Golden Dawn' and a careful reader of the *The Garden of Pomegranates* by written by Israelie Ragardie, secretary to Alastair Crowley.

Loreena McKennitt would call on the associated meanings of this symbol of the pomegranate tree in one of her first original compositions. Her original lyrics to *Courtyard Lullaby* on THE VISIT isolate the pomegranate tree in a surreal vision of a unicorn, an image based in part on the a depiction of the unicorn in a garden of pomegranates in the Cloisters Museum tapestries in New York.

Courtyard Lullaby

. . . Last night you spoke of a dream
Where forests stretched to the east
And each bird sang its song
A unicorn joined in a feast

And in a corner stood
A pomegranate tree
With wild flowers there
No mortal eye could see . . .

This image of the unicorn in the garden of pomegranates appears on the cover of THE MASK AND MIRROR, while an image of pomegranate seeds appears on the cover for her WINTER GARDEN album. The logo for Loreena McKennitt's Quinlan Road record label is a tree inside a courtyard fence, which has been slightly altered so only the top sprigs and fruit are visible, most likely a pomegranate.

In the secret rituals of the Eleusian mysteries, the goddess cult of Persephone forbade eating pomegranates and certain other fruits. These stories, told in secret, were called *aporrhetoteros logos*. Persephone, trapped in the underworld, returned to the earth annually so her mother Demeter could bring on spring. Modern Jungians suggest we spend one third of our life in sleep, or the underworld of dreams, where we receive wisdom to bring to the dawn, the spring of each new day. Persephone in the Jungian underworld is Queen of the individual and the unique. She gives value to each one of us. But Pluto offered her a pomegranate when Hermes came to rescue her so she would not stay in the upper world. The pomegranate, packed with seeds of a latent future, is connected to birth and rebirth. The pomegranate has a connection with ground, moisture, and sunlight, sprouting . . . as you plant so shall ye sow.

The ancient Hebrews thought the Tree of Life was a cedar because of its scented wood and delicate oil. The Assyrians depicted it as a date tree, which provided both food and wine used as a libation to the gods. In the Bible, the sycamore is frequently mentioned, but scholars think this is a mistranslation since the species does not grow in the Nile Valley. Most likely the fig (Greek: *sycos*) and mulberry (*moros*) were united to denote the tree dedicated to joy, fertility, and the afterlife. Whatever species the tree is, it confers immortality. In the Old Testament Garden of Eden man was given a choice between the tree of knowledge, which conferred mortality on mankind, and the tree of life, which granted immortality. And so the allusions in *The Two Trees*, the W.B. Yeats poem Loreena McKennitt set to music on her THE MASK AND MIRROR album.

The Two Trees

Beloved, gaze in thine own heart,
The holy tree is growing there;
From joy the holy branches start,
And all the trembling flowers they bear.
The changing colours of its fruit
Have dowered the stars with merry light;
The surety of its hidden root
Has planted quiet in the night;
The shaking of its leafy head
Has given the waves their melody,
And made my lips and music wed,
Murmuring a wizard song for thee . . .

Gaze no more in the bitter glass
The demons, with their subtle guile,
Lift up before us when they pass,
Or only gaze a little while;
For there a fatal image grows
That the stormy night receives,
Roots half hidden under snows,
Broken boughs and blackened leaves.
For all things turn to bareness
In the dim glass the demons hold,
The glass of outer weariness,
Made when God slept in times of old . . .

In the video *No Journey's End*, McKennitt notes that she found this poem "quite fitting from the Celtic point of view that he [Yeats] would draw on the symbolism and the imagery of trees. I felt that after the whole journey of exploring the question of 'what is religion, and what is spirituality?' that Yeats' sentiment of looking into one's own self for goodness was a very comforting one."

In the Celtic 'Wheel of Life' (like the Great Plains native 'Medicine Wheel'), the tree of life grows in the center of the sphere that connects the four elements, the four seasons, and the four directions, the turning of a life cycle for gods, goddesses, and humans. Traditionally, certain images are held in various quadrants of the wheel. But the wheel is actually a sphere, with zones of awareness above, below, and within, the living spirit of being. In the Celtic traditions are found the sacred trees of the Druids. All trees had sacred attributes: Apple, Ash, Birch, Blackthorn, Broom, Cedar, Fir, Holly. Certain trees were said to be inhabited by spirits or had spirits of their own with strong auras for a healing influence. Our expressions 'touch wood' and 'knock on wood' come from respect for this ancient power. Trees and plants were divided into classifications based on importance, as chieftains, peasants, shrubs, and herbs. Where oak, ash, and thorn grow, fairies live. But plants had symbolism also. St Patrick preached the doctrine of the Trinity to the pagan Irish with a three leafed shamrock as an object lesson. The word 'shamrakh' is Arabic. A three-leafed plant as a symbol is older than Christianity.

The Willow was seen as a Moon Tree sacred to the White Lady, its groves magical. Priests, priestesses, and artisans sat among these trees to gain eloquence, inspiration, and the gift of prophecies. Oak trees were holy — rustling oak leaves and wrens brought divine messages. The oak tree was long-lived and a host for mistletoe, their sacred plant. Rowan or Mountain Ash was sacred to Brigit; the branches used for wands, rods, amulets, and divination. The Yew tree was sacred to the Winter Solstice and deities of death. A longbow was made of yew, and yew wood was placed on graves to remind a departed sprit that death was only a pause before rebirth.

The Pine tree was magical, the highest form of life, as it is in several Native American cultures with the red hawk of wisdom flying above and the great snake of the underground moving beneath. Pine trees were also especially important in the life of Canadian settlers. Try to imagine a land with millions of trees. The trees they encountered shaped their lives. Ontario was once 97% forest. Boles rose straight up to block the sky. Settlers carved the land to make farms and homes. In three years, an immigrant could build a log house, a log barn, buy a horse, yoke of oxen, two cows, some pigs, and clear 25 acres. Not much went to mills; pine needs sap to make good lumber. Some was cut for corduroy roads; some split for rail fencing, but most demolished. The British navy used one hundred-foot long pine for masts and pitch and timbers, especially after the Baltic ports were closed by Napoleon. Masts and timbers came from the St Lawrence, the Saguenay, and Lake Ontario. Over a dozen horses were needed to pull one mast on poor roads to

Lake Ontario. The ancient pines were cleared.

To this day in Perth County, Ontario, Loreena McKennitt's home county, many farmers leave a tree in the center of a field and a large stone at the driveway entrance. *Ancient Pines* is the title of an instrumental on Loreena McKennitt's PARALLEL DREAMS album, a song she composed as the score for a National Film Board documentary called *Goddess Remembered*, a song she describes in the liner notes as evoking "the earth's yearning for release from the oppression of the human hand."

While Loreena McKennitt's interest in the 'pagan' significance of trees is clear, her tree songs are, nevertheless, rooted in this political world. She's particularly proud of tracking down *Bonny Portmore*, included on THE VISIT. An obscure ballad mourning the loss of ancient British stands of oak, once worshiped by pre-Christian tribes, it has a contemporary relevance to today's fight to save old-growth forests. On the eastern side of Lough Neagh, about a half mile from shore, lies Lough Bog, once known as the Lough of Portmore. In 1664 on this side of the lake, Lord Conwayer had a castle on the site surrounded by an ancient forest. After his death, Portmore became neglected, and in 1791, the castle and other buildings were removed. Now only a portion of the wall remains. Among the many trees sold on the breakup of the property was the Great Oak of Portmore that was blown down in 1760. This is the oak referred to in the song as the 'ornament tree'. It was huge, over 14 feet in circumference. A single branch of it sold for nine pounds. The trunk fetched 97 pounds.

Bonny Portmore

> . . . *O Bonny Portmore, I am sorry to see*
> *Such a woeful destruction of your ornament tree*
> *For it stood on your shore for many's the long day*
> *Till the long boats from Antrim came to float it away.*
>
> *O Bonny Portmore, you shine where you stand*
> *And the more I think on you the more I think long*
> *If I had you now as I had once before*
> *All the Lords of Old England would not purchase Portmore.*
>
> *All the Birds in the forest bitterly weep*
> *Saying, "where shall we shelter or where shall we sleep?"*
> *For the Oak and the Ash, they are all cutten down*
> *And the walls of Bonny Portmore are all down to the ground . . .*

Although the song does not mention the deliberate destruction for military purposes of the woods surrounding the castle, thus leaving no place for rebels to hide, McKennitt mentions in her liner notes that "over the centuries many of Ireland's old oak forests were leveled for military and shipbuilding purposes." Conwayer's estate is regarded as a major loss to the Irish, notes Sean Boyle in *Traditional Irish Songs*. A web site refers to *Bonny Portmore* as the song that wouldn't die. The song was collected in Bunting's *Ancient Irish Music*, 1840. Bunting got it from an Ulster harper, Daniel Black, in 1796, within the lifetime of many who remember the fall of the castle. In Yeats' *Collected Poems*, the woods of Arkady are dead, destroyed by troops to deprive the Celts of concealment and by English absentee-landlords to fuel the fires of the Industrial Revolution. As Loreena McKennitt explained to Anil Prasad, *Bonny Portmore* "is a couple of hundred years old, but of very contemporary relevance in terms of its environmental statement," adding, by way of describing her creative process, "I'm looking to the arrangements and the instruments to flesh out that contemporary statement.... I'm interested in expanding the contemporary relevance of this music."

The song has a curious connection to Bob Marley's *Small Axe* in its use of thematic undercurrents and levels of meaning. The song seems a simple allegory, a woodsman speaking to a tree about to be felled. References only Jamaicans would gather, obscure to others. It's a triple threat, a warning to oppressors that the people of the Third World will one day cut them down to size. It also applies to the 'Big T'ree', the three dictatorial Jamaican record companies — Dynamic, Federal, and Studio One. The central image of tree felling, following orders, refers to the plantation days when slaves were ordered to cut down the islands' sacred and gigantic silk-cotton trees. To this day, rum is sprinkled on the stumps to a woeful song to assure the spirits it was the will of the masters, not the slaves.

Spring is not the time to dig too deep, and harm the bulbs with the shovel; a reminder that spiritual gardening is for the soul, not the ego. Spring is a time of regeneration, when the seedlings stirring within the earth shoulder their way through the snow crust. Summer trees express themselves in full foliage, and emphasize the importance of weeding, pruning, clearing out, making choices. Autumn is fruition, harvest, a time of celebration. Plants connect with nature and we connect with plants with all our senses. Trees are souls. That tree you are attracted to liberates you into life.

5
WINTER IN MANITOBA

Prairie winters were scarcely mentioned in promotional literature to attract settlers to this North American utopia. What was emphasized (even today on the web sites and tourist publications) are the number of frost free days, the abundant sunshine, the healthy climate, the lack of humidity. The published images are the prairies at their most attractive, images of the short summer, not the seven or eight month long winter. Not a hard and early frost, not summer lightning bolts, not terrifying flash floods, not hail that flattens crops, not bitter cold of 50 below with strong winds on the western edge of a vast nation not a dozen years old.

The garden valley of Manitoba — Winkler, Morden, Miami — can be a cold place in January and February when temperatures can easily drop to 50 below with wind chill. A winter storm comes in on the edge of the wind, moving with speed and twisting like a snake. The snow piles hard and fast and slippery. It stings and blinds and turns the world white with nights cold enough to kill. The cottonwood trees explode as the sap expands and bursts the boles at the weakest points. Buffalo standing face down, head into the wind look like show crusted boulders. Frozen air pierces the lungs like glass. Air is crystallized. Breath congeals around heads like comic strip balloons. Tears run down cheek and freeze. Face burns. Hurts to walk to cross a street. Cars simmer and groan attached by orange extension cords to engine block heaters. Plumes of frozen exhaust and brake lights glow. Who can believe winter can be so deadly? "Like an icicle in my mind," poet Gary Geddes writes. The 'truth' is in that long dead winter where we live, Eli Mandel says. The hands quick-freeze, hard as marble.

After a storm, the ravens and magpies look for horn or hoof poking out of the snow so they can feed. Artists on the prairies are mindful of death. The hired hand who froze 10 feet from the barn door in fierce weather. Drivers carry survival kits, flares, ropes, snacks, candles, blankets, sand, and shovels. And yet, as Loreena Mckennitt recognizes in arranging Canadian poet Archibald Lampman's poem *Snow*, recorded for her albums TO DRIVE THE COLD WINTER AWAY and A WINTER GARDEN, the experience of a prairie winter world can be profound.

WINTER IN MANITOBA

Snow

White are the far-off plains, and white
The fading forests grow;
The wind dies out along the height,
Denser still the snow,
A gathering weight on roof and tree,
Falls down scarcely audibly

The meadows and far-sheeted streams
Lie still without a sound;
Like some soft minister of dreams
The snow-fall hoods me round;
In wood and water, earth and air,
A silence is everywhere

Save when at lonely intervals
Some farmer's sleigh urged on,
With rustling runners and sharp bells,
Swings by me and is gone;
Or from the empty waste I hear
A sound remote and clear

The barking of a dog, or call
To cattle, sharply pealed,
Borne echoing from some wayside stall
Or barnyard far afield;
Then all is silent and the snow falls
Settling soft and low

The evening deepens and the grey
Folds closer earth and sky
The world seems shrouded, far away.
Its noises sleep, and I as secret as
Yon buried stream plod dumbly on and dream.

In Manitoba, one thinks about the metaphors of winter — 20,000 years ago, the Ice Age glaciers were two miles thick. That mountain of ice scoured and leveled the highlands, leaving glacial debris and erratic potholes of lakes.

Moraines, eskers, sand beach ridges, and other glacial debris deposits on the otherwise flat terrain. Who can believe this was once a tropical sea, where fossils of fish and marine reptiles are excavated from quarries near Morden. The hard sharp light reveals crests of sand ridges. Colors develop uncommon contrasts across wide fields and narrow gullies. Shadows appear blue. The long straight highways dissolve in liquid mirage. A shifting, illusory pattern of images. The forms are impressionistic, abstract, hard edge. The Manitoba winter landscape is not so much about objects as it is about forces. A pressure on the mind which invites a language of experiment. Naturally enough, many prairie artists write of visionary worlds. The past has a shape and mythology.

Loreena McKennitt has recorded two albums devoted to winter festivals. In feasts and celebrations, prairie settlers found a refuge from the terrors and loneliness of the prairie. Community life was essential. In the liner notes for TO DRIVE THE COLD WINTER AWAY, McKennitt remembers that, "as a child, my most vivid impression of music for the winter season came from songs and carols recorded in churches or great halls, rich with their own ambience and tradition. In that spirit I have ventured into several similar locations that I have come to cherish in my travels. Annaghmakerrig, the one time home of the late Sir Tyrone and Judy Guthrie, nestled in the woods of Co. Monaghan, Ireland, is presently a retreat for artists. I have had the privilege of working there several times over the years. The hall in which we recorded is a rehearsal hall where Guthrie once worked with many of the world's finest actors. Glenstall Abbey is a Benedictine monastery located outside of the city of Limerick, Ireland. Through their devotion and warm sense of humour, the monks have created a tranquility amidst the surrounding green hills that I can only hope gleams through in the songs we recorded there. The recording was completed in the Church of Our Lady in Guelph, Ontario, Canada. As we recorded through the dark hours of the night, this magnificent church, built in 1877, offered a great inspiration. The arrangements are sparse but somehow I felt that reflected the dynamics of the fall and winter seasons, and that there can be much beauty in such simplicity. As it is recorded on location, you may occasionally hear sounds of life continuing on around us. We hope these are not distracting, but rather are embraced like flecks of straw in the wool sweater your grandmother might have knitted to keep the cold winter away."

During a 1994 "Christmas Interview" on KCRW-FM in Santa Monica, California, she commented, "We're a very old creature, I think, as a species and we have very primitive needs. We're now living in a society where life is moving so fast . . . that I think we find it difficult to absorb and handle all the things coming at us. So I think what is so wonderful about the Christmas season is that it represents simplicity. It represents an emphasis on community and spending time with friends and family — and that is the value of the time." Rituals and church service, even dogma, brought culture, continuity, and tradition to isolated communities. The great Christmas feast, with the evergreen pine trees and all the layers of symbolism, is congested with pre-Christian ceremonies and a clutter of minor ceremonies: Candelmas, Twelfth Night, St Nicholas, and the feast of St Stephen. McKennitt's reverence for the Christmas feast would prompt her to arrange music for the traditional song *In Praise of Christmas* (which in turn may have prompted the producers of the movie *The Santa Claus* to use her music for the soundtrack).

In Praise of Christmas

All hail the days that merit more praise
Than all the rest of the year,
And welcome the nights that double delights
As well for the poor as the peer!
Good fortune attend each merry man's friend
That doth but the best that he may,
Forgetting old wrongs with carols and songs
To drive the cold winter away . . .

Death and birth are closely related at Christmas. The CD jackets on *A Winter Garden* feature pomegranate seedpods, and on *To Drive the Cold Winter Away*, stems of grass about to burst into seed. The winter festivals are the time for singing about the Birth. A child awaited with love and respect, carrying the hope of the world. Christmas celebrates the poor, in Mary and Joseph looking for lodging. As a festival for the persecuted, the Jewish baby is the newborn of the Great Christian myth of that truth beyond us. As a festival of the animals and the holy mystery of the night, St Francis recognized the animals that we tend to forget. As a festival of the human community, a festival of joy and pathos, the pointed holly leaves and bright red berries foreshadow Easter and the crown of thorns. As a festival of the earth, Christmas is the time of winter solstice.

Winter is for seekers of revelations. The Magi are eternal seekers of revelation. The three wise men are not really kings in the Bible, nor do they have any particular class nor race. The Magi came from Persia, with their own tradition of artistry. And one, Caspar, may have been black. Balthazar ended up at the strange cliff-side village of Le Baux, southern France, where his day is celebrated with a sheep decorated with a candle. From the Middle Eastern perspective, the Magi travel to refurbish their spiritual selves; the old way paves the way for the new.

Likewise, in recording songs like *The Wexford Carol*, *God Rest Ye Merry, Gentlemen*, and *Let All That to Mirth Inclined* on to DRIVE THE COLD WINTER AWAY and A WINTER GARDEN, Loreena McKennitt 'refurbished' not only this music but also the nativity story, especially the visit of the Magi, as she explained to Lynne Walker of the BBC. "I thought it would be interesting to bring some of the Middle East back into the carols — the whole Middle Eastern dimension is something that I have been exploring for some time. And so we brought in some musicians who played in that idiom to conjure up the Three Wise Men. . . . That's been at the foundation of my quest with regard to music — it's to take some of the pieces that seem at first glance to beckon a more conventional treatment and then take them elsewhere in a cultural sense or an ethnic sense. It's difficult because it boils down to idioms and very specific instruments and finding players who have those idioms." Loreena McKennitt's tribute to the magi appears in both *The Wexford Carol* and *Let All That Are To Mirth Inclined* on TO DRIVE THE COLD WINTER AWAY.

Let All That Are To Mirth Inclined

. . . Three eastern wise men from afar
Directed by a glorious star
Came boldly on and made no stay
Until they came where Jesus lay

And being come unto that place
Where the blessed Messiah was
They humbly laid before his feet
Their gifts of gold and incense sweet . . .

Let all our songs and praises be
Unto his heavenly majesty
And evermore amongst our mirth
Remember Christ our Saviour's birth

The Christian calendar adopts January 6 as the Feast of the Epiphany to celebrate the manifestation of Christ's divinity to the magi, when God breaks through the visible and ordinary to became manifest in human lives. The homeless parents and the birth in a stable brought divinity to earth. The magi get a vision of a world transformed. A visible manifestation of something invisible

Christmas, or Christ's Mass, is also called Noel, which some say is a contraction of the French nouvelles (tidings), *les bonnes nouvelles*, or Good news of the gospel, or from Latin *natalis*, the birthday. Going back further, we find it could be a corruption of Yule, Jule, or Ule, a festival of the sun. The feast of the nativity and other major ecclesiastical anniversaries coincide with the cardinal points of the year. The Annunciation of Virgin Mary occurs on March 25, the vernal equinox. The Feast of St Michael occurs on September 29, near the autumn equinox. The birth of Christ is around the winter solstice, the return of the sun as the year draws to a close, and nights are longest. The restoration of light and commencement of a new era was kept by the Saxons in honor of Thor; the feast called Yule, or Jule. Some say the word comes from the idea of revolution or the Wheel, meaning the return of the sun. The kings came together during this holy month (Halig Monath) in Anglo-Saxon England.

The date of Christ's birth has always been controversial. Scholars point out the flocks and shepherds recorded by Luke indicate a spring birth. December 25, they claim, substitutes a Christian festival for the license of the Bacchanalia and Saturnalia, with feast and fire, and the New Year Day. Papal Rome preserved many relics of ancient Rome, so Pope Gregory, in his attempt to convert the Anglo Saxons, accommodated many so-called pagan and heathen ceremonies with the Christian ones. Christmas angels on top of the tree? The young deacon Gregory, who would become Pope, noted the white bodies and fair faces and golden hair of some boys brought to Rome by slave traders. They are English, Angles, he was told. But he thought them angels, with their Angel Faces. From where did they come? *De ira!* The country of God's wrath, *De ira*.

Before Christianity came to Britain, the month of December was called *Aeraa Geola*, 'the sun turns his glorious course'. The Roman holiday on December 25 was actually *Dies Natalis Invicti Solis*, the Birthday of the Unconquered Sun that became the Twelfth Night revels and the Adoration of the Magi. The Bacchanalia and Saturnalia of the Romans are celebrated worldwide. Greeks, Mexicans, Persians, and Chinese had special days when masters and slaves switched roles. Presents were given and received. Dolls and effigies evolved into the crib and manger figures. The feast of St Francis of Assisi often featured real animals and people in the 13th century. Nativity plays, or even the Mass itself, became a moving dance/drama in celebration. Generous hospitality was shown to the poor. Affairs of state were brought under consideration and strangers were entertained. Toward the end of the feast, when sun was presumably returning, the world was renovated. A king or ruler was chosen for an ephemeral reign.

The Druids, priests of Ancient Britons, had customs similar to the Brahmins of India, the Magi of Persia, and the Chaldeans of Syria. They worshiped in groves, regarded the oak and mistletoe as objects of veneration, and offered sacrifices. Candle flames meant the heat and light of sun, and became the symbol of Christ as light of the world, the symbol of truth. Decking the halls with evergreens, holly (with its premonition of the crown of thorns and blood), ivy, and mistletoe is a relic of Druid customs. A Norse legend related how the evil God Loki killed the sun god, Balder, with a mistletoe arrow. Brought back to life, the tree gods promised that mistletoe would be a symbol of love. The Celts saw wisdom in the diamond dark sky. At the very depth of winter, when dark was at its strongest, the makers of Newgrange, Ireland, celebrated light. Where they thought no human eye could penetrate, where no one would wander, they carved the stones. The spiral still sets the imagination alight when the light floats through the dark like a thing alive.

Of course, Christmas is not the only festival. The spring equinox at Easter, May Day celebrated in the Middle Ages by dancing in the meadows, the almost forgotten feast of St John. Oddly, summer is the only season that lacks a festival. The fireworks on July 1st (in Canada) and July 4th (in America) hint at the great solar events, and echo the ancient bonfires lit on the hills of Cornwall on this the longest day of the year, the full measure of light. Apogee, the high moment of summer, prepares us for winter, the beginning of a descent that leads to winter solstice and the cycle anew, the natural rhythm of hope Loreena McKennitt celebrates in her arrangement of *The Seasons* on TO DRIVE THE COLD WINTER AWAY.

The Seasons

Come all you lads and lasses, I'd have you give attention
To these lines I'm about to write here.
'Tis of the four seasons of the year that I shall mention,
The beauty of all things doth appear . . .

When night comes on with song and tale we pass the wintry hours;
By keeping up a cheerful heart we hope for better days.
We tend the cattle, sow the seed, give work onto the ploughers,
With patience wait till winter yields before the sun's fair rays.

And so the world goes round and round, and every time and season
With pleasure and with profit crowns the passage of the year.
And so through every time of life, to him who acts with reason
The beauty of all things doth appear.

"So it's the seasons changing that really transforms your ... umm ...," Chris Douridas of KCRW-FM asked Loreena McKennitt during a 1994 interview. "Psyche," she interjected when Douridas was at a loss for words. "For myself I spend whatever time I can in the garden, and I find the garden is this great metaphor for the birth and death cycle of life." Words well-spoken by a prairie-born woman who knows the promise buried beneath the winter snows.

6

BUFFALO GHOST DANCE

"What sort of things inspire you in composing music?" Lauren Foster asked Loreena McKennitt in *Folk Harp Journal*. "A lot of things," she replied, somewhat vaguely, before coming to the point. "I look for ancient threads, you know. I look for some threads which might have gotten broken off or lost somewhere, and try to bring them back in, whether it's through geography or time. For example, another thing or culture I've been interested in — but again, not in the 'flavor of the month' kind of way — has been North American First People's culture, because there is a lot of reverence for trees, their imagery of the salmon or the raven, and the symbolism that goes with these, their 'rootedness' to the seasons, their 'rootedness' to the earth. We're so fortunate to be this lost contemporary culture that we are, as white people in this land, and still have amongst us people of an older culture. I feel that the future is through them; it's through that culture."

Canada has been said to be a country of much geography, but little history, a concept difficult to explain to the 50 or 60 First Nations groups who have lived here for thousands of years. Over one million teepee rings have been found in Alberta, indicating long stays. Despite their differences, New World Amerindians as varied as the Peruvian Inca, the Mexican Maya, the Five Nations of the Iroquois, the Pacific Coast Haida, and the Arctic Inuit were part of a major civilization united by a cosmological view that saw a balanced world among the great and small powers of trees, animals, and humans, since they were all 'people' with minds and spirits. Even certain stones, in ritual, were alive, could speak. The key was harmony. All things — earth, sky, trees, grasses, animals, winged ones, two legged, and four legged — are all my relations, all my family, writes Black Elk. Our destiny was determined by animal spirits and powers, realized through rites of purification — fasting, prayer, dance — and a vision quest.

The straight lines of the railroad passed through Morden under an archway made from a pile of buffalo bones: hip bones, ribs curved and bare, concave shoulder blades, leg bones knobbed, skulls cold and sad, the curled horns, the knuckles and curves and furrows of spinal columns heaped together. Loreena McKennitt came of age on the ancient grounds of the buffalo, the world of the White Buffalo Woman, the Sacred Hoop, the Vision Quest, and the grand spectacle of the Great Plains hunt prepared for with Sweat Lodge prayers, the pipe and tobacco ceremony, the sacred paint on rawhide pouches, and the shaman chanting of hunts long ago. Fire dances to invigorate the tribe, the culmination of all forms of native art, music, masking, painting, storytelling, history, and legend. A dramatization of the acts of the spirits. Life was dance, dance was life. But with the near extinction of the buffalo after 1847, the dance of life too soon became a ghost dance. Forgotten history, Loreena McKennitt might say, but the stuff of the historical and mythological resonance we hear in her instrumental, *Huron 'Beltane' Fire Dance*, on PARALLEL DREAMS, where the 'old ways' of the North American native culture and the 'old ways' of Celtic culture run parallel in song.

The Plains Indians tell a legend of the White Buffalo Woman who emerged from the earth of the Cypress Hills or the Que'apelle Valley. This Buffalo woman walked into the west, outlined by the red ball of the setting sun. She stopped four times. Each time she stopped, a different colored bison was born. Black. Brown. Red. And finally the White Buffalo, the most sacred animal, seen only in dreams, was born. As the White Buffalo Woman disappeared over the horizon, the buffalo appeared in great herds. They allowed themselves to be killed so that the people would live. The buffalo gave men the sacred tobacco. The buffalo marched from grassland to grassland in a brown undulating mass. They moved north in the Moon of Flowers and south in the Moon of the Freezing Rivers. In winter they faced the icy winds, in spring the calves were born. The bulls circled clumsily to protect the herd from wolves, and when an alarm was raised the herd would gallop forward in a terrifying stampede. The Native and Metis riders followed the zig zag paths of the herds, avoiding the tangled underbrush of Ghost's lariat, a vine with bright blue flowers that can trip running horses.

Two great herds of buffalo traversed the Great Plains, the Grand Coteau (Red River) herd and the Saskatchewan River herd. The Grand Coteau most likely traveled over the ground where Loreena McKennitt spent her childhood. The buffalo of the Red River would winter as far north as Lake Manitoba, even past the site of Fort Garry, now Winnipeg. Skulls and bones have been found there, some with rattlesnakes curled in the skulls. The herds were said to have been so thick a man could walk 10 miles across their backs without touching ground. Recent scholarship suggests the areas with large herds represented contested areas of tribal dispute. Areas with large groups of animals were buffer zones. Tribal groups like the Lakota Sioux, the ones Kevin Costner befriended in *Dances with Wolves*, lived and hunted on the southern edges, and the Cree and Ojibway lived on the northern periphery. Both groups made skirmishes into the buffer zones that had large wildlife populations. Medicine wheels ringed the northern summer range, some in use for over 5,000 years.

Everything came from the buffalo. Buffalo kept the prairies fertile, cropped the curly buffalo grass back to the roots and enriched the fine-grained soil with dung that mingled with the smell of wild roses. August was the Moon of Ripe Wild Plums, and the prairies were rich in fruit and forage. Wallows where the animals rolled filled with water to create ponds for fox, wolf, badger, deer. Flocks of ducks and geese, tundra swans, cranes, and herons came to the ponds. Cowbirds, magpies, redwings, merles picked fleas and gnats off the animal's backs. Russet wrens trilled in the cottonwoods. In the rich ungrounded life of the prairie, badgers, marmots, field mice, and kangaroo rats lined their nests with the fluffy buffalo wool in the Moon of Ripe Corn. On the prairies, even the animals form large social groups.

The buffalo hunt was a sacred act for these Plains people. Before a buffalo hunt no one placed a knife upright in the ground or inside a lodge or his horse would suffer misfortune. A man could die under the hooves of the animals or be spiked on their horns. A horse could step in a badger hole. Men were told to hide behind their horse to avoid trampling by the buffalo. Imagine the day of the hunt. The shamans prayed and smoked their long pipes over painted buffalo skulls. The women sang the buffalo songs. The medicine man applied the horse medicine to give the horses power. Wild peony was rubbed on the horses' noses for energy. Red flowers were blown between the horses' ears to make the animals swift. Chewed corn was blown into the nostrils to make the horses long winded. Yellow wood sorrel bulbs were pounded and mixed into the oats for speed. Special bridles were taken from the medicine bags. The bridles were covered with red flannel, with feathers at the end and small bags of horse medicine and strips of white weasel skin. The bridle bundles were made as they appeared in the dreams of the horse medicine men. The horse bridle made the horse lively and kept it from falling. The men who received these bridles also received songs in their dreams that were sang with the other horse medicine songs as the bridles were put on the horses.

The hunters talked to their prized and pampered horses. The best horses were called buffalo runners. The owners fasted so that they would have visions about their horses. The spirit of a horse that was treated well would appear in a vision revealing the herbs or roots that would give the horse speed and cure illness. Jackrabbit feet were strung around a mare's neck to ensure the birth of fast colts, dead magpies to ensure the birth of a pinto pony. The testicles of a gelded horse were run along the backbone of a mare, and the surgeon would tie up the severed cords with deer or antelope sinew that made the horses run faster. A well-trained buffalo runner needed neither whip nor spurs. The horse would turn with just a hint of pressure form the rider's knees or shifting weight. The riders rode with bent knees and short stirrups to give more power to the lance, better aim with the bow and arrow or buffalo rifle.

Ritual guided the hunters to the herd. Special powers songs, the buffalo dance, the secret chants and prayers pointed the way. According to some, the raven that circled the camp and cawed would fly towards the herd. The scouts went looking for the herds. The horses were tense, the bright ribbons tied into their manes tossed eagerly. The hunters fanned out in an arc, like the horns of a buffalo bull. When a herd was sighted, the hunters would walk slowly, slouching behind the manes of the ponies to hide the sight of their posture from the animals. The grass whispers.

An old blind buffalo at the edge of the herd grows restless. She flips her tail and paces back and forth. An old bull lifts his head and glares down the approaching horsemen. Some new aroma over the dung and wild roses and prairie clover. Suddenly, an old cow spins and gallops away. The bull follows. The herd panics. The horsemen leap onto the back of their ponies. The horses need no kicking to begin the chase. The earth and buffalo grass is ground into muck by the herd. The air is ripe with dung and sage and buffalo grass and dust. The hot heavy black maned bulls swing their heads as they run under the sacrificial face of the sun.

Each man drops an article to mark his kill. In museums, you can see how the Cheyenne hunters had distinguishing marks on their arrows, red circles or patterns just forward of the fletching to mark ownership and avoid fights over who owns the meat. Displays show how the short curved bows or elk or buffalo ribs were exquisitely finished. The bone was boiled and shaped and flexed with deer hide handle grips. The old hunters say stone or bone kills better than iron arrowheads. The bows had tufts of horsehair to wave and mesmerize the antelopes. Then the camp moves up. Women bring out the hatchets and skinning knives and scrapers to skin and dress the meat. They cut into the belly, up to their elbows in silver tissue. Blood shines on the knives. The camp smells of sweat, leather, coffee, smoke. Stew pots were steaming. Spits of meat were roasting.

No part of the bison was wasted. The meat, fat, organs, and bone marrow provided food. The skins became tent covers, sleeping robes, cloths, and moccasins. Bones were fashioned into tools and ribs into sled runners. Hollowed out horns became drinking goblets and gunpowder horns. Hooves became glue, fat became grease, and the gall made yellow paint. The incisor teeth were used as necklaces and the vertebrae were fashioned into gaming pieces for gambling. The bladder made an ideal water bag and the tail a fly swatter. Dried dung, or buffalo chips, was a natural source of methane that provided an abundance of fuel on the treeless prairie.

With the arrival of European explorers, fur-traders, and settlers, these rituals began to change, and with the near extinction of the buffalo during the second half of the 19th century, a way of life came to an end. The birth of a Metis culture on the plains of southern Manitoba was unique to Canada, a new nation of Native peoples and European explorers who took a stand for their place in the British imperial order. The intermarriage of natives and traders brought significant changes to just about everything on the prairie, including the buffalo.

Early French explorers, *coeur de bois*, integrated into the Cree and Ojibwa communities, 'marrying' women whose children became known as 'burnt wood people', 'half-breeds', or 'Metis'. In northern Manitoba and Ontario, in the watershed of Hudson Bay, the relationships between Cree women and Irish, English, or Scottish traders created the English Metis. The French and English Metis adapted elements from both sides of their heritage to form a distinct culture and an identity, part Indian, part European, but not completely accepted by either. But the Metis became fiercely independent. They eventually declared themselves a new nation. Their resistance precipitated a campaign by the Canadian government to legislate them out of existence.

In the stereotypes, French Canadian Metis were considered merry, light-hearted, religious, generous. They made excellent guides. As superb canoemen, their distinctive clothes identified them: a blue capote and a beaded pipe bag hanging from a bright red sash. Many of the French Metis gravitated towards permanent settlements at the junction of the Red and Assiniboine rivers. In the fall of 1801, a group of Metis settled on the west bank of the Red River where the city of Winnipeg now stands. They were called 'freemen' because neither Indian custom nor fur trader law bound them. Three groups subsequently emerged: some became traders, some became voyageurs, and some became buffalo hunters. At the Royal Ontario Museum in Toronto, you can see a painting by Paul Kane entitled *Half Breeds Running Buffalo, 1840s*. In 1840, the Metis had defeated the Lakota Sioux for the rights of the buffalo hunt in North Dakota. The Metis fiercely guarded their customary rights to hunt and trade freely throughout the prairies. Rallying together under the cry, '*Le Commerce ese libre*! (Freedom of Trade!) the Metis effectively ended the Hudson Bay Company's trade monopoly.

The hunting technique of the Metis differed from their Cree ancestors. The Plains Cree and Ojibwa hunted buffalo by building fenced enclosures and driving them over cliffs in mass killings. Places like 'Head Smashed In Buffalo Jump' in southern Alberta, an enormous site estimated to be over 5,000 years old, was used by several coordinated tribal groups as a trading center until the 1870s. Archeologists have discovered over 30 mazeways where the stampeding buffalo were driven, guided by an estimated 20,000 cairns. Instead of driving the animals off cliffs or into fenced enclosures, the Metis were experts with horses and firearms. The horse made the difference. Armed and mounted, the riders were masters of craft and cunning in the dangers of a hunt. The shaggies, despite their weight and spindly legs, could outrun a cavalry pony. Many stories tell of bison outrunning teams of horses or even relays of riders. A bison can wheel and cut faster than a horse.

The hunt was a deadly game. Creating a stampede, the hunters ran their horses into the herds low enough to fire the shot. A Sharps 50-120-550 buffalo rifle — Big Fifty, Old Reliable — weighed nearly 20 pounds. It fired a slug of lead two inches long and one half inch in diameter, weighing eight to the pound. An experienced rider on a well-trained horse could down 10 to 12 buffalo in a two-hour run. Four hundred Metis horsemen could run down a herd of thousands of buffalo. With such a devastating weapon, a skilled hunter could kill 250 bison a day from 500 yards. No skill was required against such a slow-witted animal. But the Metis fired point blank at full gallop — a heart shot, just behind the shoulder or a ball placed just behind the huge head in line with the base of the horns to pierce the brain was almost as good — then turned away quickly to the side and safety. When blood foamed out of the mouth, the animal was as good as dead. At high speed the hunter moved to the next animal. A bull bison, taller than a man at the shoulder, weighed nearly a ton. The cows weighed nearly 800 pounds. Each animal had

200 pounds of meat on the humps, saddle, and loins. The Metis kept some for themselves, but the rest was sold to the fur trade companies who housed it as a staple for their traders. A good hunter could earn over a $100 a day.

The Metis Red River buffalo hunt has been called "the most heavily organized hunting party in the world." By the 1840s, the Red River colony sent 1,240 carts to the spring hunt. Guns, blankets, ammunition, cookware, skinning knives, kegs, crates, and provisions. A fully loaded Red River cart could carry nearly 600 hides. At $2.50 apiece, a load was worth nearly $1,500, a small fortune. The hunt of 1840 returned to Red River with over one million pounds of meat and hides to be used for pemmican and dressed meat to sell to the North West Company or the Hudson Bay Company. Yet there was scarcely a generation left for the buffalo — and the Indian tribes of the Great Plains were left poorer as the United States moved towards Civil War and Wounded Knee, Canada towards the Red River Rebellion and Indian reservations.

Supplying the fur trade with meat and pemmican led to the Metis becoming such a powerful political and military force. The Metis buffalo hunt also stands on record as the first form of government on the western plains. A provisional Metis council was elected for the hunt. The best known, the St Laurent Buffalo Council, elected Gabriel Dumont as its president. Ten captains were chosen with one assigned as senior captain. Guides were chosen who were responsible for the flag and to command the hunts. Some men were elected for guard duty and night patrol. Like a military operation, the hunt had strict rules and regulations. No one hunted on Sundays. No one was to lag behind, dash ahead, or breakaway from his group. No one could shoot until ordered. For a first offense, a man's saddle and bridle were cut up. For a second offense, a man's coat was cut to shreds. For a third offense, a man received a public flogging. The strict rules provided protection from rival groups, such as the Lakota Sioux of North Dakota.

During the days of the great hunts, the Metis had become a powerful political force on the prairies. When they asserted their rights to the Red River Settlement, a shoot-out called the Battle of Seven Oaks took place. A British general and 21 men were killed. A monument on Winnipeg's Main Street marks this event. The Metis flag showing the sign of infinity was flown to symbolize the eternal union of two cultures. The Metis nation was established by Louis Riel in 1869, with a provisional government created for the Red River Settlement, in response to the Metis fear of losing their land. The Metis lived on long river-edge lots, but British surveyors wanted to use the 160-acre township system with large squares of land. Riel stopped the surveyors and organized a blockade to stop the Lt. Gov. from arriving. Though the intention was to get the government to deal with the concerns and rights of the French and English Metis in Red River, diplomatic appeals were not acknowledged.

In 1869, Riel seized Fort Garry in the center of the Red River settlement and formed a provisional government to present their demands to Ottawa. But an Orangeman prisoner, Thomas Scott, by all accounts a violent bigot and racist who refused to acknowledge the new government, was sentenced to death and executed after a court martial. Riel approved the execution, which incurred the wrath of Ontario. In another strange link between Loreena McKennitt and her Ontario home, 1400 troops were organized around Stratford and Perth County to settle the Red River rebellion of the Metis. On May 21, Col. Garnet Wolsely (later General Sir Garnet) set out from Collingwood with the 60th British Rifles and Canadian Militia. On June 25th they left Port Arthur for Red River. The march was arduous. But when they arrived, they found that Riel had left the fort. The ragged Metis flag with the infinity design was replaced with the Union Jack. The insurrection of 1869/70 was over.

A year later in 1870, the territory of Manitoba was formed, with the buffalo becoming its emblem. The Manitoba Act seemed a victory for the Metis, since it was based on Riel's documents, but many of its recommendations were ignored. The Metis were promised over a million and a half acres of land. But the government reneged. Riel was twice elected to represent the Metis in the House of Commons, but because of a $5,000 bounty put on his head by the Ontario government, he never took his seat. The Metis moved west into Saskatchewan and Alberta or, like Riel, south to the Dakotas. A second provisional government was established at Batoche in Saskatchewan when Riel returned from his exile. Gabriel Dumont was elected leader of the military forces. A series of battles in 1885, known as the second Northwest Rebellion, took place, with the Metis hurling rocks and nails at the militia. Dumont fled to Montana. Riel was arrested for treason.

Now seen as a father of Confederation and the founder of the province of Manitoba, Riel probably went insane. He thought he was David, prophet of the New World, inventor of the harp, chosen by God to create an independent Metis theocracy. But despite recommendations for leniency from the jury, Riel was executed by the nine-foot drop of a public hanging on November 16, 1885. He was executed a week after the CPR drove the last spike into the railway joining Canada from east to west. After a century, a dignified statue of Riel now stands on the legislature grounds in Winnipeg, while a more avant-garde nude statue stands in St-Boniface. Place Louis Riel, an up-scale hotel in central Winnipeg, features native art in many of the rooms. The owners were inspired by Colombe D'Azur, a hotel on the French Riviera which featured works by Picasso and Matisse.

While the Metis struggled for political independence, they were losing their way of life. The last buffalo hunt was held in 1874. By 1876, the bison was nearly extinct. In 1893, the Canadian government made it unlawful to kill buffalo, but the law was never enforced. By 1900, less than 300 wild buffalo were in Canada. The total population of living bison in North America was set at 541. Buffalo hides were made into leather coats and belts for machines in factories. Buffalo bones were pulverized for refining sugar and ground into fertilizer. A sacred animal was desecrated. Ranchers' cattle ate the grass and drank the water. Sawgrass, sagebrush, and thistle crowded out the bluestem grasses. Carnivores were bad for cattle so ranchers massacred bears, wolves, coyotes, and foxes. Livestock replaced bison. Pronghorn antelope, elk, and bears disappeared. The Plains Indian and Metis ways of life ended. Strangers occupied the hunting grounds.

Perhaps in these stories of place, in these "broken threads" of "time and geography," a young Loreena McKennitt developed compassion for lost ways of life. Of cheated and displaced peoples, who were removed from their lands by treaties or forcibly removed in the face of settlement. Of animals exterminated. Of ethnic groups holding on to their language, customs, and identity. When she later visited Ireland, she would find much of the same.

Yet as the native bands of the Great Plains began to face extinction along with the buffalo, First Nation leaders re-asserted their traditional beliefs. In 1870 and 1890, the visions of Paiute spiritual leaders sparked a movement that linked these nations across North America. Their lands, their peoples, their sources of food, their cultures threatened by settlers, then 'settled' on reservations, with treaties violated, rations cut, supplies delayed, these leaders embraced the hope that by joining together in a sacred, non-violent dance, they could restore what was lost.

A dream came to the prophets to dance, because a dance was the focal point of material culture and highest expression of mystical yearnings. A dance would bring the ghosts to life again and the settlers would disappear. The dance was a vision song for the ways of the grandfathers and the lives of the children. A Paiute prophet in Nevada named Tavibo promised a revival of the old ways. The return of the buffalo and other wild game, the prairie grasses restored to their verdure, the resurrection of the dead, the end of the settlers. With knowledge of sleight of hand, hypnotism, and shaman tricks, his son Wovoka convinced many of his listeners. He returned from deep trances.

He said he had died, visited God, who had given him a message. The dead would return to a new world, as they were in their youth, and the old world would be destroyed. To bring about this new world, people must dance the ghost dance.

Wovoka learned from an almanac of a solar eclipse about to happen on January 1, 1889. He planned a 'death' at this time. Established as a great teacher, a new Messiah (he showed stigmata on his hands and feet and body), his words spread across Nevada into Oregon and the Dakotas, then north to the new provinces of Saskatchewan and Manitoba. Wovoka showed his hat, and inside, as in a crystal ball, were images of paradise: herds of buffalo and horse and grasses.

Wovoka gave specific instructions for the ghost dance. The dance would last four days, which represented the four days and nights of the catastrophe, and on the morning of the fifth, they would bathe in the river. The Sioux of the Dakotas went into a sweat lodge, symbol of renewed life, hung with sweetgrass and tobacco. Following the bathing, faces and bodies were rubbed with sweet grass. Faces were painted with images of the sun, the moon, stars, circles, and crescents. Some faces were painted red, with red, yellow, or blue paint along the line of the hair part. The paint brought about the promise of the vision. The dancers wore eagle, crow, or magpie feathers tied in their hair, near the crown of their heads, to rise above the fiery destruction of the old world. Specially decorated feathers came from people who had been in a trance.

Then they dressed in the ghost shirts and dresses of cotton muslin sewn with sinew and painted with images of eagles, sage hens, magpies, and crows, further decorated with leather fringes and eagle feathers. The medicine men prayed over the shirts, claiming their prayers made the shirts bulletproof. Word had spread to the settler's farms, government agencies, and forts that the natives were planning some kind of war dance.

In the center of the dance ground, a sprouting tree — a pine tree or a cottonwood — another symbol of renewed life, was raised. The tree was decorated with streamers, eagle feathers, claws, antlers, and a flag. At the four corners of the dance ground were placed ceremonial objects: a pipe to the west, an arrow to the north, images of rain, hail, and thunder to the east, and a pipe with a feather attached to the south. These were images of the tribes in each direction.

The dancing started at noon. A mournful chant was sung. Sacred food was passed around. A young woman, representing the Buffalo ghost maiden, brought the pipe and the buffalo, firing arrows into the four directions. The

BUFFALO GHOST DANCE

arrows were retrieved and, along with the bow, attached to the tree. The sacred hoop and hoop sticks were also hung in the tree.

Then all assembled rose to their feet. A line was formed. The chief priest passed the ghost stick, with buffalo horns painted red to form a crescent at the top and with horse tails hanging from the lower end, decorated with beadwork, over their heads. He faced the sun and said a prayer. The medicine pipe was held toward the west, from where the Messiah would come.

The dancers next formed a circle. The brilliant paintings on the ghost shirts and dresses came into view. The dancers turned to the left, placed their hands on the shoulders of the one in front, and walked in the sun circle. They sang a song about returning to the great Father.

At the end of the song, they faced the center. Some cried and wailed. Some stood straight. They asked the Great Spirit to see their loved ones. Some threw dust and dirt over their body, like ashes. Next, they formed a circle, holding hands by intertwining the fingers. A number of ghost dance songs were sung, and all were sad. The singers wept for the lost songs of the earth, for the buffalo that had gone to spirit, for the plains empty of the buffalo.

The ghost dance came last. The left foot led, lifting higher then the right, and plunging forward. The right foot dragged into position, then the left foot raised and plunged forward, advancing as the right came forward to meet it again. Modern circle dancers call this a grapevine step, and done over time, it opens up the energy centers of the body. No drum or rattle was used, and no bells.

Some circles had 300 or 400 hundred dancers. They danced in dust so thick they were hidden from view. They would dance, around and around, for hours, until some broke from the ring, staggering and falling. The priests would approach with eagle feathers, waving them in circles in front of the dancer. Sometimes the dancers would pant and groan and wave their arms and fall forward or back, twitching or quivering. Such a dancer was on a visit to the spirit world and would not be disturbed. Sometimes a hundred people would visit the spirit world at once.

Recovering from such a trance, the dancers acted as if coming out of sleep. They were permitted to take their places among the leaders. They told their stories to the head priest who shouted them to the other dancers. Perhaps one in 10 had a vision. After a rest, the dance was repeated, sometimes three times a day.

On December 29, 1890, members of the Sioux nation in South Dakota planned a ghost dance. Several camps of Sioux had formed as one large camp. This came to the attention of government agencies who sent eight troops of the Seventh Cavalry, a company of scouts, and four Hotchkiss guns to surround the camp and survey the area. The medicine man, Yellow Bird, blew on an eagle bone whistle and told his people not to be afraid and trust in their ghost dance shirts. He stooped to blow dust in the air, which in old times would have been a signal to attack, completed a circle, and sat down. While Yellow Bird was initiating the ghost dance, the soldiers apparently detained a young Native who accidentally discharged his rifle. Immediately, the soldiers with the Hotchkiss guns opened fire upon the teepees with the women and children. These men, of the Seventh Cavalry, General Custer's old outfit whose disaster occurred only 14 years earlier at the Little Big Horn, got a chance for revenge. Bodies of women and children were found as far as two miles away, shot in the back by cavalrymen as they tried to escape. Thirty-one soldiers were killed by their own crossfire.

This massacre at Wounded Knee Creek would have a profound influence on Native rights a century later. Native peoples rediscovered traditional ways. The sacred hoop of the nation. The cycle of seasons. The circle of life. The spiritual images of turtle shell, hawk, crow, and eagle feathers. Sage, sweetgrass, wampum beads. Dream catchers. Medicine pipes. The ceremonial buffalo skull that faces the sweat lodge at the western door. The halo of sundogs in a winter sky. A commitment to personal integrity and non-violence. A passionate concern for social and environmental health. A joining of purpose across political and cultural boundaries. To walk in harmony with the Earth Mother. To allow the teachings of nature to influence our daily existence. The Ghost Dance once again became the way to satisfy a hunger for the values of the Old Ways.

Such hunger is the 'parallel' Loreena McKennitt would find between North American Native and Irish 'old ways', a parallel she brought to bear on composing the *Huron 'Beltane' Fire Dance*, a song that begins with powerful fire dance drumming and chanting, then moves into a Celtic song for Beltane, celebrating the return of life after the long winter. Like the Plains Indians, the Huron band of southern Ontario was decimated by the arrival of European traders and settlers, only two centuries earlier, who brought with them the scourge of small pox. "In the *Huron Beltane Fire Dance*," Loreena McKennitt remarks, "I have tried to recall the reverence for dreams of the North American First Peoples and the early Celts. If there is a recurrent thread which runs through these dreams it is one of yearning toward love, liberty, and integration. Of all the variations of dreams we have, these surely are our parallel dreams." As she reminds us in the liner notes, "beyond the transportation into fantasy, dreams have served as a vehicle through which we have integrated our conscious and subconscious, the real and the surreal, the powerful and the intangible."

7
MULTICULTURALISM

The Native, Anglo-Irish, French, and Metis were not the only cultural groups on the prairie horizon. With the arrival of the railway, they were joined by immigrants from Western and Eastern Europe, some recruited by the government to settle the west, some arriving as refugees like the Mennonites, looking for the promised land. Loreena McKennitt has said that her chief musical influence as a child was not Irish or Celtic but Mennonite. "I feel that my musical influence really came from that extended German Mennonite community, and the festivals and operettas," she told Nick Krewen in *Canadian Musician*.

Following the Riel years, the culture of southern Manitoba changed with the arrival of settlers from Western and Eastern Europe, including the German Mennonites who settled west of the Red River. One culture replaced another. Natives recognize shared or communal territorial rights — historic rights, fishing rights, and scared places. These ideas were foreign to the new settlers' sense of territoriality and property ownership. Farmers occupied what was once the domain of hunters. Each wave of settlers brought new imprints. Tree planting and crop growing transformed the prairie landscape. Teepee and sod houses gave way to houses of pre-cut lumber brought by English settlers from Ontario, standard L, T, and A-shaped structures. The English tried to reproduce the country life with large homes. Prosperous families brought in highly decorated Victoria structures with gingerbread ornamentation. Settlers from Western and Eastern Europe built log buildings with plastered walls, and steeply pitched gables, some with thatch.

Being ethnic did not preclude being Canadian. Immigrants on the prairie provinces invented the 'multicultural mosaic' before it became government policy. The railroads recruited immigrants from Europe (and by-passed the federal Department of Immigration and Colonization) to do pick and shovel work, harvest grain, and work on farms bought on time from the same rail companies. The desire for cheap labor and wide open immigration policies meant large numbers of arrivals, often unskilled labor (called navvies) from eastern and central Europe (described as stalwart peasants in sheep skin coats), a polyglot population that set the prairie provinces apart from the rest of English and French Canada. Ethnic identities were relocated and reconstructed on the Canadian prairie. Ethic minorities persisted, in part because of rural isolation in the early years. They settled in blocks. Some historians suggest there was no clearly defined Canadian identity to assimilate to, except that of oppression and discrimination by British Canadians who reinforced nationalist consciousness.

The immigrant group that most changed the culture of the prairies was the Mennonites, who found the survey of land and the plan of small towns alien. The Red River colonists settled on long river front lots, like the St Lawrence River 'seigneur' system, but the survey of the prairies was based on a precisely measured North-South-East-West grid that imposed a geometric logic on natural features, no matter what the terrain. It also established crossroads, the sites of many prairie towns, a town plan reinforced by the arrival of the railroad. Streets were exactly the length of the rail siding. A town or village became a trading center that gave the illusion of success with false fronts.

Of the various groups who arrived in the years between 1870 and 1920 during the great settlement of the Canadian prairies, only the Mennonites objected to the square sector, which had been a contentious issue in the Riel resistance, but for a different reason. Their farm co-operative villages were unique on North America. A dozen or more farmers lived in a 'street village' and land around them was distributed into large fields according to the quality of soil, and further subdivided into long narrow strips. Each farmer was assigned a strip in each of the fields, thus getting an equitable share of both the rich and the poor land. The village of Reinhard, near Morden, was such a street village. Each farm had a doddy house, barns, stables, silos, chicken coops, corncribs, smoke house. Young girls made button boxes.

As Mennonite author Andreas Schroeder has suggested, "for sheer epic drama across four-and-a-half centuries, five continents, over forty countries, fleeing vicious persecution, utopian enticements, breached promises, and their own prophets, few histories can match the story of the Mennonite people." Their modern history begins in 1525 with the Anabaptist movement in Zurich, Switzerland. A Dutch Catholic priest named Menno Simons converted to Anabaptism in 1536 and soon became a prominent promoter of the new faith. Menno's followers came to be known as Mennonites, and since then 'Mennonite' has become a generic term applied to all evangelical Anabaptists. This new faith talked about a simple non-worldly lifestyle that rejected pride, violence, and state-sanctioned religion. It promoted pacifism and community service. And unlike the other religious expressions of the day, Anabaptism emphasized a direct personal relationship with God that did not depend on priests and organized church structure. Most of all, this new faith rejected the power of the state and of a state church. Anabaptists believed people should choose their religion when ready as adults; hence the Anabaptist practice of adult baptism.

For the followers of this new faith, there was no worse a time than the 1550s to be an Anabaptist. Between 2,000 and 4,000 Mennonites were tortured, beheaded, or buried alive by the Inquisition. After the Protestant Reformation, persecution drove the early members underground and eventually scattered them world wide. German and Dutch Mennonites fled to present day Poland and the Ukraine to establish rural communities. The state's increasing demand that Russian be taught in their schools, coupled with the threat of military conscription and government reform programs that would nationalize their farms, prompted 7,000 Mennonites to leave the Ukraine in the 1870s and settle in Southwestern Ontario near Stratford and in southern Manitoba near Morden. Some came by Conestoga wagon (named after the Conestoga River in Lancaster County, Pennsylvania), covered wagons that became known as 'prairie schooners'.

The Mennonites were enticed to Canada with a 'hamlet clause' which allowed them to live in a village away from their land. Canada was also more generous towards block settlements by ethnic groups. The Icelanders created their own 'Republic of New Iceland', with a constitution and elected government on the shores of Lake Winnipeg. The Canadian government promised to allow the Mennonites to run their own schools in exchange for their agricultural skills. This arrangement did not last 50 years, however. At the end of the First World War with anti-German sentiment strong, the government tried to enforce English-language education for the Mennonites, but many Mennonites refused to send their children to public schools staffed by English-speaking teachers. Many were jailed or fined. In the 1920s, 7,000 of the most conservative members loaded their families and farm gear onto railway boxcars and headed for Mexico or Paraguay, though many returned. Now accepted into the Canadian community and indeed revered by many fellow Canadians for their independent spirit and apparently simple life-style, the Mennonites have preserved their 'old ways'.

The Mennonites trace their ancestry to the early Celts, the Boii tribes of the Po River valley in Italy, and lay claim to the invention of iron, the alphabet, and coined money. A hundred or more tribes of Boii were part of the pan-Celtic migration from Eastern Europe. Bohemian (from the land of the Boii) culture developed along the Danube in part of what is now the Czech Republic and Slovakia. As a new culture in Europe, they brought the science of metallurgy, including the casting of bronze and making of iron, a metal known in India and China. They practiced cremation and urn burial and most likely invented the wagon and horse harness. Their migrations looking for new habitations in the iron culture transformed Europe. In Italy, they established the cities of Milan and Bologna. Living on the richest farmland in Italy, they were good farmers, experts in animal husbandry. With the Po River valley as a means of access to northern Europe, they would travel into France, Switzerland, Belgium, England, and Ireland. Known for their fierceness in battle, they disliked central government and created the first democratic state in Europe. For over a thousand years they resisted the governing power of the Roman Empire and then the Catholic Church. During the Inquisition and the Protestant Reformation, they were persecuted relentlessly not only for their religious views, but also for their refusal to bear arms or pay taxes. They took up refuge in small valleys and deep forests in Switzerland, forming three groups, the Amish, the Hutterites, and the Mennonites. The politics of central Europe led to a hundreds of years of wandering for the Mennonites that would end up in the prosperous agricultural country of rural Ontario and Manitoba.

For the Mennonites, the pine tree became the central symbol of their culture. Tree of life. Tree of peace. Tree that marks the turning point of the sun, the tree whose amber can heal. When the pine sap runs on the night of the full moon, thick and clear, it can be collected on the point of a knife and put in a little jar. The Mennonites treasure amber, the fossil form of pine resin. Most of the world's amber came from Baltic Europe or Scandinavia. In ancient times, amber occurred in such quantities that it was considered a fuel. The scent was magical and healing. An amber cult formed, with the image of amber as a sun with rays. The Greeks declared amber had a soul. After the Crusades, unemployed soldiers known as Teutonic knights monopolized the amber trade. Rights were cruelly enforced for over 500 years. Pine seedlings — pale, soft, gentle green — were carried by Mennonites as part of their folk wisdom during their migrations, and Mennonites carried amber beads with them to Manitoba and Ontario.

The Mennonites have an old awareness of their relationship to the natural world. They have charms for blessing a field, for healing a burn, for curing a rash, for scolding trees that don't bear fruit, and burying stones at the root of plum trees to ensure strong fruit. Like the Celts, they carry with them centuries of herbal and healing lore. A good herbalist could find the healing herbs that grow in abundance at the edge of wood-lots: mandrake, milkweed, rhubarb root, skullcap, cow clover, dandelion. Mistletoe is a healing plant because it grows without touching the earth from a seed lodged under the bark. The Druids cut it with a golden sickle. A divining rod, symbol of unity and diversity, is burned after its work is done. Ontario Mennonites still leave 'fire letters', spells written on paper, hidden in new barns to ensure they will not be destroyed by fire.

The Mennonites also have a long folk music history. The Mennonite hymnal, the *Ausband*, is the oldest Christian hymn-book known. First published in 1564, the songs are ancient, some written by men who died from persecution centuries earlier, symbol of a never-to-be-forgotten past and a testament to the struggle to find freedom to worship. One melody is known to be 1,100 years old. The hymns are simple, set to peasant folk-tunes, which some might call primitive. They were written in an age when people did not need to feel dominated or organized to preserve an identity. *The Martyr's Mirror* is an enormous book over 1,100 pages of history, full of tales of wandering and persecution. It was the largest book published in North America before the 18th century.

These folk songs and hymns are long narratives written by people in order to preserve their heritage. Some are so long they cannot be sung at a single service. Some have 500 lines, 75 stanzas. The complete book is called the *Thick Book*. Younger people have an abridged version, the *Thin Book*. Songs of martyrdom, of courage, endurance, conviction, and hope are created out of a thousand years of persecution for nonconformity. The Mennonites have an awareness of the homeless, hungry, ill-clad, orphaned, grief stricken. The Mennonites created the No Resistance Relief organization. The hymns retrieve a time by memory, the old ways. Ancient methods of divining. Inherited wisdom of charming, or healing with herbs and amulets that have been traced back to India.

From Morden, Loreena McKennitt carried these multicultural treasures to Winnipeg where she became part of a rich folk music movement there. In Mennonite culture and folk music, Loreena McKennitt had found another Celtic parallel, a thread she would pick up in the 1990s while exploring the ancient Celtic presence in Italy, Spain, North Africa, Asia Minor, and beyond. Today information on her quinlanroad.com website is available in multiple languages — Greek, Turkce, Francais, Deutsch, Nederlands, Italiano, Espanol, Portugues, Polske, Magyar, Cestina, Romaneste, and Svenska.

8

FROSTBITTEN FOLK

As the main Canadian city between Toronto and Vancouver in the early 20th century and a railroad center for grain and livestock shipments, the city of Winnipeg prospered. By 1919 the city had 21 merchant millionaires who had traveled to concerts in Toronto or Montreal or Europe. They knew art and music. Aspiring to cosmopolitanism, they forced culture into existence in Winnipeg. The first professional ballet company, the Royal Winnipeg Ballet, was founded in 1939. (Humorist Eric Nicol suggests they had to jump around to keep warm.) The Contemporary Dancers, one of Canada's first modern dance companies, was founded in 1964. When Loreena McKennitt moved to Winnipeg, art patrons could also attend the Winnipeg Symphony Orchestra, the Manitoba Theater Center, the activist Popular Theater Alliance of Manitoba, and the Manitoba Opera. Cultural and literary magazines like *Border Crossings* and *Prairie Fire* stimulated provocative discussions of prairie art and published new poetry and fiction by prairie artists. Artistically, Winnipeg had developed a tradition of excellence that made it possible for young McKennitt to become grounded in her art as she discovered the richness of Celtic music.

In this provincial capital, the Legislature building is located the middle of the city, topped by a golden boy, with murals and statuary inside and out, an impressive structure created by architects from Europe, the USA, and Canada. At the foot of an impressive staircase, quarried from local marble, are two golden life-size statues of the vanished bison of Manitoba designed by sculptor Georges Gardes of Paris.

Since the time of the 'General Strike' in 1919, Winnipeg has been a hotbed of Canadian populist politics. The largest and best-known strike action ever to take place in Canada was much more than a modest attempt at collective bargaining. It was, as *The New York Times* reported in six editorials, "the attempt at revolution" in Canada. In the later years of the First World War, in the wake of the Russian Revolution and the Irish Easter Uprising, inflation outstripped wages. Union activity grew. In the conflict between labor and capital, strike activity reached new heights. A violent five-week event, now called the Winnipeg General Strike of 1919, has been called by partisans Canada's 'Alamo', a revolutionary bid to destroy Western civilization.

During the late 19th-century, the economy in southern Manitoba was changing. The harsh prairie climate had proven, oddly enough, to be ideal for the growing Red Fife wheat which was in great demand in Europe and Britain. Developments in farm machinery — threshers, plows, tractors, self-binding reapers — helped the prairie economy change from fur trade to dry land farming. The completion of the CPR in 1885 allowed Canadian transport to the Great Lakes and then Europe. During the next 25 years, millions of acres of prairie land were cultivated and Canadian wheat exports soared. Grain elevators were erected every 30 miles, surrounded by towns and villages. When the CPR decided to cross the Red River at Winnipeg, the city became the hub of the west. By 1914, the Grain Exchange was the largest in North America. City officials vowed to make Winnipeg as influential as Chicago.

With these economic changes came social consequences. As a railway center, site of the Dominion Land Office and the Federal Immigration building, Winnipeg was the first stopping place for immigrants. In 1870, the Metis had represented 80% of the population. By 1884, the population was 84% Ango-Saxon. By 1921, immigrants from Europe reduced that to 67%. As a central clearinghouse for labor, unions were formed early in Winnipeg's history. In 1906, motor men and coachmen at the Winnipeg Electric Railway Company walked off the job. Strikebreakers were brought in. After two days of violence, the mayor called in the Canadian Mounted Rifles to restore order. Troops with machine guns were posted at major intersections to quell crowds.

By 1909, Manitoba grain growers, resisting federal tariffs and railway gain elevator monopolies, alleging price fixing and cheating on weights and grades, joined the unrest. They pressed for tariff reductions, control of grain marketing, political reform, and nationalization of the railways. The changes also included better schools and the vote for women.

On May 15, 1919, metal and construction workers struck for the formation of a union and higher wages. In support, half of Winnipeg's labor force, over 35,000 workers, accompanied by many unemployed soldiers newly returned from the European front, walked off the job. Women telephone operators were the first to strike in support. The Winnipeg Citizen's Committee of One Thousand, all local business and industrial leaders, believed they were fighting for Canada and the Canadian way of life. But the federal government, in the grip of a 'Red' scare and the fear of Bolshevism, saw a revolution in the making. Immigrants were suspect. The army was put on standby. In Ottawa, Arthur Meighan, Minister of the Interior, ordered in police and army reinforcements.

On the fifth and most dramatic week of the strike came the incident of Bloody Saturday. Angry strikers burned a streetcar. A fight broke out. In ten minutes of fighting, a crowd of 5,000 to 6,000 war veterans, soldiers, and strikers confronted mounted police. The Royal North West Mounted Police and Special Constables made two charges. In the first, they swung bats or batons. When they reached the end of the street, they exchanged the bats for firearms. On the second charge, three volleys were fired. Some say a Mountie was pulled from his horse, which provoked shots. Historians estimate there were 27 casualties. Two strikers died, dozens wounded. For the next five days militia with machine guns mounted on automobiles patrolled the streets.

The government deported the foreign-born strike leaders. Arthur Meighan became Prime Minister. Born in St Mary's, Ontario, his grandson is on the board of governors of the Stratford Festival, and the gardens in front of the main lobby are named in memory of Meighan. Like the displacement of the Metis and the execution of Riel, the Winnipeg Strike led to 75 years of silence. Only in 1994 was a plaque commemorating the strike placed at the Manitoba Legislature Building.

But the strike led to the formation of two Canadian institutions, the Royal Canadian Mounted Police and J.S. Wordsworth's CCF party that evolved into the New Democratic Party. With the election of the New Democratic Party in 1969 after years of conservative rule, the arts in Manitoba and Winnipeg were further fostered. Expo 67, Canada's national centennial celebration, was a fresh memory. NDP support came from working class and non-British Canadians, as well as new forces in Canadian politics: First Nation's peoples, recent immigrants, and working women. The NDP was grass roots and multicultural, advocating extensive social welfare programs and experiments in economic development, with a clear cultural ideology. Delegates from Manitoba convinced the Federal Liberal government of Pierre Trudeau of the need for a multicultural policy for the nation. Manitoba's immigration population changed. Between 1921 and 1962, the combined British and French population declined from 64% to 52%, and others increased from 36% to 48%. To the founding British, Irish, French, Jewish, Ukrainian, and Mennonite communities were added Filipino, West Indian, and Vietnamese populations. The Cree, Ojibwa, and Metis communities worked hard and publicly to bring their concerns to have their rights as indigenous peoples recognized.

Manitoba's developing cultural community insisted the government include a new portfolio, a Ministry of Culture, Heritage, and Recreation, including an Arts Council. Canada's City on the Red River adopted the motto "Cultural Oasis" that captured the soul of the place. During Loreena McKennitt's Winnipeg years, new theater companies included The Warehouse and Prairie Theater Exchange. New music was heard from the Manitoba Chamber Orchestra, Winnipeg Chamber Music Society, Virtuosi, and Music Barok consort series. The New Music Festival in January offers contemporary classical music, including neo-romanticists, twelve-tone serialists, and composers like Alexina Louie who incorporate world music. Thousands of native peoples moved to Winnipeg from the reserves, giving this multicultural oasis one of the largest aboriginal populations of any city in Canada. First Nation's theaters such as Red Roots reenacted injustice at trials and treaty signings. Heritage Proud would carry on traditional singing, dancing, and drumming, and Prairie Buffalo would do plays on historic themes. Other ethnic groups — French, Poles, Ukrainians, Italians, Filipinos, Germans, and West Indians, the latest immigrants from Central America, Somalia, Ethiopia, Eritrea — have been encouraged to start their own arts organizations and festivals. Since 1970, an annual two-week festival called Folklorama has celebrated the ethnic heritage of Manitoba. This two-week celebration in August takes place in more than 40 pavilions, operating on staggered schedules. But no event is more important in the cultural life of the city than the Winnipeg Folk Festival, which officially began in 1974 as a modest celebration of the city's centenary but has its true origin in the 'folk' revolt of the Winnipeg Strike.

The impact of cultural colonialism on Canadian artists created a "frostbite at the roots of the imagination," Professor Northrop Frye once said. Composer R. Murray Schafer, noting how musical idioms and national pride went together, complained in 1961 that musicians had scarcely begun to build Canada into cultural entity by writing truly Canadian music. Even indigenous folk songs like *Alouette* and *Squid Jiggin' Ground* had the inherent problems of metrical similarity and repeated motifs. Lacking form, these songs were as two dimensional as wallpaper. Marius Barbeau, the director of the faculty of music at University of Toronto, also expressed doubts about the folk song in Canada during the same years. "The folk music of Canada — native or adventitious — is truly gasping for breath, presumably its last," he claimed during the early 1960s. In *A History of Music in Canada*, Helmut Kallman argued that the post Industrial Revolution society had changed music from a rural to an urban setting. "Two musical cultures began to exist side by side: the declining culture of folk music and the rising culture of concert and 'popular' music. They were almost mutually exclusive. Folk music was relegated to isolated regions, while musicians and amateurs in the city tend to ignore it as something trivial and primitive."

But even while these music critics were decrying the limits of the Canadian musical imagination and sounding the death knell for folk music, young musicians were discovering their roots, so to speak. A new Canadian folk idiom began to be heard during the years Loreena McKennitt was growing up on the prairies in the lyrics and music of Ian Tyson and Sylvia Fricker, Gordon Lightfoot, Bonnie Dobson, Buffy Sainte-Marie, Joni Mitchell, Neil Young, Leonard Cohen, Bruce Cockburn, Valdy, and the Travellers, who unearthed Canada's obscure folk song heritage.

Never before had music meant so much to a generation as it did in the 1960s when a performer, an instrument, and the natural talk of people could evoke in an audience the ferment of a revival meeting. The folksinger stood for ideals. Moving away from materialism, folk singers could be political and mystical. Meeting in an informal clubs above a woodworking shop on 'Main Street' or in the basement beneath the clothing store, 'folkies' listened to Woodie Guthrie, Pete Seeger, Peter, Paul, and Mary, Simon & Garfunkel, Phil Ochs, Pete Seeger, Joan Baez, and Bob Dylan, learning the mechanics of a song, exploring the creative process, and forming a communal bond based on shared social ideals and spiritual aspirations.

Folk music represented a counter-cultural attitude. On August 9, 1974, Richard Nixon resigned as President of the United States. In Winnipeg, a 24-year-old radio producer and banjo player, with a radical left-leaning political attitude, looked over a field in Birds Hill Park, about 10 kilometers north of the city, at the first Winnipeg Folk Festival. Michael Podolak and his partner Colin Gorries had spent the previous months organizing a free folk festival to mark Winnipeg's centenary. They obtained $16,000 from CBC Radio's folk music show and persuaded reluctant civic officials to back the project, boasting that 30,000 people would attend. That first evening, not quite 1,100 arrived to see a lineup that included Bruce Cockburn, Leon Redbone, Bukka White, and the String Band. By the end of that weekend, the festival had attracted over 12,000. Leon Redbone received a twenty-minute standing ovation. Emcee Peter Gzowski promised to donate his fee to help them turn the one-time only show into an annual event. The Winnipeg Folk Festival is now the largest in North America. From Thursday afternoon to Sunday closing, the Festival attracts 40,000 fans. With over 100 acts and 150 hours of music, concert-goers need to be selective. A prairie institution, it has outlasted Ontario's Mariposa, the grandmother of folk festivals, inspiring successful folk festivals throughout Canada, including Edmonton, Vancouver, Owen Sound, and Calgary.

Podolak traces the populist spirit of the festival to his years as a young Trotskyite. A central theme of the festival has been the recovery of ethnic memory and history as a vital part of human identity. Musicians could explore the runes and ancient rhymes to invoke the psychic depths and magical strains that post-industrial men had forgotten. Another theme was the creative role of women in these cultures. Pioneer men brought a controlling will, pioneer women endured. In the small plain towns of the prairie provinces, women slowly became aware of their identities and then their rights. The women covered a wide range of folk styles from rural ballads to songs of industrial action and political protest, expressing the themes of alienation and deprivation with a more nervous sensitivity. When they protested against industry, they reasserted instinctual values. The Winnipeg Folk Festival was fertile ground to appeal for women's rights, with an audience that would support women who in their turn were developing their own unique visions.

Through the years, the festival has become increasingly multicultural, with a shift towards the emerging genre of 'world music'. Musicians began to explore neglected historical periods, especially meaningful outspoken times, the 13th and 14th century, the dances of the Sufi mystics inspired by Jalal al-Din Rumi, the texts of Tagore and Zoroaster, the Tibetan Book of the Dead. The new music was a fusion of secular and religious, medieval and modern. Sponsored by successful musicians like Peter Gabriel and Sting, the world music movement took hold in late 1970s and early 1980s.

In 1982 Gabriel sponsored the first world music concert, WOMAD (World of Music, Arts, and Dance). Someone said it sounded like a drug for menstrual cramps, and years later it was still thought by some to be a women's music festival. Like Mickey Hart of the Grateful Dead, Gabriel had been gathering tapes of music from around the world, music from Bali, music by Australian aborigines. Bands as varied as the Police, Talking Heads, and Brian Eno's Roxy Music had been listening to sounds far beyond the scope of most pop groups. With the help of local producers in Bath, England, Gabriel signed the Sabri brothers from Pakistan, masters of Qawwali, and the master drummers of Burundi, Pakistani peasant farmers, whose music had already appeared on Joni Mitchell's *The Hissing of Summer Lawns*. The three-day WOMAD festival featured 300 performers from 21 countries, with exhibitions, lectures, films, and workshops. The four stages ran concerts concurrently, with wide range of music from traditional folk to hi-tech electronic music. Though the first concert was a financial disaster, the mammoth cultural achievement provided the world with a glimpse of different musical styles whose influence was to be immense. Following his genius for world music, Gabriel created Real World Studios where artists from around the globe, including Loreena McKennitt, could co-create in a stimulating environment. He also set the pattern for a new kind of folk festival which Mitch Podolak's successor, Rosalie Goldstein, emulated back in Winnipeg.

So the ears were ready for a wider array of styles — acoustic, young, electric, country, world beat, and crossover. K.D. Lang and the Reclines stretched the idea of country and folk. Brazilian pianist Tanya Maria was among the first to cross-pollinate bossa nova, samba, salsa, and the sophisticated jazz stylings of Chick Corea, Bill Evans, and McCoy Tyner. Audiences at the festival could find acts ranging from Appalachian songwriter Hazel Dinkum to new wave punk polka group Brave Combo who did polka versions of The Doors' *People Are Strange*. A young and nervous Jane Siberry was billed with country star Lyle Lovett on the program, along with punk vulgarians Mojo Mixon and African choir Ladysmith Black Mambaso. Ian Tyson, traditional jigs and reels from Cape Breton, the urban rock of Christine Lavoir, Bonnie Raitt, cowboy acts like Riders in the Sky, Jerry Jeff Walker, the raga boogie of sitarist Ashmin Batish, the blend of African tradition and modern technology of Philip Tabane. Ali Farker Toure, the guitarist from Mali, debuted with hypnotic string work reminiscent of Delta blues guitarist John Lee Hooker. He later co-wrote an album with Ry Cooder. Wade Hensworth, Kate and Anna McGarrigle, and native dancers. Roksnoaski from Kazakstan, the avant garde drummer David Moss, Bebe Fleck and the Flecktones fusion band. The dub poetry polemics of Lillian Allen, a rock set by Winnipeg's Crash Test Dummies, the Caribbean influenced pop of Lorraine Segato and Big Jump. Clifton Chenier and the Red Hot Louisiana Band. The bluster of The BeatFarer's resident vulgarian, Country Dick Montana. The sprightly inventive blend of African tradition and modern technology of Philip Tabane and Malambo.

The backbone of the festival remained in its workshops, impromptu jam sessions that lasted till dawn, lectures on such things as The Wind Instruments of Latin America, or explanatory workshops that explained the folk music link between Minnesota, Manitoba, and Chicago. A stroll through the site might reveal a harmony workshop with Fountain, country duo Bell and Shore, and the slyly amusing Celtic Elvis. Over there was a political song-writing workshop with Salteaux Indian singer Sangoose and Stephen Fearing, a writing workshop with Jane Siberry, and Bill Henderson (former guitarist of Chilliwack), and an unlikely jam between sitarist Ashwin Batish and Loreena McKennitt.

The sounds and attitudes Rosalie Goldstein brought to the festival would appear in time in the music of Loreena McKennitt. Multicultural, open minded, inclusive, generous, reverent. The influence of world music on the folk festival transformed the events from an act of social protest to an act of religious pilgrimage, with swaying, hand-clapping, and the hush of a service. The mood song replaced the message song, the prayer replaced the protest. When words are unimportant, the music becomes anti-intellectual, spiritual. The artist is the clergy. By some of her Winnipeg fans, Loreena McKennitt became beatified as Our Lady, the Prairie Madonna.

In the Winnipeg folk world, Loreena McKennitt had been exposed to the first wave of this world sound in the late 1970s revival of traditional Celtic music. "After I heard it in the folk clubs, I felt I had to go to Ireland and hear it in its natural form," she told Nick Krewen in *Canadian Musician*. Loreena was restless. She had to leave Manitoba in search of her ancestral roots. "North Americans," she once told *Inside Borders* "having come from a whole different part of the world, feel a less strong connection to their roots, and subsequently people want to go back to where their family came from, whether it was Ireland or Scotland or Germany. The culture I was raised in was a very prairie kind of culture. There wasn't Middle Eastern music or Celtic music around the house. I first became exposed to Celtic music in Winnipeg.... Then began the process of learning, going to Ireland, immersing myself in the natural environment that this music sprang from, and also acquiring instruments that would allow me to participate and explore my own connection with it. I want to paint my own personal musical document." And so she would.

celtic
CROSSROADS

1
THE CALLING OF THE HARP

"When I went to Winnipeg," Loreena McKennitt told *Canadian Musician*, "I took my grade 12 in piano and from then until I moved to Stratford I was part of a folk club. We'd get together every Sunday and a number of the members there were from Ireland. That was really the first time I was exposed to Celtic music. They brought their recordings, and I started to tap into The Bothy Band, Planxty, Steeleye Span, and Alan Stivell." As she added in *Folk Harp Journal*, "That was when I was first exposed to music from the British Isles and I was smitten by it. I maintain it chose me."

Soon after moving to Stratford, Ontario in 1981, Loreena McKennitt set out on her first pilgrimage to her ancestral home. The McKennitt family had emigrated from County Donegal in the 1830s, and her mother's family (Dickey) from Belfast. But Loreena was looking for something more than parish records and gravestones for a family tree. Guided by a folksinger friend, she contacted John Moriarty, a west county Irishman who had taught English and declaimed poetry at the University of Manitoba in Winnipeg, the first to have shoulder-length hair. He had a passion for poetry and performance, especially Yeats and Hopkins. Through Moriarty's brother, she discovered that John had left the university to become a gardener at one of the Guinness estates in Co. Kildare. A short visit turned into several memorable weeks which Loreena fondly recalled in *Saturday Night* magazine. "It's beautiful country," she noted, "horse country. We arrive at John's abode and he comes in with a mad rush of hair. We had tea in the living room. We sat and we started to talk. He was madly in love with this woman, Eileen, from the west coast. The relationship had just broken up. He was just in a state of very serious grief. We'd sit up well into the middle of the night, talking about relationships and life and the whole thing.... I was on this mattress in the living room next to an enormous monastery table piled high with books. There was a piano there, and sometimes I would get up an play it, and I would hear him upstairs, sobbing his heart out. It was very intense."

In Moriarity's melancholy, Loreena had found the romantic world of Irish poetry, and while traveling along the west coast, taking in the sites of Country Clare and the Cliffs of Moher, she discovered in Doolin the hidden world of traditional Irish music, the object of her quest. In *Herstory 1992*, Loreena explained that her aim in traveling to Ireland had been "to track down the music not only in an historical sense, but to find the many instances where it still exists in a very living and informal way, often in a pub over a pint with a fiddle, whistle, or guitar." At the age of 24, Loreena McKennitt was born again into her ancestral culture. Within a year she found her Irish harp at a shop in England and began to compose music for W.B. Yeats' poem *The Stolen Child*, which she would record on her first album, ELEMENTAL.

Nobel laureate Seamus Heaney calls such a search an inner immigration, but because we cannot return to the origins of a culture, the traditional ways must be transformed to avoid becoming effete nostalgia. In James Joyce's in *Portrait of an Artist as a Young Man*, Stephen Daedulus leaves Ireland, paradoxically, to renew his Irishness — "to forge in the smithy of my soul the uncreated conscience of my race." As McKennitt herself would recognize in *Rhythm Music Magazine*, "I didn't buy into the conventional formula. I didn't want to be trapped re-articulating a genre that had been thoroughly mined." Even as she was transforming traditional Irish music into a new expression, she paid homage to the Celtic artists who made this possible by reviving the old ways, grand artists like Tommy Peoples and Alan Stivell, among others who were instrumental in creating a Celtic renaissance during the last quarter of the 20th century that shows no sign of falling back into a dark age.

The instrument that led Loreena McKennitt on her Celtic quest was the mystical harp of Breton artist Alan Stivell. "The whole sound of Celtic music becomes a vehicle to pursue history in a way I could never have imagined," says Loreena McKennitt, who first heard the ethereal sound of the Celtic harp on Stivell's *Renaissance de la harp Celtique* in 1975. As she told a reporter for *Dirty Linen*, "there's a versatility to the harp and a poetic sound about it that's gentle and has a lot of articulation, and can be quite dynamic. You can go from being very subtle to being very dramatic with it. A lot of these things are hard to explain. It's like trying to explain what your favorite color is and why. There are a lot of mystic things about it. In a way, I'm better to keep that mystery because I'm fearful it's a human weakness to probe into the mysteries of life so one can manipulate them to our own agenda." In *Herstory 1992*, Loreena added, "It was Alan Stivell's recordings of the Celtic harp that I was instinctively drawn to, the imagery evoked by the harp, whistle, cello and sound of the ocean which swept me to a time in the past and pulled at my primitive heart strings." For Loreena McKennitt, the harp became more than a musical instrument, taking on a philosophical and spiritual dimension, as she explained in *Folk Harp Journal*. "I'm less interested in the traditional kind of replication of the harp music. I feel that territory is so well covered by many other people who do it better justice than I would. Where my focus is, is really using the harp as the primary instrument that I play on, but also as a musical and philosophical focus point." In doing so she was following the lead of Alan Stivell.

Alan Stivell is the creator of modern Breton music and a passionate advocate for Breton, that province of France that juts out in the ocean towards England. Music is not divorced from politics in Stivell's world; it is the heartbeat. The Bretons were Celtic peoples who settled on the continent, but lost their independence to France. The harp was abandoned along with the language of the Breton culture, lost to the aristocracy and the French court. Like the Irish language, the Celtic language in Brittany remains as a trace. Some people have two names, one Celtic and one in the dominant national language, English or French. Stivell's father sought to revive the Celtic harp and built one for his son. Alan was the first man in four centuries to make the Breton harp sing again. His album, *The Renaissance of the Celtic Harp*, was responsible for bringing worldwide interest in the instrument. His style is drawn from classical and traditional motifs of the Celtic countries with modern harmonies.

Stivell explored music from the Celtic outposts — Scotland, Brittany, Ireland, Wales, and Isle of Man. He draws heavily upon the traditional songs and singing styles of Brittany. He aspires to an old tradition of singing that the Bretons call *lanteur engage*, or 'engaged singing'. In other words, protest songs — the words express Breton nationality. The 250-year-old tradition includes the writing and circulation of broadsides. Many songs are drawn from the influential 19th-century nationalistic folksong collections. Glorious moments in

Breton history and struggles against the French are celebrated in strong feelings towards the homeland and against those who try to colonize it. Breton music includes call and response (*ken hadiskan*) between two singers, which provides a liveliness necessary for dancing. Like row row row your boat, rounds have different melodic design, intensity, and diminishing of phrases, solos, and unison passages. Western singing, by comparison, is either solo or harmony. Stivell speculates this style of music has links to the long vanished past, which he calls a pan-Celtic age. He claims the purely Celtic style is the oldest in Europe, related only to Irish singing and Scottish *piobrached*, which in turn derives from the Celtic 'Grand Epoque' form 500 BC to 1200 AD and was influenced by the music of India.

Alan Stivell's influence on Loreena McKennitt is enormous. Like McKennitt, Stivell incorporates environmentalist and nationalist issues into his songs; like McKennitt, he draws parallels between native Celts and Native Americans. In *Dirty Linen*, Loreena McKennitt confided, "to be a catalyst, that's one of my life's objectives. I've been influenced by many people who in their turn have been catalysts. Alan Stivell is a good example."

The harp Loreena McKennitt found in a small shop across the street from a hospital in London was a Troubadour Lever, built by Chicago-based Lyon & Healy Co. The design dates from about 1877, when an American named George Durke began work on a new type of double action harp for the Lyon & Healy. They began manufacturing this model in 1889. About 95% of the hand made harps are still playing. Since 1959, the autograph of the maker is inside the body, on the underside of the soundboard. The harp, despite its gentle appearance, is rugged, easy to adjust, built economically as a student instrument for classical harpists, able to withstand long journeys, truck rides, and climate changes. The 19th-century model has five major parts and about 2,000 minor ones. A simple strumming shimmers the imagination.

"I have a smaller Celtic harp," Loreena told *Folk Harp Journal*, "like a lap harp, but it's more suitable for very period pieces and instrumental pieces. I find the joy of the Troubadour harp is that it has a whole bottom end section which doesn't interfere with the pitch where my voice is resting at." Loreena plays 'side-saddle' to accommodate her singing. "It's a very good position to sing in. I really need to sit up straight to get the full wind of it in the diaphragm." While she typically composes on the piano, occasionally she picks up the harp, as she did for *Stolen Child*. "On *Stolen Child*, when I wrote that piece I only had the harp. I was in England. I was actually asked to set a Yeats poem to music, so I wrote that piece on the harp." When asked if she has ever researched the history of the Celtic harp, Loreena deferred. "No, no I haven't. I would say that most harp players know far more about the structure, the history, and the nuances of the instrument than I do." Nevertheless, she sees herself participating in the history of the harp, becoming involved in the renaissance of the bardic tradition. "I feel that in the bardic tradition there were people who brought information, entertainment and so on to the people. They became a vehicle through which that could pass ... it's a form of the media ... what we've done is that we've 'ghettoized' what we now call the arts ... whereas they used to exist in a much more integrated and much broader social level.... Now the media has become radio, television, or newspapers ... and by the mere nature of doing that, we've excluded all the other functions that music and theater and storytelling and so on evolved over the centuries. Again, I feel that it's very vital to our own identity and our ability to address and deal with certain social problems and certain social circumstances, and just simply establish a sense of identity, cultural identity."

The harp, the bardic tradition, and Celtic culture are inseparable, as McKennitt suggests, almost taking on a cosmic significance. As far back in time as we care to go, music and poetry have been associated. The chief poet had an honored place at his master's table while an official known as a *reacaire* recited his poetry to the accompaniment of a harp. In Greek mythology, Hermes invented the lyre and the flute. The harp accompanies the great storytellers, the bards like Homer. Stories explain, explore, expand, and create their own realities. Though the harp looks and sounds delicate, this complex and tough instrument is a highly charged icon for politics and religion. The harp is a metaphor of the instrument of state. The wind and harp are often seen as an analogue for the poetic mind. Music rarely duplicates anything in nature or anything outside the self, so it is closest to spirit and passion. Emotion leads to motion and the strings move. The Aeolian lyre was a popular piece of furniture in the Classical era and again in the Renaissance. Some people claimed to have visions from listening to its fine sound. Made with piano or violin strings, or wind chimes and bells with ribbons, Aeolian harps were hung on tree branches, the wind vibrating the strings, sounding like angels playing harps in the trees.

Musical instruments have always connected with magic and supernatural power. Chanting is still part of shaman practice. In the Cave of Le Trois Freres (15,000 BC) is the Sorcerer or Dancing Shaman. In the same cave, a bison man is playing a bow using his mouth as a resonator. Some instruments have a sacred function within a culture. The flute is important in North America native cultures. The hooped drum, the bodhran and tar, with stretched skin is still part of the magic flight of shaman ritual from central Asia to Tibet and Siberia through the Middle East to Native America and Ireland. Spirits come from the Otherworld down the drum pattern to inhabit or possess the shaman. Certain gods have certain beats. Some drums are dedicated to certain gods and before performance require certain rituals of fire or smudge. Spirits are thought to dwell within instruments and hold the soul or ancestors of the tree that made the base or animal that provided the skin.

In the old myths, a musician was half human, half god. In that time of magic mentality, tones could bridge worlds, like magic. The Old Ways claim music and magic are the same thing, based on ritual, on repetition of patterns, on numbers, three, four, seven. In the realm of the gods, if a single note be touched, all of nature murmurs in response. The philosopher Ernst Cassirer described such a visionary experience as 'the momentary god', a single musical note so intense one can perceive a deity. The most blissful instrument to resonate with the soul is the harp. For millennia, the hand touching the strings of the harp has been an archetype of the soul strumming the eternal.

The capacity of music to disclose the inner workings of the universe has a strong place in early Christian thought, inspired by its much earlier role in Greek philosophy. Indeed, Pythagorean philosophy made much of the definition of music in terms of its arithmetic proportions. The notion of the world as an ordered realm gained expression in imagery which construed the universe as a structure of mathematical ratios, or, analogously, harmonious musical intervals. At the same time, musical instruments could themselves serve as models, one familiar comparison being that in which the world was seen to resemble Apollo's lute. The merging of music with the experience of love has a long tradition in the spiritual traditions of many cultures. The Greek understanding of the musical model of the world was subsumed under the theology of the early Christian church, in which the universe could be understood as a harmony patterned on music. Even the comparison with the musical instrument was sustained and developed as the theological tradition drew upon Greek sources.

In all cultures the harp is a celestial instrument. In some it's a bridge between heaven and earth, a mystic ladder. In the Celtic Edda, heroes wanted a harper buried with them to speed up access to the other world. And those of us who live in Stratford know there is a close connection between harps and swans. The tomb of Ramses III shows priests playing harps. In Western Europe harps are associated with bards and fairies. String tension is seen as a symbol of striving toward love and the supernatural. In Bosch's *Garden of Delights* a figure is crucified on the strings of a harp, symbol of the stress that crucifies man in every moment of the anguished expectation of this earthly life.

The harp, described as a ladder of strings linking heaven to earth, below to above, derives from the lyre of Orpheus according to myth and legend. The legends and traditions link the opposites of day and night, light and dark; darkness, underworld, night, the lyre, and singing. Hermes invented the seven-string lyre and taught Orpheus to play it. Greek modes created specific mind sets. Seven was a sacred number that linked heaven and earth, the three figures of the trinity met in the four elements, the seven days of the week, and the seven ages of man.

The Octave was known as Law of Seven; intervals created shock points at mi/fa and si/do. If the octave starts at do, the note to the left of any two black notes, and moves in steps, or half tones, or semi tones, they held meaning to the Middle Ages. Do begins. Re is the first step. Mi is the shock point whether to proceed or go back (A-men ends a hymn as a poignant return.) Fa is fullstep, but a poignant one. Sol is a triumph, a dominant note with power. La is upward, but resigned. Si proceeds, but with a resignation, to Do full union and perfection of the octave. Medieval mystics and Gregorian chanters felt re was peaceful, mi ecstatic, fa refreshing, and sol enthusiastic, the pathway that Christ used to send down his message through music. This is also the philosophical basis on the Gurdjieff system.

The musical notes on the seven strings were derived from the seven visible planets, and the notes indicated their positions from the earth. A famous orchestral work by Gustav Holst is called *The Planets*. Holst compares the psyche to a system of planets all contributing to the health of the soul. With the discovery of the musical octave came scales and modes and an endless range of tonal sequences. For Gregory of Nyssa, the musical instrument serves as an image for the human soul, "present everywhere in the body, just as an artist is present in his musical instrument," and he argues that the soul informs different organs of the body as a musician elicits different tones from different strings. Gregory understands the soul as the invisible harmony in the contrasting elements of this world.

The scale, the ladder, as it were of the lyre, climbs from the darkest tones through the subtle oscillations to the highest, the celestial, the same but different. Noel Cobb notes an octave can be played beginning at either end. The highest sounding string on the Greek lyre was the lowest, and the lowest, the highest. The high treble note given to Saturn was closet to the performer, the bass note, given to the moon, was farthest away. The player could begin heavenly or earthly, agony or ecstasy, as a Lunatic affected by the madness of love or Saturian.

The gods were always commemorated in song. Hermes first sang for

Mnemosyne, great Memory, Mother of the Muses, and mother to Calliope, who was mother to Orpheus. Calliope was known as the 'fair voiced' and the muse of epic poetry. She is crowned in gold, and carried paper, scrolls, or a writing tablet. Since antiquity, the song and the lyre have been connected to theology, spirit, and the celestial realms. In some version of mythology, the names of three muses were also names of strings of the lyre — Nete, Mese, Hypate — and were worshiped at Delphi.

The lyre was made possible by the death of a lover and a tortoise. Hermes killed a tortoise, scraped out the shell, stretched a hide over it, and affixed a bridge, two arms, and seven strings of sheep gut to it. Music, poetry, and theology, remarks archetypal psychologist Noel Cobb, were all founded on a death. The harp gives voice to pain, loss, failure, death. Tightly drawn sinews can only come from a dissected body. Orpheus sang of his love for Eurydice, but Thracian maidens drowned out his singing with harsh cries and tore him to pieces. The Muses pulled together the pieces of his body (all but his penis which had a separate life as Priapus) and buried him at Libestra, where to this day the nightingales sing the sweetest.

According to Greek tradition, the head of Orpheus continued to sing in the sanctuary of Dionysus until silenced by Apollo. Torn asunder, but not destroyed. For this mighty love, the Lyre was placed in the constellations. Why the Thracian maenads dismembered Orpheus is unknown, as befits the creator of Dionysian Mysteries, but the spirits of Orpheus and Eurydice found each other and are together in eternity. Zeus set the Lyre among the stars as a bright constellation in the summer northern sky. The constellation is also known as the tortoise, another name for the lyre.

Deaths in Celtic music are also a 'seeing-through', a different way of seeing beyond the literal. With the harp comes creation. Mythopoesis — the creation of metaphor — is going into the darkness to find a deeper light and buried significance. What also dies is naiveté and literalness. Terrible loss and suffering becomes the basis for poetry and song, the language of soul. A Greek philosophy called Platonism derives from this. The seeing through of a single literal reality to see a multiplicity of meanings. The lyre has always led away from the monotony and unity of monotheism to complexity and polytheism. Even bad poets could claim solace in their harp. One historical commentary notes, "his verse is quite lacking in the technique of the professional poet, yet it has a charm of its own. He tells how, after the loss of his dear friends, he falls back on the companions who never fail him, his books, his sword and dagger, the chess-board on which he once won many a hard match, above all his 'musical branch', a beautiful harp."

The Calling of the Harp

The archetypal God Dagda, mate of Morrigan, the Great Queen, Goddess of Ireland, had a harp called 'The Oak of Two Greens and the Four Angled Music'. With it he could play three kinds of music: sorrow, laughter, and sleep. With the sleep strains he subdued his enemies. In one battle, the Formorians carried off the Dagda's harper, whose name was Uainte. They hung the harp upon the wall of the banquet house, but the Dagda had put a spell on the melodies, which would not play until he summoned them. When he summoned them, the harp flew from the wall, killing nine men. The harp returned to the hands of the Dagda who played the sorrow tunes so that women and children wept. Then he played the smile tunes and the women and children smiled. And then he played the sleep tunes. As soon as they slept, the Dagda escaped with his harper.

In Irish folklore the great harper Craiftine played his harp so soothingly that a rival chieftain slept and was overpowered by soldiers. Craiftine was harper to the King of Leister in Ireland who had a peculiarity — he had horse ears. Only his barber knew the secret, and he was sworn to secrecy. Unable to keep the secret, he told a tree. But the tree was cut down and made into a harp, and when the harp played, it revealed the truth about the king.

On a journey, St Brigit once sought to rest in the house of a chieftain. The chieftain and the heads of the clan, including his harpers, were absent. But the remaining family members did what they could for hospitality. After a frugal meal, Brigit observed the harp upon the wall and requested the princes favor her with the ancient melodies of the country. When they protested they lacked the skill, she brushed the tips of their fingers with her own, which inspired them to perform the most powerful melodies ever heard in the ancestral hall. They could not stop playing, nor could the audience stop listening. The princes retained the power over the harp strings while they lived.

Celtic harp hymns were thought to contain spells, to give immunity against fire, poison, and wild animals. The Irish banshee known as Aoibhell carries a deadly harp; whoever hears it will die. The Celtic chant, both sacred and secular, was transmuted exclusively through oral tradition. Not a single instance of notation before 1000 has been found in any Irish liturgical manuscript. Celtic music, found in Ireland, Scotland, Cornwall, Brittany, northern Spain, and the monasteries founded by Irish missionaries, tended to be monophonic. In the 12th century, John of Salisbury, describing one of the Crusades of the previous century, wrote that there would have been no music at all if it had not been for the Irish harp. Players must surely have traveled the great (and profitable) pilgrim routes. The skill of the Irish harpers was certainly famous when Vincenzo Galilei described them in *Dialogo della Musica Antica e della Moderna*, published in Florence in 1581.

Such music as played by Irish harpers was determined as to measure by the length of a poet's lines and based on the scales inherent in the tuning of the instrument. Once tuned, the Irish harp is fixed and unalterable in pitch. (The pitch-changing pedals unknown until Harbrucker of Bavaria first introduced it, though others claim the invention.) Scales of the harp, therefore, are based on the only system possible, modes. This music has affinities with blues and jazz in its changing bars. The songs are mostly sung in AABA or ABBA. Jigs in 6/8, slip and hop jigs in 6/8, reels in 4/4, plus the involved meters of the Set Dances. No one has satisfactorily written down a song in this style.

As Loreena McKennitt has recognized, traditional Irish ballads have retained this sense of modality. "I find the melodies very, very strong," she comments in *Folk Harp Journal* concerning traditional Celtic ballads, "particulary the Irish.... The Irish, in strong ways depending on some of the music, tend to be older, tend to have this more modal type of structure. I think that's partly because Ireland wasn't conquered to the same degree that England and Scotland and Wales were. Julius Caesar and the Romans sort of stopped at England, so there are many more older dimensions left in Ireland than exist elsewhere, and that is reflected in the music. It's some of those more primitive elements, the modal system or the drones, that I find I'm instinctively drawn to. It's not like an intellectual, cerebral experience, but I do find myself very much drawn to it."

In this sense, traditional Irish music also has much in common with the ancient Greek music. Songs had essentially a pure unencumbered melodic line, linked intimately with words, especially in meter and rhythm. The Greek modes — Lydian, Phyrigian, Dorian, Hypolydian, Mixolydian, Ionian, and Aoelian — considered each octave to have a specific mood or character. Dorian was distinguished, Hypodoian was pompous, Phyrgian was violent and exciting, and Hypolydian was voluptuous. Orpheus knew the modes, not as a hobby or amusing pastime, but as a means of communicating with the gods. The lyre and the harp are always connected with the celestial realms, realms of essence. The voice of Orpheus lives among ghosts, ancestral spirits, hauntings, parallel worlds, the shades, the dead heroes, the suffering souls in Hades. To listen to Orpheus is to hear the underworld, the Celtic Otherworld. In keeping with the myth of the Dagda, Irish music has been classified according to emotional effects: Goltraige, Gentraige, and Suantraige, generally translated as Sad or Sorrow music, Joyful music, and Sleep music.

Curiously, there is no word in Irish meaning 'music'. The modes are more in common with the Hindu word 'raga', which means a specific melody

The Calling of the Harp

type associated with specific patterns and rhythms. The great Lord, Shiva, gave the world yoga and the Holy Scriptures, as well as mantras or chants which saved humanity. He made an instrument of bamboo and hollow pumpkins, with the gut strings of deer, and created the first vina or sitar. He practiced in solitude, and it is said the deer cried out, use our veins to make the strings. He then created a separate instrument played only by women, which produces sharps, flats, and semi-tones. Shiva taught that every minute of day and night had different effects on the body and so he created a special kind of music to elevate the soul both psychologically and mystically. He called this music 'raga', which means emotion.

Some ragas are played or sung before dawn; the stillness of the hour has fine vibrations. The noise of the day requires stronger notes. Midday ragas are made with natural notes; nighttime ragas with odd notes; and early morning rags with flat notes. Six ragas is considered male, creative and positive; and 36 raginis, six to each raga, is female and acutely responsive. Putras, of which there are 48, are the mingling of ragas and raginis. Like call and response in the blues, a bharja is a response to a putra. Each raga has a little government. A chief for the key note, a king for principal notes, a minister for subordinate notes, a servant for assonant notes, and an enemy for dissonance. By tuning to the external as well as the inner self, one gets 'in tune' with the essence of one's whole being. Even the smallest objects, a seed, offers as much delight as a blossoming flower.

In India, the universe is said to hang on the sound of cosmic vibration. Aum. The seers and yogis and folks in the ashram tune into Aum (or Om) to make it vibrate in the body. From this sound, Shiva created music and dance as a gift to his wife. Music was passed along to all the celestial beings. Finally Brahma, after 100,000 years of contemplation, gave the gift of music to the people. The sacred texts in the Four Vedas and music was the Fifth Veda. Music was equal to the scriptures-a direct gift from the gods and the path to salvation. All harmony has its essence in music. Shiva invented the vina or sitar, Krishna always has a flute. Sarasvati, the Hindu goddess of knowledge, is always pictured with a vina; like Orpheus' lyre, the stringed gourd has its mysteries of tone and rhythm.

The wise ones say the greatest prophets were great musicians. A legend claims Moses heard the word of God in the words, *Muse ke*, Moses hark. The revelation on Mount Sinai was of tone and rhythm and he called it Musike or music. Music grasps the structure of cosmic harmony in a way the mind cannot. Such music communicates insight into that harmony to others without passing through the limitations of mind or book. Legend claims the strings on the harp of David were made from the sinews of the ram that Abraham sacrificed instead of Issiah on Mount Moriah. The Bible has frequent references to harps. David soothes Saul, (*Samuel* 1.16.23). The belief that angels play harps in heaven is found in *Revelations*.14.2. Another Jewish tale relates how David hung his magical harp by the window of his bedroom chamber. The north wind at midnight blew across the strings and made wondrous music. David awoke, took up a pen, and in a trance, wrote the Psalms effortlessly. The tale relates how the Holy Spirit spoke through David as is he himself was a kind of harp. The legend claims that David foresaw the Temple in Jerusalem that Solomon would build, the destruction of the Temple, and the exile of the people of Israel. The legend concludes harps will be found in the upper branches of a willow tree and, in the finest willow tree of all, the golden harp of David will be found, still providing the music of the Holy Spirit as it drifts across the Holy Land.

The only thing hotter than the sun in Africa is the harp. The Ngombo harp of Africa has meaning both external in the decoration and internal in the cultural understanding. Every part of the harp is symbolic. Supernatural powers are invested in the materials, the sound, the rhythm patterns. The harp is at once microcosmic and macrocosmic. The instrument represents the microworld of the living and the macro world of the gods and ancestors. The instrument is the female body of the Great Mother in materials and voice or sound. It also represents male and female and sacred space. The harp resonator is the female principle; the neck is the masculine principle. The junction is the sexual union. The soundboard is often painted red on the left side and white on the right side to represent blood and semen. The eight strings are called four males and four females to mingle harmoniously as should humans in their rituals and society. The harpist is the guardian of the chapel, and the spirits of the ancestors enter the body of the harpist as the tunes summon ancestors to the chapel for service. The strings, like the eight sacred trees, are the primary path of communication between the worlds of the living and the gods and ancestors. The seen and unseen. To send and receive messages to the ancestors and gods. In the old tradition, the harp is music played by the dead, and for converts to Christianity, the angels in heaven. The harp is ritually honored. Certain songs are sung as the harp exits the chapel and after it has played it is danced in a procession from the chapel to a special light tight storage chamber at the end of the village.

Blues and folk musician Taj Mahal has collaborated with Mali musician Toumani Diabate, claiming there was a link between American blues and West African music dating back five centuries. Diabate plays a kora, a 21-string harp-lute that some say originated in 15th-century Timbuktu. Now considered metaphorically the most distant place on earth, several centuries ago Timbuktu was an important trading center in the Songhai Empire. Diabate is a 'griot', a historian-musician, whose role in society is to be a steward, charged with maintaining the tradition without changing the content. In his case, he maintains music that has not changed for over 70 generations.

While most African music styles, such as soukous, juju, mbalax, and Afrobeat, are drum heavy, the music of Mali relies on strings. Taj Mahal claims the finger-picking style is identical to Mississippi John Hurt. An instrument called the *ngoni* is a distant relation to the banjo, mandolin, and guitar. Like Alan Stivell in Brittany, Diambate's father has recorded an album called *Ancient Strings*, which is played on state radio in Mali to mark special occasions. Another Malian guitarist, Ali Farka Toure, had a huge hit in 1994, *Talking Timbuktu*, with music archivist and all around genius Ry Cooder. Toure also played with Taj Mahal in 1991 on an album called *The Source*. These performers have revived the tradition of the wandering bard, with harp, lute, or guitar in hand to accompany their lyrics, as has Loreena McKennitt who sees herself "participating in the history of the harp."

2

THE BARDS

In ancient Ireland, poetry was a hereditary occupation, although training at a Bardic College for a period of about seven years was also required. The method of composing was to lie in a darkened room for an extended period of time until the poem was complete. Many have commented that this seems like a relic of some type of 'otherworld' divination ceremony going back to pagan times.

When the Normans came to Ireland in the 12th century, their chroniclers noted the Irish harpers were the most skillful than they had ever heard. Music was well established as an integral part of Irish life and even a necessary part of its classical organization. Other Norman invaders even took to the composition of Gaelic poetry in native Irish rhymes. Then the harper provided music to accompany the recitation of heroic verse at the Celtic chieftain's curt.

Patronized by the aristocracy, practiced by churchmen, supported by Norman conquerors, Irish music flourished until the beginning of the 17th century. But Irish music had no part in the development of polyphonic music on the continent. Within a century, Europe had discovered the major and minor keys that attained full development in Mozart and Beethoven. With the end of modal music came modern European classical compositions. Irish modes became quaint, barbaric to the cultivated ears of the English lords.

Just as music in Europe was feeling its way out of the modes, Irish music was outlawed. Harpers, pipers, and poets were leaders in the last surge of Gaelic Ireland against the English. The defeat of the Irish at the Battle of Kinsdale in 1601 was a catastrophe for a national aristocratic order of society that had encouraged music by an intricate system of patronage. The usual slaughter was followed by English orderliness; every tenth soldier was killed as a tithe to the Lord of Hosts. In the 1603, proclamations were issued by the Lord president of Munster for extermination by martial law "of all manner of bards, pipers, etc." Within ten days Queen Elizabeth I herself ordered Lord Barrymore "to hang the harpers wherever found and destroy all their instruments." The Elizabethan enactments against bards, minstrels, pipers, and rhymers were already enforced after the promulgation of the Bull of St Pius V. in 1569, though it is said Elizabeth herself retained in her service an Irish harper called Donogh.

All through the 17th-century, harpers were banned, hunted, persecuted. In Dublin alone, some 2,500 harps were destroyed. Under Cromwell, in 1654 all harpers, pipers, and wandering musicians had to obtain letters from the magistrate of the district where they lived before they were allowed to travel through the country. The harper became a wandering minstrel, a busker, performing if invited in the big houses of the aristocracy. The passport contained full details of age, stature, beard, color of hair, and condition of life of the bearer. All musical instruments savoring of 'popery' were ruthlessly destroyed. Archdeacon Lynch, a contemporary writer, was of the opinion not a single harp would be left in Ireland. Possibly when the Earls of Tyrone and Tyrconnell and nearly 100 of the leading Irishmen of Ulster left their native land in 1607 and went into exile on the continent, they took harpers with them. The instrument was familiar, in some European circles at least, as an 'exotic' kind of harp. For example, the 1638 inventory of the Hofkapelle of the Landgraf of Hesse at Kassel included "an old Irish harp," and the earnest Lutheran choirmaster-pedagogue, Michael Praetorius, gave a short description and an illustration of an Irish harp in his *Syntagma Musicum* of 1619.

The bardic tradition was revived in the 18th century by James MacPherson, who published translations of the epic poetry of 'Ossian', a bard he claimed was as great as Homer. The book proved to be a fraud, but the image of an ancient bard like Ossian stimulated interest in the ancient Celts, invoking a vision of a Holy Land, giving a New Ireland a noble mythological heritage. This desire to discover Ireland's lost Gaelic culture addressed the growing romantic interest in novelty, nature, 'natives', and primitive cultures, replacing the mythology of ancient Greece and Rome as source for poetic imagination. As a result, so-called Irish Vision Poetry became popular. In the Gaelic poems known as 'Aisling', a poet wandering alone at twilight or at dawn sees a beautiful maiden with long curling locks of red hair, who identifies herself as one of the Sidhe or fairies, the personification of Ireland known as Eire. She delivers a message and disappears. The other style of vision poems are the 'Reverdies' written by poets who believe the maiden is supernatural, only to discover she is mortal.

At the same time laws against pipers and harpers were relaxed. Collectors imbued with the antiquarian spirit began collecting music in a haphazard manner. Gaelic lyrics and music were rarely recorded together for Gaelic was considered a dead language. Wordless transcriptions were the rule. Anthologies of music began to appear the titles like 'Ancient' or 'Old Music of Ireland'. Collections of traditional Irish airs were translated into major and minor keys, including airs written in keys harpers could not have used.

To rectify these problems, a harping convention was held in Dublin in 1792. The organizers engaged Edward Bunting, the young organist at St Patrick's Cathedral in Dublin, to transcribe the melodies. Volumes of influential harp tunes were published in 1796, 1809, and 1840. The 30 strings of the harp, based on the Brian Boru harp in Trinity College, are tuned from C below the bass clef to D above the treble clef. Tuning was by octaves and fifths, generally in the scale of G, but by altering one string a semi tone with the aid of a tuning hammer, the scale might be changed to C. Once in a while, the pitch might be changed to C or even F sharp. With modal thinking, the pitch of modes alters from G Doh to C Doh and D Doh. But Bunting did not understand this. Ignorant of the Gaelic lyrics, publishers commissioned an Irish poet named Thomas Moore to fit words to the music. Thomas Moore's lyrics in English were based on old songs set to Bunting's harp music. Moore, with Whig patrons and a connection to the Prince Regent, wrote exquisite lyrics meant to be sung. Though he often further altered melodies, already forced into conventional scales, and altered yet again by fashionable bravura passages in the Italian manner by later composers, Moore's melodies have endured in a number of long lasting ways.

Moore's work cast a romantic look backward to the faded glories of ancient Ireland. Although critics have complained correctly that the wild harp became a musical snuffbox, listen closely and see how history and myth inspire the songs. More than half of his first edition referred to the past glories and miseries of Ireland. Some songs gave Ireland a feminine persona, Caitlin or Erin. The songs lamented lost freedom, embedded with words like chains, slavery, and bondage. The opaque or oblique dedications to dead revolutionary friends gave his melodies a unique character. Many of Moore's friends, Trinity graduates from Dublin, had died in the failed Wolfe Tone uprising of 1798. "Oh Breathe Not His Name" referred to Moore's friend, Robert Emmet, one of the last men in England to be hanged and beheaded for treason. Moore's lyrics, his love songs, drinking songs, odes to music and friendship, and nostalgic laments are often patriotic allegories masquerading as love songs. But the main characteristic of 19th-century Irish writing is perpetual mourning. This continual remembering of the dead, keeping faith with their memory, gave Irish tunes their lingering melancholy. Songs were nostalgic, tales of joys lost, time slipping away. "The language of sorrow ... is best-suited to our (Irish) music," Moore said.

Moore's songs were daring. He projected the Spanish rebellion of 1803 into the hope of Irish emancipation, linking the shamrock of Ireland with the olive of Spain. He saw Irish music and politics as deeply entwined. Moore's songs celebrate the sense of place and beauty of the Irish countryside, linking the character of the people to the land and an abstract spirit of the nation, a concept that did not offend the British imperial sensibilities.

Moore's influence over the next century was enormous. The image of Ireland as a lost utopia became even more pronounced as the Irish faced political oppression, famine, and exile during the 19th century. By 1900, over 30 editions of his *Melodies* had been published in America alone, presumably treasured by Irish immigrants. The lyrics and music of the bard in *Sean nos* (the old style) became a source of communion and identity. Moore had established the symbolism of Ireland — the color green, the shamrock, and the harp. The United Irishmen chose green as the emblematic color of revolution in Ireland that was sang out in ballads like *The Wearing of the Green* or *Green Above The Red*. Moore even invented a story about an undersea siren, in love with a mortal, like the little mermaid, who turned into a harp. The woman as a harp on the cover of his *Melodies* became a resonating icon of Celtic spirit.

In 1893, the Gaelic League was formed to teach, learn, and speak the Irish language. A man named Carl Hardebeck devoted his life to taking down words and airs. Traditional Irish singing is unique, usually solo, unaccompanied. For the first time, the songs, called *Gaeltracht*, were heard with the free rhythms and changes in time signatures. Hardebeck provided the first written versions of that style of traditional singing now known as *Sean nos*. A *Sean nos* singer reflects the stresses of poetic meter in performance, but is not bound by it. In this style one syllable can be sung several ways, so the singer can move from stress to stress at a pattern determined by the feeling put into the words and by the amount of ornamentation and number of stops chosen to grace a tune. This style of singing would have great influence on the poets of the so-called second Celtic revival, namely William Butler Yeats and George Russell (a.k.a. AE).

In 1865 Matthew Arnold delivered his lectures on *The Study of Celtic Literature*, describing the romantic and feminine character of Celtic poetry and speculating that a study of Celtic language would unearth a missing link between races, especially Saxons and Gauls, a social and political affinity that links such diverse peoples as Germans, Norman, and Celts. Arnold prophesied that the Celt would influence European literature of the next generation. These lectures, too, would have a profound influence on W.B. Yeats.

Yeats picks up this idea of a Celtic renaissance in his book *The Celtic Element in Literature* (1897), refashioning the argument to save the spirituality of the Celt for the poetic imagination. The Celts were close to nature, like all primitive peoples. The Celts preserved the ancient religions, the natural magic, the power of nature, hence the immortal. When W.B. Yeats linked the words 'Celtic' and 'Twilight' in his book, he depicted a race in decline with dying traditions and arts. The Celts have a streak in their character that veers from melancholy to wild self-destruction. Yeats also instigated a revival of Celtic traditions which have came to life once again a century later. 'Celtic' is one of those moth-eaten words that somehow connects literature, politics, music, and art. In Ireland the Celtic revivals are models of nationalist ideals that resist imperialism. The strongest Celtic 'substance' is said to be found in western Ireland, that free Gaelic countryside bursting with color and vitality, where the hardest rain is called soft, haunted with fairylore, where herbalists quaff a mug of porter in the long nights after Samhain. The revival of Celtic traditions moves in hand with politics. Take the magnificent example of Boadicea, the warrior Queen who took on Nero's Roman troops around 60 AD. The Celts wanted full and equal participation in government. Rather than be taken prisoner to face further defeat and humiliation, Boadiciea poisoned herself. That is the paradox of the Celts: they are a proud warrior people destined to lose, which may explain the eternal melancholy of the Celt, even more so than bad weather or famine.

In the 1890s, dreams of a New Ireland were ennobled with the heritage of the ancient Celt. Revive our birthright, said W.B.Yeats, and Ireland will be great again. Other poets and scholars and politicians followed his lead. The founding of the National Literary Society in 1892, the Abbey Theatre in

1899, the poetry of George Russell (AE), the plays of Synge, O' Casey, and Beckett, the fiction of Joyce — the Irish certainly took front stage in western literary life in the early years of the 20th century. As Yeats proclaimed his Celtic pride in his cherished poem, *Under Ben Bulben*, his fellows artists turned to the national heritage, drawing inspiration from the triumphs, tragedies, joys, and sorrows of their people that hovered between fable and fact. Some thought Ireland's Sacred Book was Yeats' *A Vision*, with its theory of gyres and revelations of Spiritus mundi inspired by William Blake, swans as emblems, water as the soul, the moon an astrologers diagram. Dressed in black with a flowing cape, Yeats adopted the aura of the ancient. He restored a rotted tower called Thor Balylee that is now a museum.

"All sounds, all colors, all forms either because of their preordained energies or because of long association, evoke indefinable and yet precise emotions," Yeats wrote, "and when sound, and color, and form are in a musical relation, a beautiful relation to one another, they become, as it were, one sound, one color, one form .... an emotion that is made out of their distinct evocations and yet is one emotion." Yeats thought that art would replace religion. He saw Celtic literature as central to European literature, quoting Renana, who believed St Patrick's pilgrimage in Lough Derg inspired Dante's *Divine comedy*, an idea which perhaps inspired Loreena McKennitt's *Dante's Prayer* on THE BOOK OF SECRETS album. The arts were a priestly vocation; poetry and song had the saving power. "A lyric impulse, conceived in the dark, is the frailest of things," he wrote, "a spark, a candle, and a match flame. But it grows, by encountering other impulses, ideas, thoughts, flames, to engulf the world, flows out, a 'power among power.' Creative thought, a flash, an insight, an intuition, comes to someone in a moment, and finally 'makes and unmakes mankind.' A single small act, small, seemingly impractical, can change the world. Art, small and useless as a little song, is the most powerful action a human can create."

The Irish might have been nostalgic for some sense of Celtic past, but Ireland was part of the British Empire. Politicians grasped that Celtic heritage could be used to throw off the yoke of British rule. The Celtic revivals brought back the memories of other political and military heroes like Hugh O'Neill and Red Hugh O'Donnell of the Tyrone War (1594-1603), Owen Reo O'Neill who led the Catholic Confederacy against Cromwell (1642-49), Wolfe Tone and Robert Emmett of the ill-fated United Irishmen of 1798. The heroes of 1916 Easter Uprising — Pearse, MacDonagh, Plunkett — had their political ancestors. The Irish are proud of their heroes who took up the case of the Gael against the foreigner — the Norse, the Normans, and the English.

Pictures of CuChulain hang above the doors of schools. Brian Boru united the clans and overthrew the Norse at the Battle of Contar on Good Friday, April 23, 1014. The emblem of his harp appears on the state seal, the coins, and the presidential letterhead of Ireland, based on the model in Trinity College, Dublin. (The word 'Ireland' does not exist in Irish, but in the constitution of 1919 that established the Republic, the Irish word 'Eire' was attached to the English word 'land'.)

In Dublin, you can ponder these things while standing in line at the chipper for smoked whiting and bright green mush peas, lime green, electric green. A harp on the so-called Green Flag has always been the national emblem of Ireland. A gold harp on a field of blue has been the arms of Ireland since the 16th century. The Society of United Irishmen, a Republican movement led by Wolfe Tone in 1798, used the gold harp against a green field. The green leaves of the liberty tree and shamrock that were used as Republican emblems in the Rebellions of 1798 and 1803. The flag was unofficially the national flag from 1798 to 1919. Sometimes the motto *Eiregobrach* (Ireland forever) is inscribed below the harp.

The Green Flag has been in continual use for four hundred years. First raised during the repeal of the Act of Union in the 1830s and 1840s, the flag was later viewed as a seditious emblem by the British. Its use faded in the 1850s when the radical group called Young Ireland adopted the tricolor green, white, and orange flag, modeled on the flag of the second French Empire. In the 1860s, the Irish Republican Brotherhood (the Fenians) reverted to the Green Flag with the gold harp, and several Irish battalions in the American Civil War flew the Green Flag. Nationalist politicians who campaigned for Home Rule used that flag. By 1880, the Green Flag was officially tolerated so that no one was likely to be arrested for displaying it.

Both the Green Flag and tricolor were used by insurgents in the Irish uprising against the British in 1916 and raised above the post office, an appropriate symbol of communication, where the nation was born. Today at the General Post Office there's a statue of fighting Cuchalain, bound to a standing stone, facing death on the plains of Muirthemne. A black crow named Badb perches on his shoulder whispering the secrets of the Otherworld. After the rebellion, the Sinn Fein used the tricolor, and the Irish Republican Party (which advocated Home Rule) used the Green Flag. Alternative national flags became flags of competing political parties, until Sinn Fein won the general election of 1918.

The tricolor is green on the hoist side and represents the island's Catholic population, while the orange opposite represents the Protestants, supporters of

William of Orange. A field of pure white unites the two, symbolizing peace and unity. The Irish Free State was established in 1919, and the tricolor adopted as the official emblem of the Republic.

But the historic Green Flag with the Golden Harp continues to be used as a secondary national emblem, and often, during events which demand partisan support, such as World Cup soccer matches, the Green Flag represents Ireland. The Green Service jack is based upon the Green flag but uses the official Brian Boru harp adopted as the state emblem in 1922.

The harp has thus become the emblem of Celtic culture, the symbol of Celtic poetry and politics, the bard and the warrior. In the 1950s the Irish harp featured prominently in popular Irish entertainment and was promoted throughout the world in the tourist industry. The Irish harp organization, *Cairden Cruit*, was established in 1960 in Dublin. Dedicated to an ongoing discussion of the Irish harp, it provides newsletters, classes, publication of suitable music, and a great number of summer schools, festivals, and workshops. By the 1960s, it was part of folk music revival and rediscovery.

Harpers are now relearning the instrument from such groups as the Belfast Harp Orchestra and the Irish National Harp Ensemble. Clarshee, a smaller group within the Belfast Harp Orchestra, perform on harp, harpsichord, uileann pipes, flutes, whistles, concertina, and bodrhan. *Clairseoirinah Eireann* (The Harp Foundation) offers harp players in Belfast a similar range of activities. Using a 1,400-year-old method of teaching by ear, performers are taught to be infinitely creative within an Irish style. They are also learning, like Loreena McKennitt, from contemporary masters of the harp, most notably, Alan Stivell.

3
ELEMENTAL CELTIC

From her visit to Ireland, Loreena McKennitt gained a "deep feel for the Celtic tradition," as she explained in *Folk Harp Journal*. "Celtic culture is more rooted into the seasons ... integrated to the earth ... and a lot of the songs reflect that. I feel that, as a species, we've removed ourselves so far now that we've set up a very unnatural position in relationship to the earth.... The Celts ... felt that the souls of their ancestors ... resided in the trees, so they held trees in great reverence. Oh, and the lunar cycles of the year and the solar cycles ... It sounds ... I don't know ... some pie in the sky, I suppose to some degree, but again, I think that we as a species on the earth have got to reacquaint ourselves with the fundamentals, and that exists by reintegrating ourselves. And it all hinges on natural phenomena, the natural sciences and the natural elements . . ."

This reverence for the Celtic tradition finds expression in Loreena McKennitt's song *The Old Ways* from her album THE VISIT.

The Old Ways

On a dark new year's night
On the west coast of Clare
I heard your voice singing
Your eyes danced the song
Your hands played the tune
T'was a vision before me . . .

Suddenly I knew that you'd have to go
Your world was not mine, your eyes told me so
Yet it was there I felt the crossroads of time
And I wondered why . . .

As you turned to go I heard you call my name
You were like a bird in a cage, spreading its wings to fly
"The old ways are lost," you sang as you flew
And I wondered why

The thundering sea is calling me home to you, home to you
The pounding seas is calling me home to you, home to you . . .

What Loreena McKennitt calls the 'old ways' of the Celts pre-dates the dualism of the Christian world where the material and the spiritual worlds are separate. For the ancient Celts, the natural and supernatural are inseparable. A good Celt sees spirits and deities in trees, groves, rivers, bogs, and mountains. The entire countryside pulsates with spiritual significance. Earth is the divine mother goddess, the land is fruitful, animals are nourished. The Celtic wheel-cross surrounded by a circle symbolizes the balance of male and female forces, the four Elements, the four winds, and the four cardinal directions. In the center, where the lines cross, is the hidden fifth element, spirit. In prehistoric cultures, spirit was often personified as any number of sun deities. Mithra from Babylon. Zas from China. Oirus and Horus and Ra from Egypt.

Dionysus from Greece. Vishnu from India. Tammus from Syria, Merodath from Assyria. The Cornish name, Cymbeline, is Celtic for Lord of the Sun. The sacred Light is embedded in names as varied as Luke, Lew, Lucius, Lucy, Lorne, Lorraine, Loren, and Loreena.

In her song *The Bonny Swans* from THE MASK AND MIRROR, Loreena McKennitt draws on these elemental Celtic beliefs. The story of the Bonny Swans, she explains in her video *No Journey's End* is "a great, metaphorical kind of fable and the song was also inspired by a wonderful book I have traveled with for several years based on the Unicorn Tapestries and the metaphors and iconography woven into those tapestries. Elements that tap into very pre-Christian elements that had a lot to do with nature and the natural world. The Celts didn't make a large distinction between this world and the next, and it [the story of the Bonny Swans] is certainly a great example of that idea. A story where a young sister is drowned by an older sister and becomes transformed into a swan (which in the Middle Ages was a symbol of death) and then in turn becomes transformed into a harp, and the harp is brought to her father's hall."

The Bonny Swans

There came a harper passing by
the swans sing so boony o
He made harp pins of her fingers fair
hey hee ho and bonny o
He made harp strings of her golden hair
the swans sing to bonny o
He made a harp of her breast bone
hey hee ho and bonny o
And straight it began to play alone
the swans swim so bonny o . . .

The cover art for Loreena McKennitt's THE MASK AND MIRROR is from a tapestry masterpiece, *The Hunt of the Unicorn*, preserved in the Cloisters Museum in New York. Once owned by John D. Rockefeller, the seven tapestries in this series are huge, some twelve-feet square, red, yellow, and blue in color from pigments derived from plants. They date from the beginning of Francis I's reign, the same era as Michelangelo, and may have been woven to celebrate the marriage of Anne of Brittany to Louis XII in 1499. The tapestries form a long cycle devoted to the story of the hunt and capture of the unicorn, the symbol of purity and perfection. The sixth panel shows the slaughtered unicorn presented to the royal couple, while the last panel shows the unicorn resuscitated, captive in a fenced garden tethered to a pomegranate tree by a gold chain, not unlike the 'unicorn' gardens painted by Sandro Botticelli in his *The Hunt of the Unicorn* and *Spring,* now hanging in the Uffizi Gallery in Florence. Some art historians say this 'Captive Unicorn' panel is a symbol of the Risen Christ, a symbol of rebirth and eternal life, at home in paradise. The ideal Renaissance garden was home to the unicorn.

The unicorn is one of the most rich and perplexing symbols of Western art and mythology. Greek writers, including Aristotle and Pliny, claimed the small horse-like animal with the single horn came from India, Egypt, or China, where it represents wisdom, good fortune, and purity. In Greek mythology, the god Zeus was nursed by the she-goat Amalthea (which was later transformed into the star 'Capella' — Latin for 'goat — because of the gratitude of the god). In one version of the myth, the god broke off one of her horns, from which food spilled out. This became known as the 'horn of plenty'. Another story tells of the horn being cut in two to reveal living beings. The unicorn image appears in the fanciful creatures on the Ishtar Gate of Babylon (in the Pergamum Museum in Berlin) and the one dimensional (thus one-horned) 'antelopes' on Egyptian pyramid art. Curiously, an Irish harp and a unicorn are portrayed on the coat-of-arms of Canada. Hebrews believed the unicorn guarded the Tree of Life (which explained why it was not on Noah's Ark). When transformed into Christian iconography, the unicorn appears as a fierce and dangerous creature, which became submissive when captured by a virgin, on whose lap the creature would lay its head, an image of purity and chastity which early Christian writers associated with the Annunciation, the Virgin Mary, and Heavenly Love. The patron saint of Padua and Venice is St Justina, who is associated with a unicorn. The unicorn also carries the double meaning of Courtly Love. To see a unicorn strengthened the soul. The occasional beautiful ivory spiral of a seven-foot narwhal horn would come to Europe from explorers in the Arctic Canada, proof enough the unicorn must exist somewhere.

The image McKennitt uses on THE MASK AND MIRROR is 'The Unicorn at the Fountain', the most puzzling of the series. Hunters surround the animal in a dazzling Garden of Paradise, richly illustrated with botanically accurate plants, and real and imaginary animals, perhaps symbolic of humanity in harmony with all of creation. A lion, lioness, panther, rabbit, hyena, civet (or leopard), stag, dogs, rabbits, and birds encircle a fountain. From the fountain in the center, water pours from lion's mouth, and the unicorn dips its horn in the stream. Sir Kenneth Clark, in *Animals and Men*, speculates the unicorn cleanses its horn from the poison of the serpent in the Garden of Eden. Like Christ, the unicorn serves others, puts itself in danger, and sacrifices itself.

Besides the rich iconography of these unicorn tapestries, Loreena McKennitt may also have found inspiration in the fact they were woven by women. Queen Mathilda created the Bayeux Tapestry with the ladies of court while William was conquering England. Woven by women, 'The Lady and the Unicorn' series hangs in the Musee de Cluny in Paris. While most women in the Middle Ages were married by 14 and burdened with domestic chores, documents exist that show specific art works were assigned to women, usually embroideries, tapestries, and illuminated manuscripts. English women in the 13th and 14th centuries developed ecclesiastical embroidery called *Opus Anglicanum*, cooperative work that eventually led to the first organized guild workshops. As a form of highly developed medieval art, women's embroidery equaled painting and sculpture. That Loreena McKennitt should choose the unicorn as a personal logo is thus not surprising, nor is her choice of wardrobe, richly textured wool fabrics and yarns woven in unique patterns and embellishments, evoking memories of ancient legends, patterns we see repeated on her CD jackets, on her website art, and on her show sets. For THE MASK AND MIRROR tour, she borrowed two enormous tapestries from a Toronto-based medieval troupe, Poculi Lundiqua Societas, which flanked the stage among rows of candles.

Ancient Ireland was occupied 7,000 years before Celts arrived. Literally pre-historic, the country has no written records. Extensive archeological evidences, especially in Newgrange and Cleide Fields, revealed a lost fabled world only beginning to be understood by archeologists. Archeological finds suggested the Celtic Goddess was dominant in the Bronze Age. The so-called 'Bog People' discoveries found Mother goddess and Mother Earth figurines in several small representations in bronze. The goddess was known in the ancient cultures of the Middle East as the Asiatic goddess, Ishtar or Astarte, the Greek goddess of love, Aphrodite, and a whole array of fertility goddesses played a role in the great ritual drama of crops from seed to harvest, the cycle of the seasons. Her images appear on pottery vessels, in amulets as slender ornaments carved from schist, a fine crystalline rock, and on heavy necklaces and brooches worn to ward off evil spirits.

The ancient Irish believed the soul combined the four elements — earth, air, fire, and water. The supreme spirit is idealized as an immutable fire, a pure and elemental flame. A fixed point of dazzling luminosity. The spirit fire of the universe. A wheel with rays. Primal light. The subtle fire, the vital fire, the mystic element that permeates the streams, quivers in the trees, pervades the universe, burns a red path like the flaming tail of a fox streaking into the underbrush. In the Celtic traditions, the male and female aspects of nature were the White Moon Goddess and the Horned God united as one. In Celtic herb magic, alder shoots were hollowed out for whistles to entice the Air elementals. Ash leaves, laurel, or hops were put under a pillow to stimulate dreams. Fresh basil protected each corner of a house already purified with pine branches. Briar rose tea gave prophetic dreams, burning broom at the spring equinox protected ritual areas, the leaves of catnip promoted fierceness and marked pages in magical books. Ivy protected a house, with marigold rubbed on the eyelids a person could see fairies. Irish moss attracted money.

Around 500 BC the Celts appeared. Called Keltoi by ancient Greeks, they probably come from central Europe, then spread across Italy, Greece, the Balkans, Asia Minor, Gaul, Spain, Britain, and Ireland. While the Celts were dominant in culture, they were not in politics. Celtic Ireland was not a great civilization like Assyria or Babylon or sophisticated like ancient Egypt. The Celtic Irish had no cities. Monasteries were the first population centers for art, prosperity, and learning. Simple homesteads, some inscribed coins, stone circles, and a few remains are scattered here and there across the British Isles and Europe. Celts were illiterate in the sense they left no written record, though some limited information exists on coins, inscriptions on stone work, and a few place names. Nevertheless, they were highly educated and cultured, with a profound oral literary tradition expressed in folk tales and songs. These took the form of sagas, tall tales of sorcery and enchantment, told by Druid priests, bards, and harpists who guarded Irish lore.

The other remnant of this prehistoric pagan culture are the over 1,200 megalithic monuments found in the Irish countryside and on the Orkney Islands, including the Standing Stones, which Loreena McKennitt alludes to in the title of her song of the same name on PARALLEL DREAMS.

Standing Stones

Standing Stones of the Orkney Isles
Gazing out to sea
Standing Stones of the Orkney Isles
Bring my love to me . . .

These stone circles, menhirs, dolmen, and pillars are approximately contemporary with the age of the Egyptian pyramids and symbolically connect earth and heaven. Many have ritual use, possibly astronomical. The Druids claim the stones were raised by levitation. Some dolmens weigh over 200 tons. At Uisneach, the exact center of Ireland, the island's navel, stands a cairn marking where four provinces meet, each with a unique character. Warfare to north. Affluence to east. Learning in west. Music in south. These are the qualities of the isle of Celtic saints and scholars.

But Ireland is also home of the prehistoric 'Bog People' un-earthed by archeologists. Tollund Man and Grauballe Man were well-preserved in peat and clay that resisted decay, despite their unnatural deaths by hanging and throat cutting. Bog people found in Scandinavia were human sacrifices to guarantee good crops. A rope noose twisted like the necklaces sacred to the corn goddess was found around the neck of a young man whose final meal forensic scientists deduced was of spring time grains and seeds. These, too, are the qualities of Celtic culture.

Though no Celtic museum exists to exhibit the artifacts of this culture, we can imagine that a show on Celtic art might have included bronze stags, gold models of boats, shields of bronze with enameled ornaments, bronze brooches in the shape of birds, glass dogs, roosters of silver with coral inlay, multi-colored glass ornaments, cast bronze bracelets and bronze figures glass inlaid eyes. Some of the finest examples of Celtic artistry bronze mirrors, intricate status symbols with a precision of workmanship that was as delicate as the Celtic illuminated manuscripts, found only in southern Britain, with designs based on three circles linked together in delicate basketry motifs. The Celtic museum might also display pictures of bog burials, chariot burials, images of the white horses cut into hillsides by removing turf, such as those found at White Horse Hill, Oxfordshire, and Bratton Down, Wiltshire. Models of four-wheeled carts and two wheeled chariots, terra cotta heads, bronze figurines of winged creatures, brooches, cloakpins, bracelets, scabbards with engravings, dancing figures and lute players incised on pottery, spearheads with bronze decorations, grooved swords with jeweled hilts, helmets with enamel inlay, bronze bird crests, and a variety of horns. Antlers carved with faces, cups engraved with carnyx players, cauldrons, iron anchors, Celtic calendars on bronze plates, and faces carved on oak heartwood. Celtic jewelry, brooches decorated with gold filigree, cuttlefish shell, garnets, lapis and other stones, buckles of gold filigree, pins and linked pins with animal stylings, necklaces of amber, cheeks reddened with roan, eyebrows darkened with berry juice, cloths dyed in bright colors of clear red, green, blue, or yellow. Natural plant dyes of wood for blue, acorns for brown, Queen Anne's lace for yellow-green, and alder shades, red from bark, green from flowers, brown from twigs.

The Celts celebrated their culture and exercised their faith during a host of annual festivals or holy days. Wiccan meetings were held at or near the full moon, the highest point of psychic power. The word Wicca, or witch, means wise one in Anglo-Saxon. Eight festivals called Sabbats were observed during the year. The Four Greater Sabbats are Imbolc, Beltane, Lammas, and Samhain. The four lesser Sabbats are fire festivals celebrated at the equinoxes, where the flow of power is strong, and at the solstices, a quieter time for regrouping energies. They also represented plowing, sowing, growing, and harvest.

The feast of Imbolc or Candlemas, which occurs in early February, around 'Groundhog Day', used to be a bear festival, notes Joseph Campbell in *The Way of the Animal Powers*, when the ancient bear goddesses connected the hibernation of the animal with the Great Bear constellation. The god is young and arrogant, demanding that the goddess show herself to him. Nothing happens at the first, second, or third, quarter candles. At the fourth candle, the goddess announces she has been there since the beginning, but is not to be commanded. The god continues on his journey until the spring equinox when he finds the young maiden goddess and celebrates the rites of spring with a joyful dance.

At Beltane, all people and creatures gather under the symbol of the May blossom in the green wood for a great celebration. Also called Lady Day or May Day, Beltane occurs on May 1, during the first full moon of Taurus. This is a special time for the Horned God, the Lady of the Greenwood, and house guardians. Beltane is a time of trial marriages for a year and a day. Green is worn at this time to honor the Earth mother. The Celts celebrated this fire festival of May 1 with energetic dancing and games throughout the day, ending with bonfires. As a pagan festival with disputed religious associations, May Day possibly derives from the Roman festival of Maia, mother of Mercury. The opening of the month of May is a busy time for rituals worldwide. Vesakha, the full moon, celebrates the birth and death day of Buddha and his Enlightenment beneath the Bodhi tree after 49 days of meditation.

In *The Mummer's Dance* from THE BOOK OF SECRETS, Loreena McKennitt captures the tree iconography and reviving spirit of this festival.

The Mummer's Dance

When in the springtime of the year
When the trees are crowned with leaves
When ash and oak, and birch and yew

Are dressed in ribbons fair
When owls call the breathless moon
In the blue veil of the night
The shadows of the trees appear
Amidst the lantern light . . .

As she explains in the liner notes, this song is "a musical painting of the traditional custom of mumming, which has its roots in the tree-worshiping peoples who inhabited great regions of a forested Europe now long gone. Mummers, dressed in masks and costumes bedecked with ribbons and rags, are performers who parade through village streets to neighboring houses, singing songs and carrying branches of greenery. Though such celebrations appear to be relate to our Hallowe'en, they usually occur at different times of the year, particulary the New Year and close to May Day."

J.C. Frazier, in *The Golden Bough*, links this festival to pagan tree worship celebrated as maypole dancing. In Medieval and Tudor England, May Day was a public holiday marked by a parade where boughs of sycamore and hawthorn were carried in the procession and a young tree about 25 feet high was stripped of all branches except the top bough, sometimes topped with a floral garland in the shape of a crown with and long ribbons, sometimes with dolls, representing Flora, the Roman god of flowers, though some accounts also suggest a Dionysian phallus topped the tree. During the Renaissance era, James I banned maypoles, the celebrations of May Day, and Christmas as excessive and wanton. The Restoration of the Stuarts restored maypoles, but the festival was limited and by 1800 almost disappeared. May Day received a renewal of interest in 20th century. In my hometown of New Westminster, British Columbia, all the elementary schools participated in intricate dances using colored ribbons formed by steps of dancers. The idea came from Alfred Lord Tennyson, William Morris, and John Ruskin, who made it a children's day which included the crowning of a six-year-old Queen of the May. (This ritual day is not to be confused with a day for the working people, chosen in 1889 by the Congress of the Second International as Labor Day.)

At Lammas, or Loaf-Mass, the first bread from the first grains of the harvest is celebrated in a great dance that celebrates the circle of life from seed to harvest. With the return of autumn, comes the winter aspect of the God, the balance of light and dark, left and right, celebrated at the feast of Samhain or Halloween. This festival marks the coming of the Dark Time, the end of the agricultural year and the preparation for winter. Once celebrated on November 1, the day marked the return of cattle from high pastures, the end of summer, start of winter. In the depths of winter, the Sun God is asleep, renewing energies; his other Self, the Dark Lord, is in attendance with the Lady, protecting her, calming her, diverting her with tales, songs, poems, while she awaits the birth of the Child of Promise who will set forth on his journey, seeking the Goddess, once the days lengthen, and Imbolc will be celebrated again.

The Celts celebrated Samhain as the end of the year and the beginning of the New Year. Samhain was a time of courting and weddings, promises and renewals, a late autumn feast of thanksgiving for the harvest with the sun worshiped by lighting a bonfire. This is also the time of apple harvest. Avalon (associated with Camelot) means place of Apples, a tree sacred to Celts because when an apple is cut crosswise, a pentagram or five-point star is visible. The Romans added the festival of Pomona, goddess of fruit. The star was a symbol of the underworld goddess of death and regeneration, a reminder everyone journeys to the land of death. The custom of bobbing for apples at Halloween was once seen as a symbolic cheating of the death goddess.

For Loreena McKennitt in her song *Samain Night* from PARALLELL DREAMS and then again in *All Souls Night* from THE VISIT, this festival revives memories of the old ways when the collective soul comes to rest.

Samain Night

When the moon on a cloud cast night
Hung above the tree tops height
You sang me of some distant past
That made my heart beat strong and fast
Now I know I'm home at last . . .

All Souls Night

Bonfires dot the rolling hillsides
Figures dance around and around
To drums that pulse out echoes of darkness
Moving to the pagan sound . . .

I can see the lights in the distance
Trembling in the dark cloak of night
Candles and lanterns are dancing, dancing
A waltz on all All Souls Night . . .

Samhain is the most complex Celtic holy day. Under first full moon of Scorpio, the time of the thin veil, a festival of the of the dead. Spirits and mortals pass back and forth. Samhain called together the souls of the wicked who were condemned to inherit the bodies of animals. The Old Irish called this day *Oidche Shamna*, vigil of Samain. All Hallows Eve or Halloween (October 31), All Saints Day (November 1), and All Souls Day (November 2) came to replace Samhain in the Christian era. The souls that returned to earth on the 31st were prayed for the next two days as Hallow tide. The Church remembers those who have died on All Soul's or All Saints' Day. All Saints Day celebrated saints known and unknown and those who might have been sanctified but were not. To these pagan and Christian associations was added Guy Fawkes Day, November 5, complete with bonfire, fireworks, and the burning of effigies of the man who conspired to blow up the British House of Lords in the so-called Gunpowder Plot. Joyful at the deliverance of the King and his Parliament, the English celebrations have continued since that time. And now Samhain is reduced to a children's holiday called Halloween, a night for spirit walking, thoughts of black magic, a time for dressing up in orange and black, wearing masks, telling ghost stories by the weird shadows of Jack O' Lanterns.

4

THE BOOKS OF THE CELTS

The Roman Empire and the Roman Church did not extend to Ireland until the 5th century. Christianity in Ireland evolved as a monastic rather than an episcopal organization, with the monasteries open to a variety of ideas. Open to Celtic fables and legends, to the Greek and Latin texts, the Scriptures, the hagiographies of the martyrs. Literature and religion were one in the celebrated Irish illustrated manuscripts and scriptures. The monasteries saved the *fild*, the professional poets, from being expelled from Ireland, where they remained a privileged group until the final collapse of the Gaelic order a thousand years later in 1603. In the so-called Dark Ages, as the Roman Empire collapsed, literary culture flourished in Ireland, as Thomas Cahill recounts in his study of the Irish monks, *How the Irish Saved Civilization*.

The Irish monks mastered Greek, Latin, Hebrew, and their own oral literature. On specially prepared calfskin, monastic scribes and artists wrote the Irish codex using reeds, quills of geese and crows, cutting the feather to a chisel point to make thick and thin lines. Animal fur brushes, knives for

The Books of the Celts

scraping mistakes, and inkwells of cow horn, were attached to scribe's chair. A desk had wooden compasses, rules, templates, plant and mineral pigments, lapis lazuli from Hindu Kush of Afghanistan. Scribes used ink made of iron sulfate and crushed oak apples or a type of red insect from the Mediterranean. Other inks derived from oak galls, hard as crab apples from the gnawing of wasps into the bark, crushed in rainwater and vinegar, thickened with gum Arabic, with iron salts added to color the acid. Called encaustum (from Latin *caustere*, to bite), these inks bit into the springy velvety surface of the parchment. The skin was pressed between heavy wooden covers to keep from curling.

The Irish codex were magical books. Unlike a scroll that rolled up, the codex was cut and folded into leather quires, the length and breadth of a sheep, then pressed between covers. The Irish script, called minuscule, became the common script of the Middle Ages. The text model came from the megalithic tombs of the Boyne Valley, the spirals and zigzags, the wave of complexity moving in a unity. Some carvings may be sky maps or calendars. The great decorated manuscripts of early medieval Ireland were copied by monks on obscure outposts like Inis Murny and Skellig Michael. Decorated with spirals, geometric patterns, interlaced ribbons and animals, miniature pictures, these elaborate designs were meant to attract and convert pagans. The large clear script and pictures from the gospels were displayed to the congregation. The oldest manuscripts are the Cathach, Book of Psalms, from the 6th century. *The Book of Kells* was called the work of angels. *The Book of Ballymote*, from the 14th century, collects Irish sagas, law, genealogies. Celtic mythologies can be found in the *Books of Lenister, The Dun Cow, Ballymate*, and the *Yellow Book of Lecan*.

This was the golden age of Irish scholarship. Scholarly communities flourished at Derry, Durrow, Iona, and Skellig Michael, centers of holy learning that honored professional poets and women, the Druid teachings of the Bards (poets) and Ovates (philosophers) whose tonsure was copied by Christian monks. Abbots and abbesses ruled equally. In the 5th century, Colmcelle (Columba) founded the great monastery of Iona for women with Druid associations like Ciarin, Brendan, and St Brigit, who worshiped under the sacred oak trees and could hang her cloak on a moonbeam.

In her song *Skellig* from THE BOOK OF SECRETS album, Loreena McKennitt recreates the life and death of one such Irish scribe, which symbolically marks the end of this golden age of Celtic scholarship.

Skellig

I joined the brotherhood
My books were all to me
I scribed the words of God
And much of history
Many a year was I
Perched out upon the sea
The waves would wash my tears
The wind, my memory . . .

Beneath these jasmine flowers
Amidst these cypress trees
I give you now my books
And all their mysteries
Now take the hourglass
And turn it on its head
For when the sands are still
'Tis then you'll find me dead . . .

That Loreena McKennitt should look to books for inspiration for her music is not surprising given her reverence for these Irish scholars. As she explains in her press release, "the lyrics to this song tell the story of an elderly Irish monk in the 7th century. Having spent most of his life in the isolated religious community of Skellig Michael on the west coast of Ireland, he then travels with his fellow monks to Europe, perhaps to Italy. On his deathbed, he passes on to a fellow brother the responsibility of continuing his work: the copying, and thus the preservation, of ancient texts. Those illuminated works, it has been argued, were crucial for reintroducing classical literature to the European continent after the decline of the Roman Empire. Despite their weighty content, the manuscripts handed down to us also display the lively personalities of their long-ago scribes. Many are embellished in the margins with irreverent asides, comments to the lonely monks' far-off loved ones, and charming drawings of birds, mice and other small creatures." Loreena McKennitt gleaned the information for this song from Thomas Cahill's book, *How the Irish Saved Civilization,* as she acknowledges in her liner notes. "I set out for Bobbio in Emilia-Romagna, which Cahill says was the first Irish monastery to be established in Italy when renegade Irish monks were banished to the continent. How strange it was to view these very early

Irish times in the museum at Bobbio and see the name of Saint Columbanus. . . . With these ruminations fresh in my mind, I find myself returning to Trinity College for yet another look at the beautifully illustrated *Book of Kells* on display there." This is one more elemental Celtic tradition Loreena McKennitt discovered during her travels in Ireland.

This great age ended as the Irish melded with Normans and the Church aligned with the episcopal power of Rome. Celtic history became confused and chaotic as it blended with different cultures: Danish, Norman, and English. When Anglo-Norman knights arrived in Ireland, Henry II claimed the island and so began centuries of English colonial rule. Beneath the official accounts of the English Crown trying to civilize a conquered nation was a moving chronicle of tragic heroism and suffering under foreign oppression, a spirit of persecution some compare to the Jews of Europe.

5
COLONIZATION

While the Irish bards struggled to keep alive the legends and lore of druids, saints, and scholars, England began to build the British Empire, first exploring and then colonizing the Americas, Africa, and Asia, not without conflict with other colonizing powers, namely Spain and France.

In the 16th century, Henry VIII had thought Ireland was England's back door, vulnerable to attack from 'Catholic' France and Spain. On the sailing route from Europe to North America, Ireland was equally important to Spain, France, and England. Henry VII had sought to secure Ireland, as he had England, from the Pope by banning Catholicism and burning monasteries. The English began placing subjects in Lough Foyle, Shannon, and Dingle on the west coast, Bantry, Cork, and Youghal on the south. At the same time, the Spanish had intelligence outposts in Cork, Wateford, and Exford. By the time of Elizabeth I's reign, the Irish, apparently more sympathetic to the Spanish, had become a problem to be solved in true colonial style.

The Elizabethan army of 20,000 invaded Ireland and began a systematic conquest, attacking the last of the great Gaelic chieftains, Hugh O'Neill, Earl of Tyrone, and Hugh O'Donnel, Earl of Tyreconnell, who were defeated at the battle of Kinsalein, Co. Cork, Christmas Eve, 1601. This was to be the final solution. Kill the chieftains. Plant the country with English settlers and landlords.

Scots Presbyterians replaced the Irish Catholics on the land. Jail or hang the poets and bards. Destroy harps, books, manuscripts. Send the children to England to be educated. Eliminate the Irish language. This is the plight alluded to in Loreena McKennitt's *Bonny Portmore* through the memory of those sacred Druid oak forests destroyed by the English army for military purposes.

The Irish rebelled in 1640, which only brought 'the curse of Cromwell'. The invasion of Ireland by Oliver Cromwell's Roundheads, followed by famine and plague, killed a third of the Irish. But the Irish Catholics rose four decades later, in a fight with William of Orange at the Battle of the Boyne, still celebrated in Orange day parades on July 12. The Catholic forces were defeated again and many were exiled. The 'Wild Geese', as vanquished soldiers were called, went to France or the New World. Irish convicts were sent to penal colonies in the southern United States. Indentured servants went as slaves to Barbados and Jamaica.

During the 1700s, The Penal Laws were instituted by the English in Ireland, designed to stamp out the threat of Catholic resurgence by barring them from the land, the army, the electorate, commerce, and law. Ninety percent of the land, and all of the power, was in the hands of Anglo-Irish Protestants. The business of the nation was conducted in English. Irish speakers were marginalized, unable to defend themselves in court, banned from public office, all professions. The only book published in western Ireland was a Bible to help Protestant missionary groups at conversion. It took 200 years, but the English finally had a victory. Ireland was called the first and the last of England's colonies.

Though most of Europe watched in horror, the French Revolution in 1789 offered startling new ideas to the Irish: the inalienable rights of the individual, the concept of Liberty, Equality, Fraternity. The Irish, through mercantile ties with France, were well informed about the French Revolution and its progress. The ideas of democracy and the rights of the common man were impetus to people humiliated by 150 years of imperial rule. The leader of the United Irish Movement, Wolfe Tone, asked Napoleon for help, securing 50 French warships, 14,500 troops, and over 42,000 stand-at-arms for an assault on England. But the small expeditionary force was driven back by a gale, close enough to be seen from shore. The Society of United Irishmen was the most thoroughly prepared and nationally organized revolutionary movement in Irish history. Unfortunately, Wolfe Tone was betrayed by spies, arrested, and hung himself. On his person were two manuscripts of novels and a manifesto.

On June 21, 1798, the last great battle took place on Irish soil around Enniscort on the Salney River in Co. Wexford. Over 20,000 English troops killed an estimated 30,000 Irish. The Act of Union and the 500-year old Irish Parliament was dissolved. The final blow came in the 19th century when the English government introduced a National School System with free school, available nationwide, but in English only. To speak Irish was a punishable offence.

To this day, keeping Wolfe Tone's name alive is itself a political act. The popular Irish band, the Wolfe Tones, now in their third decade of recording, celebrate with whistle, banjo, mandolin, and drum kit the Irish Republic, the IRA, and their close ties with France. Though seen as a novelty act by the record industry, they sing old rebel favorites like *'Til Ireland A Nation* and *Rifles Of The IRA*. They have a fierce, loyal following. The Wolfe Tones regarded themselves as Ireland's answer to the folk protest movement in the USA. As Afro-Americans fought for civil rights, the Wolfe Tones spoke for Catholic civil rights and supported the aim of a united Ireland.

In her own way, Loreena McKennitt has given voice to this dream in her song *Breaking The Silence* from the PARALLEL DREAMS album. As she comments in the liner notes, the song is for "those who dream of freedom" and a "tribute to Amnesty International," an organization she believes is "vital to the whole concept of democracy," as she declared in *Dirty Linen*, and an organization she has supported through benefit concerts.

Breaking The Silence

I hear some distant drumbeat
A heartbeat pulsing low
Is it coming from within
A heartbeat I don't know
A troubled soul knows no peace
A dark and poisoned pool
Of liberty now lost
A pawn, an oppressor's tool . . .

May the spirit never die
Though a troubled heart feels pain
When this long winter is over
It will blossom again

As cultural critic Terry Eagleton has remarked, "the Irish can't forget their history because the English refuse to remember it."

6
THE GREAT HUNGER

1847, the year of the last great buffalo hunts on the North American Great Plains, also marked the greatest disaster of modern Ireland, the potato famine. The 'Great Famine' is the single most important event in Irish history and a defining moment in 19th-century European social consciousness.

Five hundred years ago, looking for a route to Asia, the Europeans discovered America. In the ground, dirty and valuable as truffles, was the potato. The potato came from the Andean countries in South America and native bands had cultivated many hardy, hearty, and tasty varieties. Sir Francis Drake and Sir Walter Raleigh first brought potatoes to Europe. A statue to Drake still stands in Offenberg, Germany, holding in his hand a complete potato plant, with blossoms and tuber. At first, the merits of the potato were debated furiously. Potatoes and corn were only good for pigs. Evangelists argued that since potatoes and corn were not mentioned in the Bible, they were incarnations of satanic spirit. Some said eating a potato would cause leprosy. In Diderot's encyclopedia, he states that potatoes produce flatulence, which Diderot adds is not a problem for peasants as they work outdoors.

But others saw differently. Phillip II sent potatoes to the Pontiff explaining they were a tonic, though he did not mention they were considered aphrodisiac. The Pope shared the potatoes with the cardinals. Parmentier, the pharmacist at Les Invalides, presented Louis XIV with a basket trimmed with potato blossoms. Marie Antoinette put a sprig in her hair. Land was set aside for growing potatoes.

Due to the vagaries of politics, Sir Walter Raleigh was forced to spend some time in Ireland living in the guardian's house at Dominican monastery in Youghal Bay. Having already brought tobacco to the fashionable court, he now introduced the potato, but of the many varieties of potatoes — Bintje, Kerr's Pink, German Butterball, Red Thumb, Katahadin, Carola — the English brought only one, the Lumper or Horse potato, which was susceptible to blight. A coarse, white, watery potato, it was rich in nitrogen, minerals, and vitamin C. With a dash of butter or milk, an egg, and a bit of herring, a healthy worker could eat pounds a day. Bland, unlike the turnip, the potato could be eaten month after month. Country people grew a long fingernail to peel the potato skin.

In the 18th century, potatoes replaced bread and meat as a staple of the Irish diet. Like rice in Asia, potatoes were the sole sustenance of a third of the rural population and a staple for many more. Potatoes were easy to grow. They flourished in bog marsh and on 'lazy beds' or self-draining layers of sod or seaweed covered with a little earth or manure. The 'lazy beds' were ironically named; they required the lifting of many tons of heavy stones. Potatoes were so plentiful they were used as fertilizer and to fill gaps in stone fences.

When Ireland's population doubled from around four million in 1790 to almost eight million in 1845, Irish farmers and peasants sub-divided leases among their children and were encouraged by absentee landlords to expand their rents by carving up the dwindling plots of land. Few plots of land were as large as five acres. Many were half or even a quarter of that. On the eve of the Famine rural Ireland had a population density some have compared to modern day Bangladesh. A farm in Co. Clare that had one tenant in 1793 had 96 tenants in 1847.

From 1800 on, a series of crop failures hinted at the impending crisis. In 1845, the summer brought unusual thunderstorms and heavy rains. The first sign of the blight was a spot on the leaf. The leaf turned brown and then purple. When the tuber was dug, small round spots appeared on the tuber with the appearance of a running sore. The starch within turned to sugar, with a sharp sweet taste, but it was inedible. The 1846 crop was entirely wiped out. In Co. Sligo Holy water was sprinkled on the fields. People in Co. Mayo said it was the work of malignant fairies. The cause, a parasitic fungus that rapidly spreads on the damp winds, was not discovered for seven years. Mycology, the study of fungi, was a new science. The antidote, a mixture of copper sulfate and lime, was not discovered for 30 years.

Sir Richard Peel, the Prime Minster of Great Britain, ordered emergency supplies of maize, the cheapest grain on the market, to be shipped to Ireland. The first shipments were not milled — it was like eating raw popcorn — because there were no gristmills in Ireland. The resulting concoction was known as 'Peel's Brimstone'. But cornmeal eventually did save thousands of lives. Rich agricultural interests forced Peel from office over his repeal of the grain laws. In Hansard aristocrats remarked that the Irish could eat grass — and some bodies were found with grass stains on their mouths. Indeed, anti-Irish feeling increased with the famine. Benjamin Jowett, Master of Ballilol College, Oxford, feared the famine would barely kill a million people, scarcely enough to do much good for English landlords. After visiting workhouses,

Thomas Carlyle asked, "Can it be a charity to keep men alive on these terms?" Novelist Charles Kingsley coined the phrase 'white niggers' for the Irish and captured two prejudices at once.

The Great Hunger began in 1847 and caused the death of over one million Irish. Half the population just disappeared. Nobody left records. Those who died were largely Irish speaking peasants. Their bodies went into unmarked graves. Coffins were built with trapdoors and hinges so dozens of bodies could be buried from the same box. Empty granaries became morgues. Stories are told of bodies of dead children stacked from floor to ceiling. The Irish died in ditches. The Irish died in fever hospitals. And the Irish died in 'coffin ships' on their way to Canada and America, dumped overboard to be 'buried at sea'. The 'coffin ships' lacked food (of course), water, and sanitation. Not only starvation but also typhus and cholera took the passengers on voyages that lasted three weeks to three months. In 1847, over 20,000 Irish died at Grosse Ille, Quebec. French Canadian families adopted many orphaned children, but many of the children have kept their Irish surnames to this day.

Travelers' accounts tell of the dreadful silence that greeted visitors to Ireland in 1847. The land of song had no tune. "The only human sound," notes one report, "was a feeble or depressing wail for the dead." The traveler notes the silence was awful. Men could not shout, children could not cry, dogs could not bark.

Some 360,000 one-room mud cabins known as 'bothies', which housed over two million peasants, simply disappeared in less than a decade, though their name lives on as Tommy People's Bothy Band. Land holdings were consolidated. The social structure and landscape of rural Ireland changed forever. In one decade, half the population died or was forced to emigrate. Over one million people starved to death, nearly two million emigrated, with another four million or more leaving before the end of the century as they faced similar hardship in Ireland. Social critics call this the emptying of Ireland.

The Great Famine killed nearly everything: poetry, music, dances. A culture was nearly lost, but when the Irish left they held fast to memories of age-old Celtic traditions. In Canada and America, they kept together, joined by their language, politics, poverty, Roman Catholicism, peasant folkways, clannish concentration, tragic history, and deep nostalgia for the old ways which found expression in sentimental stories and songs. The power of these stories and songs soon shaped the quality of North American culture. Tom Hayden calls the Irish the Indians of Europe. Like the Indians, the Irish gave to North America a rich oral culture where song, dance, and storytelling are prized art forms.

The Great Hunger

After the 1850s, a famine consciousness fueled Irish nationalist anger for decades leading to the 1916 Easter Uprising, the creation of the 26-county Republic of Ireland, and even the 'new' Ireland of the 1990s. In 1994, the Irish held the first national 'Famine Walk' in remembrance of this social crisis. The Republic of Ireland officially commemorated the 150th anniversary of Black '47 in 1997. The Famine Museum was opened in Stokestown where passengers departed on the coffin ships. Public statues to the famine were raised in New York, New Jersey, and in Boston's historic Cambridge common. A conference on Irish emigration held in 1998 at University College Cork was entitled 'The Scattering'. UN High Commissioner for Human Rights and former Irish President Mary Robinson spoke of the Great Hunger during state visits to famine-torn countries like Ethiopia. As part of the peace process in Northern Ireland, British Prime Minister Tony Blair personally acknowledged British responsibility for the catastrophic policies of 150 years earlier.

In spring 2001, the *Jeannie Johnston*, a replica of a 19th-century 'famine' ship originally built in 1847 at Quebec City to shuttle Irish refugees from Ireland to Canada and the United States, set sail from Tralee in Co. Kerry. The first *Jeannie Johnston* made at least 16 voyages from 1847 to 1855, but unlike many other vessels involved in this 'trade' that become known as coffin ships because of disease and overcrowding, the *Jeannie Johnston* never lost a passenger to disease or the sea. The replica ship would retrace the original routes, calling on more than 20 ports in North America, bringing the hope for an end to the long 'famine of peace' in a still-troubled Ireland.

The Great Hunger has been called the most powerful metaphor in modern Ireland by John Waters in his studies of contemporary Irish culture and music, *Rage of Angels: Ireland and the Genesis of U2* and *An Intelligent Person's Guide to Ireland.* For example, Sinnead O'Connor's rap song *Famine* piled into this metaphor religious and colonial rage as she blamed her abuse by her mother on her Roman Catholic upbringing, dramatically tearing up a photo of Pope John Paul II on *Saturday Night Live*. O'Connor spoke out against the Famine, citing Ireland's treatment by the English as 'domestic' abuse. She calls herself a professional 'keener', a singer who mourns the dead, howling and wailing as a counterpoint to a starved land, knowing full well that keening (from the Gaelic *cavineadh*) is admonished by the Church as pagan.

Keening after the Great Hunger and the loss of the old ways also gave emotional depth to the so-called Celtic revival of the 1990s whose most visible manifestation was the music and dance review *Riverdance*. The Irish tradition of song and dance had shaped the traveling minstrel shows of the early 20th century; indeed, the Irish dominated the 'black face' tradition in

America. Al Jolson, Bert Williams, and hoofers like George Christy, Billy Whitlock, and George 'Yankee Doodle Dandy' Cohen were Irish Americans disguised as African Americans. This Irish-African connection goes back to the 1600s when African slaves worked alongside Irish men and women who were deported or exiled from Ireland to work the sugar plantations in Jamaica, Monserrat, and the southern United States. As Michael Ventura suggests, "the major studies don't mention that Africans weren't the only slaves who had a Pre-Christian cosmology." In the 1650s, after Oliver Cromwell had conquered Ireland in a series of massacres, his brother, Henry, was the island's governor. In the next decade, Henry sold thousands of Irish people, mostly women and children, as slaves to the West Indies. The Irish slave was mated with the African. Irish-American poet Bob Callahan presents an image of a hybrid culture of music and dance evolving from a century of working alongside each other in the plantations of the West Indies. "You get Ibo men playing Bodhrans and Kerry men playing Jubi drums. You get set dances becoming syncopated to African rhythms and your basic Celt turned into a full blown voodoo ritual."

Eventually hundreds of black-faced minstrel groups traveled throughout America, creating one of the most fascinating American art forms, influencing the blues, old time mountain music, New Orleans jazz, bluegrass, gospel, music hall styles, and eventually Broadway tap dancing and network television variety shows, all descendants of the jig and hornpipe, which culminate in the extraordinary success of *Riverdance*.

Composer Bill Whelan, a former member of the Irish band Planxty, came up with the title 'Riverdance'. His extensive career includes writing scores for film and television, including a celebration of Dublin's millennium in 1988, and production credits with most of Ireland's leading musicians. He is also well known for setting the works of Irish poets to music, having served as a composer to the W.B. Yeats Festival at the Abbey Theater. Yeats, that compulsive mystic, considered theater an intricate combination of dance, music, and drama. In 1992, Whelan worked on an album that explored Irish, Bulgarian, and Macedonian music, including time patterns not found in traditional Irish music. He learned about the eastern European mystic tradition in such instruments as the gadulka, kaval, and gaida. He completed a large scale commissioned orchestral work, *The Seville Suite (Kinsaleto La Coruna)*, about the flight to Spain of Red Hugh O'Donnell after the disastrous defeat at the Battle of Kinsdale in 1601. The piece included many of the band members who would appear in the original cast of *Riverdance*.

In 1993, he wrote *The Spirit of Mayo*, an 85 piece symphony orchestra with

the GREAT huNGeR

200 voices, a battalion of drummers, part of the celebration of the 5,000-year-old Ceide Fields. The megalithic tombs in northwest Ireland are the most extensive Stone Age monuments in the world. The producers of *The Spirit of Mayo*, John McColgan and Moya Doherty, felt the world was ready to hear the mix of Irish, Eastern European, Spanish, and North African rhythms of *Riverdance*. They added dancer Jean Butler, who had toured with The Chieftains, Irish American tap dancer Michael Flatley, listed in the *Guinness book of Records* as the world's fastest tap dancer, Anuna, a Dublin choir of seven men and seven women, who had recorded with Sting, Sinead O'Connor, and Maire Brennan of Clannad, who specialized in long forgotten Celtic music.

Riverdance made its debut as a seven-minute program in a three-hour Eurovision song contest before 300 million viewers on April 30, 1994. Jurors came from Africa, Europe and Asia. The program was gimmicky, even kitsch, and its intention was to promote tourism to each participating country. But the show was hugely popular. The public demanded a video, a one-hour special, and a Christmas show. The video, the best selling in Irish history, raised 300,000 pounds, the proceeds going to charities working with victims of the war in Rwanda. As the project developed, it involved research in Spain, Hungary, and Moscow. The one-hour show would include a flamenco dancer, dancers from the Moscow Folk Ballet Company, a gospel choir from Georgia, and tap dancers from Harlem. *Riverdance* also featured 30 former world champion Irish dancers.

To the mix of traditional Irish instruments — fiddle, accordion, Uileann pipes — came bass and electric guitars, soprano and alto sax, midi keyboards, masses of precessions instruments, including bodhran, dumbek, spoons and bones, and eastern European instruments gadulka, kaval, gaida, and flamenco guitar. Irish traditional music meets music from other cultures. The integration of Irish, Russian, Spanish, and American cultures, meant, as the producers craftily reasoned, something for everyone. At one level, the show was simplicity itself: an evening of music, singing, and dancing such as could be found at any Irish house party. But the presentation was on a par with the sophistication of Broadway or the West End. After opening in February 1995 to critical acclaim, Prince Charles invited the cast to perform at the Royal Gala to celebrate VE Day at the London Coliseum, with 20 million viewers. Later that summer, the cast performed again at a charity evening in the presence of the Queen and Princess Margaret. When the show arrived in New York, Senator Ted Kennedy booked a block of 60 seats at Radio City Music Hall.

The show is a symbolic short hand for Irish history and culture. According to the official book on *Riverdance*, "Act One is internal. The songs praise the elemental forces of fire, water, wood, and stone, cultivating the earth, dealing with spiritual and human relationships, culminating in a bond with home. The spirit of a river-woman is summoned from the water to reawaken the land. In the final scene water and land come together. A uileann pipes solo is the highlight of the first set. Act Two: American Wake is a poignant depiction of poverty and famine, parting and separation, and how millions of Irish were driven from their homeland to immigrate to the US in the mid 19th century. The Irish way of death, the wake, celebrates the new life with drinking, singing, dancing. 'Lift the wings' is the highlight of the set with its melancholy undertone of men and women and children driven by war, slavery, and famine, to the New World. Here meets diverse cultures that shared uprooting, dislocation and resettlement, the common suffering of oppressed peoples, African, Russian, Macedonians, Slavs, Celtic Spaniards, now integrated and transported back home, if only symbolically, as Ireland celebrates its new place in the post modern world."

While Loreena McKennitt may not have a direct connection to the Famine since her family immigrated to Canada in the 1830s, she has deep sympathy for the plight of the hungry Irish child, as she expresses in *Dickens' Dublin (The Palace)* on her PARALLEL DREAMS album, a song set in time just prior to Black '47.

Dickens' Dublin (The Palace)

I walk the streets of Dublin town
It's 1842
It's snowing on this Christmas Eve
Think I'll beg another bob or two
I'll huddle in this doorway here
Till someone comes along
If the lamp lighter comes real soon
Maybe I'll go home with him . . .

Maybe I can find a place I can call my home
Maybe I can find a home I can call my own

As she explains the genesis of this song to Lynne Walker of the BBC, "I first heard it when I traveled to Ireland in 1981 and met a veterinarian up in Donegal who had this cassette at the time, and at the time that I heard it I was interested in playing and creating a piece based on the plight of homeless people, then shifted my creative focus to writing a piece based on homeless children." The child's 'keening' recitation that opens and closes the song comes from a series of recordings broadcast on Radio Eireann in the 1960s, where inner-city Dublin children were invited to tell their version of popular stories, in this instance, Charles Dickens' *A Christmas Carol*.

And in setting W.B. Yeats' *Stolen Child* to music on her first album, she clearly understood the keening at the heart of the Irish experience.

Stolen Child

Come away oh human child
To the waters and the wild
With a faery hand in hand
For the world's more full of weeping
Than he can understand . . .

When Loreena McKennitt traveled to Ireland to discover the "romantic Ireland" of Yeats, she seemed to have found a place she could call home. She would return to Ireland several times during the 1980s, deepening her appreciation for the old ways with each visit, often staying at Annaghmakerrig, an artists' retreat in County Monaghan, the former home of Tyrone Guthrie, founding artistic director of the Shakespeare Festival Theatre in Stratford, Ontario, where Loreena would record traditional Irish songs for her ELEMENTAL album and found her Quinlan Records label while acting on the Stratford stage. Eventually she would buy her own Irish home, "a very modest cottage on the west coast," she told *Inside Borders*. "It's been a kind of anchor, in a way." She would need such an anchor in the old ways during the next decade as she followed her calling, assuming the role of the bard of Stratford, busking at the St Lawrence Market in Toronto, and touring the country with her Troubadour Lever harp.

celtic quest

Loreena McKennitt

celtic quest

Loreena McKennitt

celtic quest

Loreena McKennitt

celtic quest

LOREENA McKENNITT

QUINLAN ROAD

1
STRATFORD

The year before her first pilgrimage to Ireland, Loreena McKennitt had moved to Stratford, Ontario, a sturdy little agricultural town, not unlike Morden, Manitoba, but with a cultural difference. Stratford is home to the world-renowned Shakespearean Festival Theatre where Loreena would work for three seasons as a singer, performer, and composer before founding her own recording company, Quinlan Road, and releasing three albums, ELEMENTAL, TO DRIVE THE COLD WINTER AWAY, and PARALLEL DREAMS. With the release of THE VISIT in 1991, a decade after she moved to Stratford, Loreena moved beyond Quinlan Road out to the world stage in a new record deal with Warner Bros, negotiated on her own fiercely independent terms.

Stratford presents two faces to the world. 'Welcome to Stratford', the sign at the city limits says, 'Home of the World Famous Festival Theatre and the Ontario Pork Congress', an agricultural fair held each June to celebrate the swine industry. (A local joke claims Stratford has two kinds of ham, four legged and two legged.) The Festival Theater, built in the shape of a tent and situated beside the Avon River with overhanging willow trees and resident swans, is attached to an agricultural and small industrial community of 30,000. The prime industries are suitcases, toilets, 'soft' auto parts (dashboards, paneling), feed and seed, corn and hogs, with a disproportionate number of elegant restaurants and a host of bed and breakfast business situated in grand old southern Ontario buff brick houses and contemporary homes. The largest employer makes ball bearings for the aerospace industry; the coat of arms for the city features a pair of swans.

Stratford was founded in 1832 by Scots settlers who thought the ideal community should be no more than 35,000 in population so citizens could wander to the city edge and contemplate God's natural handiwork in the temple of the world. As the eastern mystics might put it, each time a human being attains enlightenment, a flower opens in the garden of the universe. Stratford today fits this ideal, with rich agricultural land acting as a greenbelt surrounding the city and curtailing excessive industrial development. Stratford is also situated in the 'Snow Belt' of southwestern Ontario on the windward side of Lake Huron, some 45 minutes drive west, and at an elevation of 1,100 feet. The winters are bracing, though not so nearly as cold as a southern Manitoba winter, with a cutting northwest wind, in part caused by the devastation of nearly 95 percent of the natural forest, cleared to make way for farms or harvested for furniture manufacturers. Local farmers say the last snow is mid May and the first frost-free week begins June 1st. In late spring, the large maple trees lining the streets and farm fence lines lose their keys and the air is rich with little green propellers. The aspens produce catkins, and dandelion, milkweed and thistle fill the air. The summer brings forth acre upon acre of corn and soybeans to feed the cattle and swine, the autumn a burst of color as the deciduous trees prepare to drop their leaves.

Socially, southwestern Ontario is the world portrayed in the stories of celebrated Canadian writer Alice Munro, who lives just up the road from Stratford, near Wingham. Quiet introspective lives of strong women resigned to the patriarchal and sometimes brutal ways of farming men, where the chief cultural event is a quilting bee at the local United Church, organized by the WCTU (Women's Christian Temperance Union), or the hockey game at the arenas found in almost every small town. Munro characterizes these communities as having few writers, few painters, and few musicians, other than the church organist and choir leader. Even fewer who would admit to liking the arts. Small 'c' conservative politics, small 'i' imagination, with a Gothic touch.

But agriculture and culture, industry and artistry miraculously meet in Stratford, at least during the Festival and growing season from May to October. Miraculously so because the city is relatively isolated from the cultural capital of Canada, Toronto, 88 miles from city hall to city hall, which was quite some distance on a two-lane highway in 1953 when the Theatre was founded. This isolation prompted the first artistic director of the theater, Tyrone

Guthrie, to remark: "It makes attendance at a play something of a pilgrimage. The Wise Pilgrim is not in much of a hurry." Loreena McKennitt would spend considerable time during the 1980s retreating to the Tyrone Guthrie Centre in Ireland and recording songs for TO DRIVE THE COLD WINTER AWAY there. She would also adopt the attitude of the 'wise pilgrim' during the 1990s as she journeyed across Europe and Asia, tracing the travels of the ancient Celts in Spain and Italy, even the through the Russian Steppes on the Trans-Siberian railway.

Perhaps as a record of our search for a place in the universe, Stratford has pleasant gardens hinting at other worlds, perhaps a reminder that the original garden was the Greek 'paradeisos, from the Persian 'pairi-daeza', an enclosure divided into four equal parts by artificial waterways as a model of the universe. A short excursion around town leads admiring visitors to a pretty garden with classical symmetries (once a pottery factory) and over 500 herbs, plants, and flowers mentioned in Shakespeare's plays. A forest of endangered trees is called 'Burnham Wood' after a scene in *Macbeth*. Streets, like Romeo and Falstaff, are named after Shakespearean characters. The public schools are called Avon, Hamlet, Romeo and Juliet, Falstaff, and King Lear. Schools do class projects in Shakespeare, a celebration of children discovering the magic of a writer whose work embraces magical charms and fairies, great sword fights and the kings of history, and moving love stories. A Grade Two class presents an abridged version of the season opener in the city hall auditorium. The associations of Shakespeare with Stratford go back to 1832, when the first hotelier hung a picture of the Bard. A fine lending library, one of the original Carnegie libraries, celebrated its centenary in 2001. Their holdings are unusually strong in Shakespeare and the theater arts.

Some two dozen reptilian Stratford swans have more bones in their necks than a giraffe (25 to 7). Swans are heavy birds, mythological speaking, associated with divinity, air, and blood in occult thought, symbols of eternal and supreme knowledge and power. The Greek god Zeus sometimes hides in a swan disguise, which meant trouble for Leda, but gave W.B. Yeats inspiration for his great poem, *Leda and the Swan*, and Loreena McKennitt for *The Bonny Swans* on THE MASK AND THE MIRROR album. The swan is symbol of the lasting values of Greek civilization. (At the end of the Greek era, the Christian era begins with the Dove of the Holy Spirit.)

When Loreena McKennitt moved to Stratford, the Festival Theatre was undergoing a crisis so intense that it nearly destroyed the institution. The growth of alternative theatre in Canada in the 1970s came about in part because of the assertion of Canadian identity. Theatre productions made plays about 'here' and how it was different from 'there' and 'elsewhere'. Canadian plays immediately brought up arguments about non-Canadian plays as expressions of a post-colonial culture. How is Canada different from the imperial power, the ideology that sponsored it, and how is Canada different from the United States or Britain? How to make Shakespeare, or for that matter, the classic and contemporary theatre repertoire relevant for Canadians in a way that went beyond Tyrone Guthrie's RADA style of acting, or mounting classic American productions from Eugene O'Neill or Tennessee Williams to even Gilbert and Sullivan to bring in the US traffic? Actor Cedric Smith once quipped that Shakespeare was a Canadian cultural worker who had to go overseas for employment. Should the Festival have an Artistic Director from the UK? These debates, instigated by the choice of a British director instead of a Canadian, truncated the 1980-1981 season. While the crisis was resolved, the question broods uneasily unanswered in the background of every season.

But Stratford created for Canada the possibility of an artistic industry. The Stratford Festival generates $110 million in services, goods, and accommodation. No other artistic organization in the world is the central source for a region's economic well being. The Stratford Festival can proudly boast it is one of the three best classic theatres in the world, after the Royal Shakespeare Company and the National Theatre in London, England. Stratford has a chef's school and many fine restaurants with frequently changing menus as the nature of cuisine and creative dining has evolved from meat and two veg to a celebration of the world's culinary traditions. Chutneys, salsas, curries, and sweet and savory barbecue sauces accompany wildly innovative foods, the newest of fusion cooking, and other gastronomic delights. Traditional livestock ranching has also been revolutionized; nearby farms raise elk for the antlers, emu for oil and meats, potbellied pigs and red deer for the Asian export market. More than a local industry, the festival operates in the international marketplace.

Why Loreena McKennitt moved to Stratford is clear, but how she ending up staying remains somewhat of a mystery, even, apparently, to Loreena herself. "I was invited to be part of the theatre's Gilbert and Sullivan production," she told Nick Krewen in *Canadian Musician*. "I left all my household effects in Winnipeg thinking I'd be here just for the summer." The story goes that she was encouraged to move to Stratford by legendary musician and actor Cedric Smith, a founding member of the Perth County Conspiracy, the name given to a 1960s and '70s farming commune and folk band. Smith had gone on to act on the Festival Theatre stage and would eventually become a television star on the highly successful *Road to Avonlea* series, based on the Lucy Maud Montgomery 'Anne of Green Gables' stories and broadcast on the CBC in the 1990s. Smith would collaborate with McKennitt on the recording of ELEMENTAL, providing guitars and vocals on *Carrighfergus* and *Kellswater*. Smith may also have been instrumental in the choice of *Carrighfergus* for the soundtrack of the movie *Bayo* (1984), which opened a career door for McKennitt as a composer of music for other films in the 1980s, including *Heaven on Earth* (1986), *To a Safer Place* (1987), *A Wake for Milton* (1988), *Adam's World* (1989), *Bridging the River of Silence* (1991), *Mother Earth*, and a trilogy of films on women's spirituality produced by Studio D of the National Film Board of Canada, *The Goddess Remembered* (1989), *The Burning Times* (1990), and *Full Circle* (1993). In *Heaven on Earth* McKennitt also played a small role, and she appears as one of the musicians playing at the wake for Milton Acorn, the 'People's Poet', in *A Wake for Milton*.

Loreena was not new to the stage. She had acted in mini-Broadway musicals on a small stage at a Winnipeg dinner theatre club called The Hollow Mug as part of a cast of five, and had participated in local productions of shows such as *My Fair Lady*. She had taped a television commercial for the Manitoba Liquor Commission, requiring her to say the line, "I don't drink gin and tonic." When she left agriculture studies at the University of Manitoba, she enrolled briefly at the Manitoba School for Theatre and Allied Arts. McKennitt had been a contestant in the Manitoba division of the Du Maurier Search for Talent competition, making a short list of 15 semi-finalists who received a prize of $2,000 and the honor of being featured on CBC-TV. From these 15, five were chosen by votes cast by television viewers as well as a panel of judges. For her final performance, McKennitt chose a scene from *My Fair Lady*. As one of five finalists, she received another $5,000 cash prize and the opportunity to work for future CBC productions.

Despite such acting promise, Loreena did not make the 'cut' for the Stratford production she auditioned for, though she did play a small role in the chorus of *HMS Pinafore*. She stayed on in the city, nevertheless. In 1982, she was cast in the singing role of Ceres, goddess of agriculture, in Shakespeare's *The Tempest*, a play she would return to when composing *Prospero's Speech* for her THE MASK AND MIRROR album. In 1984, she composed music for the Festival production of Shakespeare's comedy *The Two Gentlemen of Verona,* then a year later she studied briefly with Guy Wolfendon, composer-in-residence at the Royal Shakespeare Company in Stratford-on-Avon, England. Indeed, her roles at the Festival Theatre took her in the musical direction she had first envisioned on her pilgrimage to

Ireland as she found work in composing scores for dramaturges like Elliott Hayes, who was producing a Festival play about the life and art of the romantic poet and visionary William Blake.

So, in Stratford, Loreena McKennitt found a way to make a living, however spartan, a congenial theatrical and musical community, and a town not unlike her hometown of Morden, Manitoba, where everyone knows everyone. As she commented on her adopted home of Stratford in the Toronto *Globe and Mail*, "there's a comfort and a confidence that comes with shopping, going to the bank or post office or whatever and if you don't have any money in your pocket, you can pay them tomorrow. It's great because there are a lot of forces in business that project you in unnatural and therefore unreal corners and I'm not interested in that. Living in this community keeps me, I hope, more normal." Here she has created a studio in the loft of a local church, " a very comfortable space," she commented in *Canadian Musician*, which features rows of antique and exotic instruments with richly colored tapestries and curtains hanging from the ceiling to improve the acoustics. Through the past two decades while living in Stratford, Loreena has remained loyal to the town, naming her record label Quinlan Road after a concession road just north of the city where she lives, using Beacon-Herald Fine Printing, a division of the local newspaper, for producing her album sleeves and booklets, employing Hypertext Digital Publishing to design her very attractive yet highly functional web site, calling on the Festival Travel agency to handle her touring needs and adventures in search of Celtic history, and giving back to the community as a volunteer member of the Stratford Heritage Trust. Most recently, she has purchased a heritage school building, 'The Falstaff School', saving it from the wrecker's ball. Loreena McKennitt has become a source of immense pride for the fair citizens of Stratford, Ontario, taking her place in the Stratford pantheon alongside hockey legend Howie Meeker, Thomas Alva Edison, who lived briefly in the city during the 1860s about six blocks from the offices of Quinlan Road, and the Bard of Stratford himself.

2

THE FESTIVAL, THE THEATRE, AND THE DANCE

The Festival Theatre is one of Stratford's public faces, one civic mask. That the theatre season coincides with traditional agricultural festivals, opening in May (Beltane) and closing in October (Samhain) may be a quirk of the calendar brought on by a north temperate climate, but nevertheless significant. For the first three years, the Festival Theatre was staged in an outdoor tent, in part to capture the spirit of ancient festivals and performances.

The word festival originally refers to the feast, a ritual meal, at the time of dryness before the winter rains. Over time, it has become associated with renewal, a joyous occasion, and communion. The words communion, communication, and community tell us something about the nature of feasting and festival. A festival is about sharing words, images, and concepts. Twentieth-century thinkers like Carl Jung, Mircea Eliade, and Joseph Campbell have studied the links between staging festivals and mythmaking. Much as myths can be seen as stories expressing the deep and complex inner workings of the psyche, so can festivals and their progeny, the theatre. Masks and costumes express ancestral spirits, theatre reenacts these in the form of ritual drama. We don't attend the theatre to see how the story ends — we know that MacBeth will die, we are confident that *All's Well That Ends Well* will indeed end well. We attend to partake in these tragic or comic rituals. The role of audience is to be a chorus, part of the community. In a society that often lacks meaningful rites, theatre re-establishes the ancient and the supernatural with the contemporary and the actual, connecting us to cultural and moral orders.

Theatre is an act of symbolic disclosure stripping away false masks and seeing through illusions. As an instrument for enlightenment, theater is a place for ideas, philosophies, and the most intense discussion of our fate. To unveil the intricacies of mind, unravel the skein of human existence. Yes, theatre must entertain, but only so as to find the most appealing way of presenting these thoughts and ideas. Excitement, illumination, and discovery, however fleeting, that is theatre. To the gods of Pity, Terror, Tenderness, and Mirth, the theatre is a temple. Deeper than acting style, content, and story is the ritual of movement, dance, and song. To evoke the essence of something greater than ourselves, we respond with emotion, mind purged of the trivial, and live for an instant at our highest imaginative peak. Ritual brings a strong sense of wonder, beauty, horror, tenderness, and glory.

Among the greatest acts of the theatre are, of course, William Shakespeare's plays, whose genius combines classical themes and with traditional folk rituals, among them re-enactments of medieval morality plays, mystery plays, ancient fertility masques, and the so-called 'mummers' plays, a form of theatre Loreena McKennitt began to explore as a means of musical expression while working with the Stratford Festival Theatre, long before recording her most successful song, *The Mummer's Dance*, on THE BOOK OF SECRETS album. Her first journal entry concerning the mummer's dance, published in her liner notes, reads: "January 1, 1985, Stratford: I just read an account of a mumming troupe which boarded a Polish ship stranded in the harbour in St John's, Newfoundland, on New Year's Eve to entertain the sailors. According to James Frazier in his book *The Golden Bough*, mumming has its roots in the tree-worshiping of the peoples who inhabited great regions of a forested Europe now long gone." As she goes on to explain the ritual, "mumming usually involves a group of performers dressing up in masks (sometimes of straw) and clothes bedecked with ribbons or rags, and setting out on a procession to neighboring homes singing songs and carrying branches of greenery. It is primarily associated with springtime and fertility, and it has a cast of stock characters, like the Fool, which recurs in some form or another from Morris dancing to the shadow puppet plays of Turkey and Greece and even the morality plays of the Middle Ages." In subsequent journal entries from September 1995, May 1, 1997, and May 15, 1997, McKennitt traces the presence of this form of theatre in the Halloween rituals on the "island of Inishmore, off the West coast of Ireland," in the Padstow May Day festival at Padstow, Cornwall, even in a "Sufi ritual associated with St George." The Padstow May Day dance is especially colorful, beginning "with a ritual carol, sung *a capella*, rich with references to springtime and St George. May Day morning's rendition of the song adds a full complement of accordions and drums which accompany a procession of the 'obby oss,' a 'horse' figure costumed in a large hooped skirt and an almost African-looking mask."

This ancient ritual of song, mask, and theatre resonates in the lyrics and music of *The Mummer's Dance*.

The Mummer's Dance

We've been rambling all the night
And some time of this day
Now returning back again
We bring a garland gay . . .

'A garland gay we bring you here
And at your door we stand
It is a sprout well budded out
The work of Our Lord's hand'

In the medieval English countryside, mummers' plays were a dramatic ceremonial performed by men. Traditionally, only men (even if the play has female characters) perform the mummers' dance, the crossed sword dancing of the Highlands or the Morris dances. To be seen as priests or agents of magic, the men wear disguises, simple masks of straw, rags, and paper, leather strips, or, sometimes, elaborate headpieces. Horns are symbols of fertility. On certain nights of the year, men would disguise themselves and form a troupe, which visited certain prearranged stations. At each one of them, the men perform a little play of about 20 minutes. The performers create a half circle or full circle with a broom to sweep back the spectators. In the play, one of the men is stricken down, but lives to fight another day, symbolizing autumn and winter bursting to life again in the spring. Some say the circle is made clockwise, a ritual portrayal of the sun's passage across the heavens in winter between Christmas and Twelfth Night. The plays ensure the return of the sun. The concept of magic is essential in the mummers' dances. Each detail contributes to the feeling of a primitive kind of magic. Inside the circle the players are charmed and safe.

The mummers' plays differ from conventional theatre in several ways. The play comes to the audience. The plays are short, less that half an hour. The performance space will be a house, more likely, a pub, or even the open road. The ceremony is seen as a 'visit'. Nobody communicates with the audience to tell a story or explain the action. What words are spoken or chanted, if any (mum's the word, hence, mummer), have a magical purpose. Spectators, viewing mumming for the first time, will possibly see it only as slapstick humor, but this is part of an underlying primitive ritual. Many argue mummers' plays are rooted in early sympathetic magic, and the simple death and resurrection plot is associated with the primitive idea of death of winter and rebirth of the summer. The purpose of the performance is familiar the world over — 'to drive the cold winter away' by asking for a blessing on spring crops and livestock. The mummers' rituals summon fertility for the land, health for the body, grace for the soul.

So the plays have direct ritual purpose. The origins of mumming lay in pagan rites concerned with the eternal struggle between good and evil, winter and summer, death and resurrection. Ritual sacrifice may have been an ingredient. What matters is the ritual, not the acting, from station to station, creating a magic circle, reenacting death and resurrection.

Although there are no records earlier than the 16th century, both the season for the plays and their apparent great age offer suggestions as to their origins in the dark nights of winter with a calling upon magic for light and spring. Historically, in England, the drama was performed in the old style winter months commencing at All Souls, or the Irish Samhain (31 October), and ending at Easter. Mummers were once found in nearly every village in

England. The Christian church frowned on these 'sinful' practices and staged its own dramatic presentations as miracle, mystery, and morality plays grouped in cycles, plays which are still performed at York, Coventry, Wakefield, and Chester. Antiquarians like the Folklore Society collected these plays for publication in the late 19th century. By the end of the 19th century, however, appearances were most common at Christmas when players collected money to augment low winter earnings. The Christmas mummers' plays have a Father Christmas as central character, as players move from one hostelry to another, presenting their play with characters that include St George, a doctor, a Turk, Robin Hood, Little John, a brave soldier, Tom the tinker. Wounds are healed, the dead brought back to life. Since the beginning of the 15th century, St George has been a favorite as one of the heroes up against a cunning Turkish Knight. Many legends of St George involve a dragon, which some say symbolizes summer defeating winter. All the plays, despite certain differences, are seasonal, and all contain a death and ritual resurrection of one of the characters.

The mummers' plays and other folk rituals were celebrated in the court of Henry VIII. Dozens of players were kept on his household rosters. The king had a corps of 16 trumpeters, their instruments hung with banners and tassels, minstrels, and royal lutenists. He owned a vast collection of instruments, some masterpieces: a recorder, lutes, keyboards, and even a silver organ studded with jewels. He himself was skilled on virginal, recorder, lute-pipe, cornet, and organ. And he practiced harpsichord day and night. As a serious amateur musician, he composed love songs and instrumental pieces, melancholy songs of parting, the suffering of lovers, and true love. His hymns, such as *O Lord The Maker Of All Things*, are part of the canon of English church music. As a composer he was part of a broad transition in concert music, from the ornate traditional style of the Middle Ages to the more fluid Italian style of *pavanes* and *galliards*. He left written notes on sheet music. He had a fondness for the harp. One of the events of his social season was called 'Harping and Carping' when court minstrels recited long poems of old adventurers in a medieval fashion. *Greensleeves*, the song Loreena McKennitt recorded on THE VISIT, is credited to him. Music was an indispensable part of the learning of servants, and children sang his works at mass, vespers, and compline. He wrote a song for every event, significant or mundane. His songs were sung in alehouses, inns, at court, and with sermons.

This is the spirit of play Loreena McKennitt captures in her arrangement of this standard English folk song — and in the recording of the song, as she explains in an interview with the BBC. "We began the tracks for PARALLEL

The Festival, the Theatre, and the Dance

DREAMS in 1988 through an artist development deal with Polygram. In that session, the mandate was to come out of the studio with four pieces. While we were working on "Silent Night," the phone rang and the engineer had to chat on the phone for awhile. I was set up in the control room with the vocal mic and keyboards. The guitar player was set up in the booth and the cello was set up on the floor. I said to them, 'While he's on the phone, why don't we try something with *Greensleeves*? I want to send Tom Waits up doing it.' So, I started playing it and we didn't get very far — maybe through the first verse. The engineer got off the phone and said, 'That sounds kind of interesting. Why don't we roll the tape just for sport and see if you guys can get through the whole piece?' So, I looked at Brian [Hughes] and George [Koller] on the floor and said, 'Okay, fine!' And we rolled tape and went all the way through it. So, that cut on THE VISIT is a totally spontaneous thing. We never went back to fix anything. This is that moment captured like a photograph. I didn't know where I was going with it in terms of chord progressions or verses, so it's a very special piece for that reason."

While Henry VIII would have enjoyed such musical revelry, what he most enjoyed was an ancient spectacle called mumming, disguising, or masking. The American Heritage Dictionary says the medieval word "mummer" comes from the Old French "*momer*" meaning to put on a disguise, wear a mask, or pantomime, especially at a festival. The mummers at court were elaborate. The king, a graceful and agile dancer, often disguised himself, to perform intricate and demanding dances at a court transformed into a theatre with movable props, elaborate dress, complex masks and headwear, creating the fashion show of its day. The London of Henry VIII had 500 conjurers, purveyors of white magic, prophets with potions and conjuring books, horoscopes, talismans, magic signs, and all manner of sorcerers who claimed their brew of lime, horse bones, rabbit skin, chalk, and powdered glass would make a cloak of invisibility.

Even today many of these folk customs linger on as part of the collective wisdom of village communities, welding the population into a tight community with dancing, plays, and ritual. Mumming plays have proved to be most persistent of ancient folk theatre rites. The mummers plays have connections with Tibetan Festivals and others as varied as the Mexican flying festival, Australian Intichima ceremony, the Easter celebrations in Russia, the American Zuni initiation ceremony, and other primitive dances and ceremonies. Similar traditions with the common theme of death and resurrection have been noted in the Pyrenees, through the Swiss-German border area, in Rumania, Thrace and Macedonia in the Balkans, Skyros in the Aegean, and in the mythology of ancient Syria, Greece and Egypt. The Swiss troupe, Mummenshantz (which means mummers dance or masquerade), began as a fringe act at the Avigonon Festival in 1972 and have celebrated nearly three decades of mime, mask, dance, and costume. Mummer's plays are still performed in some parts of England and outports in Newfoundland. Short story writer Alden Nowlan wrote a fine collection, *Will Ye Let the Mummers In?* And in Newfoundland, folk singer Simini had a hit in 1982 with her *The Mummer's Song*.

While the mummers' plays are not performed per se on the Stratford Festival Theatre stage, a wandering group of Morris Dancers appears each summer, and in the various masques at the center of Shakespeare's comedies and romances the mummers' plays resonate. These masques are uniquely theatrical to the degree that the thoughts and meanings they express are beyond the reach of spoken language. Mummers' plays give viewers a chance to rediscover the relationship between ritual and drama and explore the terrifying possibilities of existence. Like the ritual elements of the Stratford Festival, the plays establish a relationship in the 'space' shared by actor and audience. The purpose of the performance lies in an immediate and imaginative change from a secular to a sacred space. In this context, think of Loreena McKennitt's video of *The Mummer's Dance* as a little theatre piece. Beneath the 'dark other' is the veiled world of heroes, gods, goddesses, little people. Initiation into this veiled world beneath our ordinary reality is what we seek. As a popular song rooted in an ancient ritual, Loreena Mckennitt's *The Mummer's Dance* is an extraordinary musical and theatrical success.

3
DEAD POETS

Not surprisingly, Loreena McKennitt's music has been significantly influenced by the works of William Shakespeare, as well as two other 'Williams', William Butler Yeats and William Blake, not to mention other greater poets like Alfred Lord Tennyson and Dante Alighieri. Loreena McKennitt is one of the most 'literary' musicians to have ever recorded. Her music resonates with the collective force of the world's best literature. Her performances, one critic playfully remarked, send her audience "racing home to dig out the *Norton Anthology of English Literature*." When she released THE VISIT in 1991 featuring one of her most popular songs, *The Lady of Shallott*, based on the lyrics of Alfred Lord Tennyson, she found herself accounting for her 'literary' influences in many interviews she gave. On this album she also set to music a passage from Shakespeare's romantic play *Cymbeline* and would return to Shakespeare's *The Tempest* for *Prospero's Speech* on THE MASK AND MIRROR, where she also composed music for St John of the Cross' *The Dark Night of the Soul* and W.B. Yeats' *The Two Trees*. On ELEMENTAL she had already called on Yeats (*Stolen Child*) and Blake (*Lullaby*). And on THE BOOK OF SECRETS she turned to Alfred Noyes for the lyrics for *The Highwayman* and Dante Allighieri for the inspiration for *Dante's Prayer*.

When one interviewer asked her, "What made you want to set *The Lady of Shalott* to music?" Loreena responded, "People have kidded me about drawing on the Dead Poets' Society because I've set some of Yeats' poetry to music. For people who aren't familiar with it, *The Lady of Shalott* is set in the Arthurian time of Camelot. It's an epic poem in terms of performance because it has about 15 verses. I just liked the imagery of it. There's a rural imagery that I tap into because I live on a farm just north of Stratford. When the sun sets, I look to the west and see it setting over this wonderful field. So, the verse 'the reapers reaping early' had imagery that really caught my eye. I found the whole story quite romantic and thought it would be an interesting piece to have in the recording. It's different from a lot of other things on THE VISIT. I've tried to cover a wide thematic territory with the album's imagery and arrangements."

Again, during an interview on the BBC she was asked, "How do you choose the adaptations you do of poems and literary works, and what sort of particular problems do they present in adaptation?" Her reply suggests that she was drawn to these poets for more profound reasons than their imagery. "In 1985 I had been asked to perform at an authors' festival in Toronto," she explained, "and to set an Irish poem to music as a tribute to one of the Irish writers who was visiting at that time. Once I had done it and looked back, I felt that having another voice other than my perspective strengthened the recording. The recording itself — at least my recordings — are not all about me. I'd like to think they're about all different themes and subjects. And one can expand the perspective on a subject by adding more voices into that. So that's been one of the driving motivations in including other writers' work." In a similar vein, she commented to Nick Krewen in *Canadian Musician*, "the reason I've used other writers in a classical domain in the past is I wanted more classical perspectives and voices woven into the work. I felt it gave it more body, more significance. It was a narrative, not of convenience, but I wanted to hear how Yeats feels about a certain subject, or Shakespeare or Blake." In *Pulse* magazine she commented, "What Dante was writing about in the 14th century about the human condition, I can see certainly applies to the Russians in 1995 or the West. ... The material that I'm attracted to are universal themes that are not really restricted to a particular place or time. One of the strengths of Shakespeare's work is that he understood the human condition so well and in such a sophisticated way that his work has tremendous resonance even in our times."

Shakespeare's works do resonate through Loreena McKennitt's music. In her most beautiful song, she breathes into an organ pipe to end *Prospero's Speech* — the final speech of Shakespeare's final play. The breath is numinous. McKennitt's interpretation of the speech literally evaporates as it ends and fades from existence, returning to the place where breath has its beginnings, where language resonates in the body, where drama gets its start.

Prospero's Speech

And now my charms are all o'er thrown
And what strength I have's mine own
Which is most faint; now t'is true
I must here be confined by you

But release me from my bands
With the help of your good hands
Gentle breath of yours my sails
Must fill, or else my project fails

Which was to please. Now I want
Spirits to enforce, art to enchant
And my ending is despair
Unless I be relieved by prayer

Which pierces so that it assaults
Mercy itself and frees all faults
As you from your crimes would pardon'd be
Let your indulgence set me free

In THE MASK AND MIRROR liner notes, Loreena offers a dated journal account of the genesis of this song: "March 9, 1982 — Stratford ... have just begun rehearsals for the Stratford production of *The Tempest* ... I am singing the part of Ceres, goddess of agriculture, in the masque ... enchanted by the magic and the function of the masque as a conduit to the worlds of the gods and nature. The cast has an interesting discussion with a psychologist on the nature of Caliban and what qualified as 'the civilized world' . . ."

The Tempest, Shakespeare's greatest romance, was first performed at court in 1611, at Hallowmas, the feast of winter — a play 'to drive the cold winter away', we might say to use the title of Loreena's second album. Critics note the final plays of Shakespeare from *Midsummer Nights Dream* to *The Winter's Tale* follow a seasonal pattern, another 'parallel' to McKennitt's work. No doubt, this element of a seasonal festival behind *The Tempest* drew her to the play. But there is more, much more, in the play that has parallels to Loreena McKennitt's art.

The Tempest is exotic and symbolic, a series of rituals and ceremonies, masques or allegorical plays. A ship is wrecked by a storm, and Prospero, the deposed Duke of Milan, and his daughter, Miranda, are washed ashore on an enchanted island, an arcadia inhabited by an ethereal spirit named Ariel and a subterranean monster, Caliban. Ceres, goddess of agriculture, blesses Prospero's world so as to be without winter. As sung by Loreena McKennitt, Ceres joins Juno in blessing the marriage of Miranda and Ferdinand during the pageant or masque of the gods:

> *Earth's increase, foison plenty,*
> *Barns and garners never empty;*
> *Vines with clust'ring bunches growing,*
> *Plants with goodly burthen bowing;*
> *Spring come to you at the farthest*
> *In the very end of harvest!*
> *Scarcity and want shall shun you,*
> *Ceres' blessing so is on you.*

Various groups of passengers are involved in a number of subplots or masques tracing ancient rites of passage, the sufferings and ordeals the human soul passes through in quest of knowledge and freedom. The initiation rites of heroes often involve labyrinthine journeys. Some characters learn, some don't. Prospero educates the shipwrecked Italians, ends the civil war, and forgives his enemies. *The Tempest* shows Shakespeare's desire for Utopia, a golden world, whether it be Ferdinand's "Paradise," Miranda's "brave new world," or Gonzalo's social utopia where "nature should bring forth /... all abundance / to feed my innocent people." The play revolves around this vision of a golden, pastoral world tempered by the reality of our mortal, even immoral, world.

Prospero, possibly Shakespeare's self portrait, interrupts these dreams at the end of the play to remind us of our mortality and thus our humanity. His final multi-leveled speech explores the relationship between the real world and the world of imagination, nature and civilization. Does art mirror the real world or should the real world mirror art. "We are such stuff as dreams are made on," Prospero ventures, but he concludes, "Our revels now are ended" and "Now my charms are all o'erthrown." We cannot simply chose between the perfection of art and the limitations of life. Characters like Ferdinand and Miranda see the marvelous in each other; the spirituality they embody is half matter, half spirit. Prospero, a man once concerned more with alchemy and philosophy, learns what it means to be human. What he loses as a magician he gains as a man.

The play ends — Shakespeare's final play — and he asks the audience, in a prayer, to set him free and let him return home. Loreena McKennitt remarks in her journal notes: "April, 1993 — Stratford ... once again, I am drawn to Shakespeare for insights into the human condition ... Have not created the piece relative to 'the masque', but rather chose Prospero's closing speech, which is delivered with the sense of the actor removing his mask as an artist ... the illusion has ended, and reality and god are left for us to determine ourselves ..." And so with THE MASK AND MIRROR: the album ends, the artist prays for release, and the audience goes home.

Prospero's speech was not the first time Loreena McKennitt had set Shakespeare's lyrics to music, though. On THE VISIT, she mined another of his later romances for the lyrics of the dirge Guiderius and Arviragus sing in honor of the supposedly dead Imogen who is 'disguised' as Fidele in this tale of virtue and innocence tested.

Fear no more the heat o' th' sun,
Nor the furious winter's rages,
Thou thy worldly task has done,
Home art gone and ta'en thy wages.
Golden lads and girls all must,
As chimney sweepers, come to dust.

The sceptre, learning, physic, must
All follow this and come to dust.

DEAD POETS

Fear no more the frown o' th' great;
Thou art past the tyrant's stroke.
Care no more to clothe and eat;
To thee the reed, the reed is oak . . .

Fear no more the lightning flash,
Nor th'all-dreaded thunder stone;
Fear not slander, censure rash,
Thus hast finished joy and moan.

All lovers young, all lovers must
Consign to thee and come to dust.

This song has been called Shakespeare's crowning lyric achievement, a song Loreena McKennitt often uses to close her concert performances, a song she has sung in memory of her father.

The two voices we hear at play in this song from *Cymbeline* and in Prospero's speech from *The Tempest*, voices of innocence (with a boundless imagination) and voices of experience (with a mortal wisdom), are perhaps what attracted Loreena McKennitt to the work of William Blake, arguably the second greatest poet in the English language, though some would reserve this place for John Milton. The lines "Golden lads and girls all must, As chimney sweepers, come to dust" resonate through the works of Blake, especially his *Songs of Innocence* and *Songs of Experience*.

Before recording Blake's *Lullaby* on her ELEMENTAL album, Loreena McKennitt worked with the late dramaturge Elliot Hayes in Stratford on the score for a stage version of a play called *William Blake*, based on the life and art of this 18th-century Romantic poet and mystic visionary, one of the strangest yet grandest figures of English art and literature, who claimed the poetic imagination was God operating in the human soul. Born in 1757, in London, about where Picadilly Circus is today, young Blake had a gift for seeing visions. At the age of four, he claimed God pressed His face against his bedroom windowpane. On rambles in London, past the Thames River with its banks the color of mud and saffron, he claimed he saw angels in trees who looked like thoughts. But he also saw charity schools with half-starved children who were flogged and poorly educated. He witnessed the hypocrisy of a clergy who praised God but permitted chimney sweeps as young as eight to be sent up burning chimneys where they died.

Blake's most famous works are *Songs of Innocence* and *Songs of Experience*, engraved poems, the first series spoken in the voice of the 'Piper', the second in the voice of the 'Bard', the first presenting a vision of the world from the innocent eyes of the child, the second from the wizened eyes of the fallen man — "the Two Contrary States of the Human Soul," to use Blake's words. The pastoral world of *Songs of Innocence* begins with the poet playing his pipe or lute:

> *Piping down the valleys wild,*
> *Piping songs of pleasant glee,*
> *On a cloud I saw a child,*
> *And he laughing said to me:*
>
> *"Pipe a song about a Lamb!"*
> *So I piped with merry cheer . . .*
> *And I made a rural pen,*
> *And I stain'd the water clear,*
> *And I wrote my happy songs*
> *Every child may joy to hear.*

Through such well-known songs as *The Echoing Green*, *The Lamb*, and *The Chimney Sweeper*, Blake portrays a world of "Mercy, Pity, Peace, and Love." Innocence in these lullabies is not so much the state of childhood as an image of the soul in eternity. Children have their own particular kind of energy and unique perceptions. The 'republic of childhood', as children's scholar Sheila Egoff called it, has secret societies, vision quests, ritual renaming, romance and poetry, rebellions against the elders of the family and distant politics, their own dance and music and sense of the occult.

In *Songs of Experience* the republic of childhood has been lost; the mood has changed as Blake announces the prophetic voice of the Bard calling out the tune of the "lapsed Soul."

> *Hear the voice of the Bard!*
> *Who Present, Past, & Future, sees;*
> *Whose ears have heard*
> *The Holy Word*
> *That walk'd among the ancient trees,*
>
> *Calling the lapsed Soul*
> *And weeping in the evening dew;*

That might controll
The starry pole,
And fallen, fallen light renew!

Echoing the Biblical account of man's fall from Eden, Blake declaims, rather than sings, such 'songs' of experience as *The Tyger* ("What immortal hand or eye / Could Frame thy fearful symmetry"), *London* ("In every voice, in every ban, / The mind-forged manacles I hear"), and an 'experienced' version of *The Chimney Sweeper* ("A little black thing among the snow, / Crying 'weep! 'weep! In notes of woe!"). While Blake still held out hope that the golden world, an arcadia, could be restored by an act of the imagination in such poems as *America: A Prophecy*, his response to the democratic promise of the American Revolution, he became increasingly more tormented by the problem of God's 'fearful symmetry'. How could God create the innocent child only to be exploited or corrupted? How could the Creator show such love but then exercise such righteous anger? After *Songs of Innocence* and *America*, Blake assumed the voice of the prophetic bard in satiric poems like *The Marriage of Heaven and Hell* and visionary epics like *The Book of Urizen* and *The Four Zoas*, where he rehearses the fall of man from innocence.

This voice of the bard, the voice of experience, angry and prophetic, is the voice we hear in *Lullaby*, Loreena McKennitt's final song on ELEMENTAL, adapted from a verse fragment of the Prologue to Blake's unfinished play, "Intended for a Dramatic Piece of King Edward IV," his turn on Shakespeare's "Oh for a muse of fire" verse in *Henry V*. The title 'Lullaby' is surely ironic.

Lullaby

O for a voice like thunder, and a tongue
to drown the throat of war! When the senses
are shaken, and the soul is driven to madness,
who can stand? When the souls of the oppressed
fight in the troubled air that rages, who can stand?
When the whirlwind of fury comes from the throne of God,
when the frowns of his countenance
drive the nations together, who can stand?
When Sin claps his broad wings over the battle,
and sails rejoicing in the flood of Death;

> When souls are torn to everlasting fire
> and fiends of Hell rejoice upon the slain,
> O who can stand? O who hath caused this?
> O who can answer at the throne of God?
> The Kings and Nobles of the Land have done it!
> Hear it not, Heaven, thy Ministers have done it!

On the album, this song of experience is declaimed by renowned Shakespearean actor Douglas Campbell while Loreena sings softly behind him, echoing a voice of innocence announced earlier on the album in her adaptation of W. B. Yeats' song, *The Stolen Child*.

Indeed, ELEMENTAL takes on the structure of a 'Songs of Innocence' and 'Songs of Experience' cycle, especially evident when we look to McKennitt's adaptation of *The Stolen Child*, one of the first poems Yeats published in his collection *Crossways* in 1889, which, significantly, opens with an epigraph from William Blake: "The stars are threshed, and the souls are threshed from the husks." Like Blake in *Songs of Innocence*, Yeats opens his collection by summoning the pastoral muse in *The Song of the Happy Shepherd*, only to find this voice muted by 'Grey Truth':

The Song of the Happy Shepherd

> The woods of Arcady are dead,
> And over is their antique joy;
> Of old the world on dreaming fed;
> Grey Truth is now her painted toy;
> Yet still she turns her restless head:
> But O, sick children of the world,
> Of all the many changing things
> On dreary dancing past us whirled,
> To the cracked tune of Chronos sings,
> Words alone are certain good.

Yeats holds out hope for a return to this lost arcadian world in poems like *The Stolen Child*, where the world of innocence takes on a distinctively Celtic tone in references to faeries and fauns, a tone Loreena McKennitt underscores with her harp arrangement of this song. Here the faeries try to steal back the child from the world of experience.

The Stolen Child

Where dips the rocky highland
Of sleuth wood in the lake
There lies a leafy island
Where flapping herons wake
The drowsy water rats
There we've hid our faery vats
Full of berries
And of reddest stolen cherries

Come away, O human child
To the waters and the wild
With a faery, hand in hand
For the world's more full of weeping
Than you can understand . . .

Loreena McKennitt's ELEMENTAL, like Yeats *Crossways*, integrates these songs of innocence and experience with traditional Celtic folk songs and ballads — *Blacksmith, She Moved Through the Fair, Carrighfergus, Kellswater*, and *Banks of Claudy*, for example, on ELEMENTAL; *Down by the Sally Gardens, The Ballad of Father O'Hart, The Ballad of Moll Magee*, and *The Ballad of the Foxhunter*, for example, in *Crossways*. And like Yeats, McKennitt deliberately set out to 'revive' these Celtic standards after discovering them during her travels in Ireland.

Yeats' poem came from his research into the 'old ways' of Irish legend and poetry written in a national tradition. A deceptively simple poem often included in children's anthologies, the poem is enriched with hints of the occult, psychic phenomena, and Indian philosophy. Yeats was serious about faeryland. He respected the ways of ancient times, believed in the supernatural as part of an inclusive account of the universe.

When asked in *Innerviews* the question, "What do you take into consideration when choosing and arranging traditional material?" Loreena McKennitt gave this insight into her creative process in reviving these traditional Celtic songs and ballads. "The theme of the song and lyrics," she explained, "and also the melody. It's hard to find striking melodies like *Come By The Hills* or *She Moves Through The Fair*. It's always the melody that attracts me. Sometimes, there are lyrics that I find very exciting, but the music isn't so exciting. For example, *Standing Stones* from PARALLEL DREAMS was a case where I found the music in a wonderful little collection. I had never seen it before. I liked the story very, very much, but the music didn't do very much for me. So, I took the lyrics and set my own music to it. That's something I'll do as well." Throughout the recording of ELEMENTAL and PARALLEL DREAMS, she mined the catalog of traditional Irish songs to compose in this way, looking for 'parallels' between the themes of these songs and contemporary concerns, transforming the music when necessary. Yeats, likewise, thoroughly researched the muse of Ireland, seeking an original poetic style while reviving the Gaelic language. "I thought one day," he relates in his essay *What Is Popular Poetry?*, "if somebody could make a style, which would not be an English style, and yet be musical and full of color, many others would catch fire from him, and we would have a really great school of ballad poetry in Ireland."

From studying ballads and sitting by turf fires in Connach where he heard Irish folktales, Yeats learned to combine the written and oral traditions of poetry. He learned from French Symbolist poets like Baudelaire and Paul Verlaine stylistic techniques that included urbanity, lightness, wit, and double entendre. A verbal shrug with a precise statement and a pure melodic line gave his poems a change in tempo and technique. When he cleared out stuffy sentiment, he achieved poetry of insight and knowledge, not longing and complaint. He also learned an abbreviated theatrical method of flashing an impression upon a reader through metaphor, image, consonant patterns, and internal rhymes. And he explored the deeper meaning of symbolism, visions, dreams, and a belief in the unseen world. The soul of a singer is apprehended by the soul of the listener, Yeats believed. He had a fine sense of things unseen, imagining all life as "an image in a looking glass." Following the publication of his early ballads and songs, Yeats explored in poetry, plays, and essays like *A Vision* this image of the looking glass, or mirror, and the mask, which would seem to inform Loreena McKennitt's THE MASK AND MIRROR album and also THE VISIT.

In her autobiographical video *No Journey's End*, Loreena McKennitt comments on the impact of Yeats' Celtic subject, symbolist method, and spiritual musings on her work. "I've always tried to infuse different perspectives into my music, and so I subsequently go to other writers. I've used the poems of W.B. Yeats, and Shakespeare, and William Blake. *The Two Trees* is actually a W.B. Yeats poem that I set to music. I also thought that it was quite fitting from the Celtic point of view that he would draw on the symbolism and the imagery of trees. I felt that after the whole journey of exploring the question of "what is religion, and what is spirituality?" that Yeats' sentiment of looking into one's own self for goodness was a very comforting one." *The Two Trees* is also rich with Yeats' most characteristic symbols, the gyre and the glass: "The flaming circle of our days, / Gyring, spiring to and fro," for example, and "Gaze no more in the bitter glass / The demons, with their subtle guile."

The ideas of William Butler Yeats flow through the Irish songs of Loreena Mckennitt. He loved the west country of Ireland, especially Co. Sligo, the childhood home of both his parents. The mountains form a half circle around Sligo town, dominated by Ben Bulben, and the legend haunted Knocknarea, with its rough stone circle, the tomb of Queen Maeve. The kind of place, with island lakes, rippling waters, quivering bushes, and bird prints in the sand that set a boy to dreaming. As a student Yeats discovered Shakespeare, the Romantic poets, the Pre-Raphaelites, and the French Symbolists. He explored eastern mysticism. Call it a new Romanticism. An editor of London's *National Observer* described Yeats during his attendance at an arts fair in the 1890s as a mystic: "Another mystic looking booth, flying a green flag with an Irish harp figured upon it, was presided over by a cabalistic young poet, Mr. W.B. Yeats, musically talking of Rosicrucianism, fairies, Celtic folklore, and an Irish theatre, and backed by Irish scholars proclaiming the revival of the Gaelic tongue as the certain cure-all for Ireland's wrongs.'

Yeats attempted to create a literature that was Irish in subject matter and tone. He wanted to reawaken a sense of the glory and significance of Ireland's historical and legendary past. He saw the loss of the Irish language after colonization and the famine as a loss of nationhood. Nothing was done in Irish except to bring turf from the peat bog and say prayers. Yeats tackled the task of providing a Celtic movement with enthusiasm. Two years after his first book of verse, he founded the National Literary Society, and seven years later, the Irish Literary Theatre in Dublin. Drawing from Irish folklore, Yeats created a lyrical romantic peasant figure, as playwright J.P. Synge did with the comic and tragic characters in the language he heard in the Aran Islands and Co. Wicklaw. Although of different political convictions, both turned to Irish folklore to find a tradition, almost a religion, upon which to build a new literary movement. Paradoxically, Yeats' occult interests, aesthetic tastes, and social success were based in London. As a cultural commuter, he is said to be the originator of the intellectual anti-immigration scheme. In 1923, he won the Nobel Prize for Literature.

Yeats turned mythical figures into private symbols, and found a way to translate his life into mystical events presented by the symbolism of Irish mythology. Fantasy, mysticism, and the unknown were used as analogies to explain and examine the human condition. "I always sought to bring my mind close to the mind of Indian and Japanese poets, old women in Connacht, mediums in Soho, lay brothers whom I imagine dreaming in some medieval monastery the dreams of their village, learned authors who refer to all antiquity to immerse it in the general mind where mind is scarce separable from what, we have begun to call 'the subconscious'," wrote Yeats. Once the world fed on poetry, he believed; now it feeds on science and reason. Only poetry, almost lost to us, can celebrate the ancient worlds, he claimed. Poetry should be more than a chronicle of loss. He uses the image of shepherd, a time when poetry and modern world were unified.

In his esoteric essay *A Vision* (1925), Yeats presented his own mythology to counter science and reason. To vastly summarize: as a soul goes through various incarnations, such as Will, Mind, Mask, and Fate, it gets to know itself and the universe. The Will has drive. Mask is the image the soul strives for, all that is admirable accrued from past lives. Through Will and Mask, the soul shapes itself from within. The sum of everything that happens is the Body of Fate. Two processes are at work here. Will tries to become Mask. Mind tries to understand Fate. As one grows, the other weakens. Yeats calls this the two gyres, whirling against each other in opposite directions. Each aspect faces its opposite, like a lunar calendar or wheel. The conflicting pulls create the diversities of human personality. The goal, if possible, is to live in balance as the wheel turns through each phase. In such a moment, the self is renewed, or even created. The experience is more important than any interpretation of the 'meaning', greater than a simple religious conversion, open to wider meanings which increases its power, radiance, and luminosity. We need to realize two kinds of time here, ordinary or chronological time and imaginative time, *chronos* and *kairos*. In these luminous moments in kairos, clock time is defeated — by poetic agents like the song and harp.

Building on the perspectives on the human condition and the creative imagination offered by Shakespeare, Blake, and Yeats, Loreena McKennitt would begin to create her own mythology, more and more writing her own lyrics for her songs on THE MASK AND MIRROR and THE BOOK OF SECRETS.

4

INDIE ARTIST

Despite her dramatic Ariel-like, ethereal stage presence and abiding interest in the spiritual and mystical musings of Blake and Yeats, Loreena McKennitt is an extraordinarily practical musician whose grasp of the intricacies and machinery of the recording industry has become legendary among independent artists. She is duly proud of her 'indie' spirit and business acumen, quick to tell the story of making it on her own terms whenever asked by journalists, willing to write at length about the 'business' in trade magazines, even going so far as to speak at business lunches to the Stratford Women in Business group at the Stratford Country Club. For young D.I.Y. (Do It Yourself) artists and women entrepreneurs, her 'career' has become inspirational. Sounding the rallying cry of most indie musicians, she once told the Toronto *Star*, "I have an insatiable curiosity and desire to know how things work. There have been many times when I wanted to divest myself over to a manager, but I couldn't find the right one who could understand the project, because what I do doesn't fit on commercial radio. So I built my own infrastructure."

As she tells the story of her indie days in an interview on the BBC, "I got very interested in Celtic music about the late '70s, early '80s, and I traveled to Ireland and sat in on some music sessions, learned how the music sprang from a very indigenous kind of need and informal kind of capacity. I became so interested in it that in 1985 I borrowed $10,00 from my family and I recorded my first cassette in a week, and I ran off about 50 cassettes and I went down to the market in Toronto on Saturday mornings and busked on the streets and sold the cassettes. By 1989 I was traveling across Canada with three musicians and sound engineer. I had sold 35- 40,000 copies at that point. By that time I was already able to make a very good living in so far as that I was able to do what I liked, what I found interesting on my own terms. It's a culmination of a very brick-by-brick kind of process." While describing her life as a busker, she told Jenny Tucker on BBC's Woman's Hour, "I sort of took my destiny into my own hands, feeling that I didn't want it thrust upon me. I was interested in the Celtic music. I borrowed some money from my family to make my first recording, and after I had done that and produced about 30 cassettes, I found that busking in the street was a way to sell them and make a bit of money. As it turned out, I found that it was a very important point of independence, not just financial independence, but saying that even though I wasn't doing commercial top-40 kinds of material, there seemed to be a lot of people who were actually interested in what I was doing."

Obviously proud of her achievement — and duly so — McKennitt has always been quick in any discussion of her business career to acknowledge the seminal influence of a book by Diane Rapaport. "I took it upon myself to teach myself as much about the business as I could. One of the great books I used was the one called *How to Make and Sell Your Own Recording*, by a woman, Diane Rapaport, but it was brilliant. It was a fantastic map of the processes involved, all the mechanical processes, but also publicity, copyright, all those tangential issues."

Indeed her championing of this book led her to write a preface to a new edition in 1999, as reported in the newsletter of the Canadian Country Music Association (CCMA). "Sixteen years ago, Loreena McKennitt was an early morning busker outside a down-town Toronto market," the CCMA News report begins, "and attended a conference, organized by CAPAC (one of the predecessors of SOCAN) at which the keynote speaker was Diane Sward Rapaport, who introduced her book, *How to Make and Sell Your Own Recording*, to Canada. Using the book as a blueprint, McKennitt took her own career in her own hands. In 1999, with world-wide sales of more than eight million albums. Her last three records are all multi-platinum in Canada, and gold or platinum in the United States and many foreign territories. Her companies own the masters of her eight albums, she controls her own publishing, and she has built a team of co-workers who have helped bring her music to international audiences. She contributed a special forward to mark the 20th anniversary — and the fifth revised edition — of *How to Make and Sell Your Own Recording*, and we are pleased that she and the author have allowed us to reprint an edited version of it in this edition of CCMA News." The excerpt from Loreena's foreword to this book was printed under the headline, "Eight Million Albums Later, Canada's Most Successful Independent Artist Urges Her Contemporaries: Take Control of Your Own Destiny."

With a backward glance at the course of her own career, McKennitt states, "I have long taken the view that I would rather work towards seizing my destiny than having it thrust upon me," then sets out to dispel some myths about the music business. "There is much misinformation and myth about what artists themselves can and should be doing on the 'business' side of their careers. In my more cynical moments, I have wondered whether some record companies, managers, agents, lawyers, and promoters have a vested interest in artists remaining ignorant of the forces which directly influence their work. People in all professions, restauranteurs to shop owners, rightly see creativity as a vital ingredient of their work, but would never dream of completely abdicating their business responsibilities and passing them to somebody else. In my experience, artists do exactly that, far too readily and frequently. I can understand why many of us are initially daunted by the prospect of becoming more hands-on in the execution and administration of practical matters, including that of creating a recording itself. There are budgets, timelines, and mechanical and technical matters galore, but they are not beyond comprehension, particularly taken piece by piece at a point in one's career when there is time to learn, and the volume and complexity is not as great as it will be when the pace quickens. Learning business is not unlike learning music; you start modestly, with simple steps, and as you reach one plateau, you acquire the skills and the confidence you need to reach the next level."

In navigating these plateaus, "having a map such as this book is vital," she comments with reference to Diane Rapaport's work, but even if you master the art of recording and grasp the business skills needed to market, promote, and distribute your music, "reaching out more directly to those who might be interested in our work, and maintaining and expanding that connection, is one of the most significant components in developing a lasting career. . . . A greater understanding of the music business will let you discover the fact that there are certain musical genres and scales of operation that are far more likely to be successful and lucrative outside the boundaries of a major label than within them. The perceived notion that a major label deal is necessary needs constant and vigilant re-evaluation; for the vast majority of those that become recording artists, making and selling your own record is, indeed, the way to begin. The main ingredients in building a solid and successful career," McKennitt concludes, "in addition to your talent and vision, are curiosity, tenacity, determination and a fondness for creative problem-solving."

In another of the many interviews that have focused on her business acumen, Loreena described her step-by-step approach to making Quinlan Road a successful independent label, attributing her business sense to those days she spent in Morden and Winnipeg working in her father's livestock business. "I took the money the money I was raising on the street," she told the BBC, "and put that into my second recording, and then my third recording. I started to produce my own concerts, hired a publicist, hired the venue, the sound equipment and so on. Sold the recordings at those performances, then started touring across Canada. So, it was that — the money that can be made if you are manufacturing and then selling to the people, there is quite a substantial profit margin. When you have all the rest of the retail and record company and so on, it diminishes. So at that point of the game I was going directly from a producers standpoint." When asked, "Where did the business acumen come from?" McKennitt responded, "Well, I would attribute that to working in my father's office. He was a livestock dealer, in Winnipeg in the middle of the Canadian Prairies. I would go into his office in the morning and I would do basic secretarial and accounting skills, and then at three o'clock I would head out to the Auction Ring, and round up the cattle and sort them into pens. So I was exposed to an office environment and budgets and that kind of thing." In the press release accompanying the release of THE BOOK OF SECRETS, she added, "I think coming from a farming and rural background gave me the insight into being self-sufficient. You become familiar with creative problem solving. If you want something badly enough, you will roll up your sleeves and start chipping away."

Despite her business 'cool', Loreena still finds herself amazed at the course of her career. "I had always dreamed of becoming a veterinarian," she commented in a internet interview, "but here I am a musician with my own business. No doubt most people have encountered this humbling phenomenon: no matter what plans you make sometimes, life just comes pouring down on top of you, in ways and at times when you least expect it. It can carry you off in directions you could never have imagined or hoped for." To the *Edmonton Journal* she likewise stated with a sense of wonder, "I dreamed of being a veterinarian and I would say my first and strongest passion is the outdoors and hiking. Music was a sideline: if I wasn't going to be a vet, maybe I would be involved in forestry or wildlife conservation. . . . I never dreamed this could happen."

Loreena McKennitt's rise to business independence was not without a few rough roads, as she confessed to Peter Feniak in *Saturday Night* magazine while describing those early mornings busking at the St Lawrence Market in Toronto. "I would drive in on Saturday mornings, early, early, early in my little Civic just to get a god spot there. In the old building, in the front foyer, there's a real resonance. . . . I remember a tiny woman named Celeste from Winnipeg emerging from the crowd after I'd finished this piece, and I was really enjoying what I was doing. But tears were streaming down her face, and she said, 'Oh, Loreena, has it come to this!'" While Loreena is now able to look back with good humor on her busking years following the recording of ELEMENTAL, at the time she had misgivings about her career choice, finding herself depressed at her prospects of becoming a recording artist. "It lasted about three months,' she told Feniak. "I didn't have any money, I didn't want to eat. I couldn't sleep. Tuesdays, just to force myself out of the house, I'd go down and quilt with the ladies at the Red Cross. The depression was a very dark place. It scared the hell out of me.'" Besides becoming involved in the social outreach activities of the Red Cross, she became involved with the Stratford Heritage Trust during these years, a cause she still hold dear, finding in this preservation effort a parallel with her own work in the Celtic tradition. As she explained in an interview with Daniel Durcholz, "here in Stratford, I've been involved in architectural preservation and heritage. I guess I have an appreciation for the merits of an archival process, where you're not trying to make a finished piece of art like a studio recording . . . With that in mind, you don't go and fix it up too much. At best, if you're dealing with an old building, you might want to blow off some of the old grub and grime and dirt and everything, but you don't want to replace anything."

Loreena McKennitt not only extended her civic interests but also began to diversify her career during the 1980s by composing music for film, including the films *Bayo* in 1984 and *Heaven on Earth* in 1986. Between 1987 and 1993, she composed scores for seven National Film Board of Canada productions, including a trilogy on women's history and spirituality by Donna Read. When asked by the BBC how she composed the music for two of the films from this trilogy, *The Goddess Remembered* and *The Burning Times*, McKennitt offered a practical explanation. "Usually in film they come up with the fine cut," she stated, "or they'll give me a copy of the film, a rough cut, which is quite close to the length of the film. When I get the rough cut I work on musical ideas and textures and so on, while they're working towards the fine cut, which means the final edited version of the film. . . . I work with a copy of the film that has the time code burnt right into it. Then I tailor each scene; I tailor the music to fit the picture. It gets to be very, very tricky because each piece of music has its own sense of flow, and has a whole sort of life of its own. . . . you feel like is has to have a natural flowing completion that doesn't sound disruptive." When asked to elaborate on her approach to the soundtrack for *The Burning Times*, McKennitt gave greater insight into the rhythms of her career. "*The Burning Times* is a film set in the Middle Ages of Europe when women were burned as witches, supposedly. I worked quite closely with the director when doing the film. We talked a lot about the intent, and when you get a rough cut, you try and get a feel for its essence and the period. You try to augment the scenes, not take them over. You try to illuminate scenes that need a bit of a push. I really quite adore working on films. It's a very challenging kind of medium. It's very stimulating in ways that performing isn't. It's quite fascinating to see how music affects visuals and vice-versa. There's an interesting chemistry there. A lot of people have said that when they hear my music, a lot of images come to mind. So, my musical style lends itself to film work. I like to do at least one film a year. Similarly, I like to perform one piece of theatre a year and then do a recording and go off on tour. I find that diversity quite exciting and stimulating."

To her portfolio, McKennitt added a stint in 1986 as musical director of the Blyth Summer Festival, an 'off-Stratford' theatre west of the city which features Canadian plays. In 1988 she was involved in composing and performing music for a production of *St Stephen's Green* at the Abbey Theatre in Dublin, the theatre co-founded by W.B. Yeats. And then in 1989 she composed and performed the score for *Kidnapped* at Toronto's Young People's Theatre. She has also composed music for the Royal Winnipeg Ballet. In and around these efforts, she wrote, recorded, and promoted ELEMENTAL, TO DRIVE THE COLD WINTER AWAY, and PARALLEL DREAMS, with a spirit that seemed indefatigable.

Besides her own talent and ambition, McKennitt's career as an artist during the 1980s was made possible by the women's movement. The feminist movement created a listening atmosphere for women, and for men who cared to support them, especially for an album like ELEMENTAL where we sense what might be called a feminist primitivism. McKennitt's first recordings coincided with the 'revolution in archeology' inspired by the women's movement, led by such investigators as Marjita Gimbatus and Reine Esler who revived the role of the goddess in our Western culture and consciousness. Although the Judeo-Christian created the myth that Eve was born of Adam's rib, in most other creation myths, this is reversed — man is born of the Great Goddess. In re-imagined Biblical stories, a bone flute is fashioned by God from Adam's rib and given to Eve as a symbol of her creative powers. What was derisively called sinful and pagan (from Latin *pagus*, country or village, rural and agricultural) becomes women's wisdom. The so-called crafts, like the plates and embroidery re-visioned by Judy Chicago, celebrate women's art across centuries of neglect. Crafts, medicine, herbs, and animal husbandry — what was low becomes high. The pagan woman restores the crafts. Unlike the outer world of the patriarchal classicists whose scientific objectivity, controlled prose, and concise knowledge stopped with the Greek and Roman myths, this revolution went deeper into antiquity, to the inner world of ritual and folklore.

A women's tradition was discovered. A women's culture. Journals, letters, quilting, gossip, (originally the conversation exchanged between women at the cross roads), bedtime stories, embroidery, jewelry and sometimes-forgotten sometimes-silenced cultures within cultures. When a whole culture is silenced or forgotten, knowledge is lost. The straw weaving of St Brigit's cross contains worlds of meaning, old ways of being, old wisdom. And the values of those that made the culture, the life and thoughts of those people. The publication on the same day in 1979 of Margot Adler's *Drawing Down the Moon* and Starhawk's *The Spiral Dance* heralded the rebirth of the religion of the Great Goddess, introducing a generation of women to long-lost female spirituality and ecofeminism.

On ELEMENTAL we sense a longing for this woman's world. To revive the myth of earth goddesses and the wisdom of the ancient matriarchs, to revive women's songs of complaint like *Blacksmith* and *Banks of Claudy*, to recover ancestral matriarchal memory — this was elemental. Because of this revolution in archeology and recordings like Loreena McKennitt's ELEMENTAL, a qualitative shift occurred for women in the performing arts during the 1980s. Women found a voice after decades of silence. Loreena McKennitt was not only one of these voices but also an embodiment of what an independent woman could achieve outside the traditional patriarchal world of the recording business.

"You are your own manager and agent?" Loreena McKennitt was asked during an interview in *Folk Harp Journal* in 1991, "... and record label," she interjected. "So I not only produce my recordings but I supervise the distribution of them, and I've several accounts set up across the country, and that, in itself, has become a full-time business. But there's just a lot of work ... here I am traveling with three other musicians and two crew, and we're doing 25 dates across the country, and it's just ... you know ... accommodation, equipment, rental of vehicles, negotiation, servicing of contracts, publicity, interviews ... it just goes on and on. So, there gets to be very little time to just practice technique, but I'm hoping to delegate more of these other responsibilities, so I can practice more, and create more." Handling everything from creating the songs to booking the tours was vitally important to Loreena McKennitt because her business independence guaranteed her creative freedom from the shaping hands of a record label or the demands of a musical trend or fashion, as she was quick to point up in an interview on BBC's *Woman's Hour* in 1996. "I sort of took my destiny into my own hands feeling that I didn't want it thrust upon me. ... As it turned out, I found that it was a very important point of independence, not just financial independence, but saying that even though I wasn't doing commercial top-40 kinds of material, there seemed to be a lot of people who were actually interested in what I was doing." So interested, in fact, that by the time she came to record THE VISIT, she was able to call her own tune in negotiations with Warner Music.

Negotiations with Warner were conducted on Loreena McKennitt's terms, as her lawyer, Graham Henderson, explained in *Saturday Night*. "A lot of acts go into a record company for their 'deal' and the label basically says, 'Here it is, take it or leave it.' We scrap and fight, but there's not a lot of bargaining power. People want access to the marketplace and the record companies provide it. Loreena, on the other hand, has developed her own access. She was selling 30,000 records. She could sell out the Winter Garden for two shows. Her questions was, 'What can you do for me?' I have to say she walked out of Warner with an exceptional contract."

During an interview on the BBC, Loreena discussed at length her decision to sign with Warner. When asked if this deal would affect her approach to the recording of her next album, she responded, "I know there can be a temptation when you enter into a larger deal with a major company to think 'Well, I'm really going to expand my market' or whatever, but I'm not a very market-driven person. I have a creative agenda before me and I keep my eye on that ball. The ideas of THE VISIT had been brewing well over a year. A year ago, I spent a week at an artist's retreat in Ireland. I remember putting down the first draft of notes, ideas and themes there that I wanted to encompass in this recording." She did confess to becoming overwhelmed by the success of her indie career. "PARALLEL DREAMS sold between 25,000-30,000 copies independently. In the big scheme of things, that's not a vast number of units, but in the independent realm it's considerable. So, the demand for things was reaching a level I wasn't able to service. Various companies approached me and I spoke with them. They interviewed me and I interviewed them. It was like seeking out a marriage with each other. This deal with Warner is a licensing deal with my label. At Warner, there was a group of people who seemed to me had an appreciation for the whole concept of music. There wasn't a lot of rock'n'roll attitude around the place. There were a lot of down-to-earth people who had difficult jobs to do, but were there for the right reasons as far as I can tell." Loreena also allayed fears that Warner would 'pigeon-hole' her music in some larger marketing trend. "I don't think the average punter on the street is concerned," she remarked. "They're only concerned when they have to go to a store and ask for the title. That's where the categorization pitfall can come in. There's no question about categorization when I see the people who come to my concerts. It ranges from New Age and folk people to kids who listen to hard rock to people who are grandmothers. I've met children who are five and six years old who know all the words to *Blacksmith*. But I know it's necessary to catalog pieces in a store and to serve an industry function in order to reach people who are unfamiliar with my work. People may say, 'I've heard of this person. What kind of music does she do?' They will then draw from other names as points of reference. Hopefully, eventually that won't be necessary."

    Loreena received an enhanced royalty rate on the sale of her records and retained the rights to sell her CDs direct from the stage and by mail, thus maintaining the close contact she has had with her audience since those early days busking at the St Lawrence Market and selling cassettes of ELEMENTAL. Her artistic freedom was ensured and she was free to devote more time to creating. Before the deal with Warner, she told *Saturday Night*, "eighty percent of my time was spent administering. The workload was unbelievable. The stage was like a sanctuary. As long as I was playing, I knew there wasn't going to be a phone call." In the deal with Warner she was able to adjust this creation:administration ratio, as she told the Stratford Business Women. Warner "was the sole company that was prepared to throw out the rule book and prepare a contract related to what I was bringing to the table.... I'd rather create for 70 percent of my output and spend the rest of my time looking after that creation, making sure it's properly represented and properly placed." As she told *Pulse* magazine, she hoped the Warner deal would free her to create more music and avoid the transformation from being primarily a musician into being an independent record 'executive' like Windham Hill and Imaginary Road founder Will Ackerman. "I personally have been so consumed by my own career," she commented. "I have an office in London, England; five people work for me there. An office in Stratford, Ontario; five people work for me there. And sometimes there are inner voices that tell you that you need a change. For me, the most significant gift I can give myself is to release myself from a lot of the responsibilities that I've created for a while and see what happens. I have a sneaking suspicion that it'll be similar to the unfettered, psychological environment I enjoyed 10 years ago." She even imagined that she might return to busking.

In October 2000, McKennitt wrote an article called "Lessons, Revelations, and Just Good Business Practices" for *Indie Nation*, a publication for independent recording artists distributed by HMV record store in Canada, summarizing her indie philosophy in face of the conforming forces of the major labels. "It's a daunting task to find a point of departure when asked to offer some constructive thoughts on the music business these days," she began. "Nevertheless, as an independent artist, no matter how chaotic the path may be, it has afforded me lessons, revelations and ultimately philosophical positions which serve as rudders, litmus tests, and ultimately, a point on the compass when the chaos becomes too great." She then set out a series of 'philosophical' positions.

"My first philosophical position was a commitment to exhaust every avenue which might allow the realization of whatever potential I had. In fact, every person owes at least that much to him or herself in life. As a recording artist, I knew that along with working on the creative process, this meant teaching myself at least some of the ropes and rolling up my sleeves, administratively speaking, whether that meant trucking around to record stores, finding busking positions, packing cassettes (this was 1985 after all!), attending to my mailing list and consequently learning about how I wanted to define my own concept of success."

McKennitt's definition of success has not changed significantly from those early years as the artist who recorded ELEMENTAL and founded Quinlan Road. "Knowing that goals and success can be measured by internal means as well as external riches (the second philosophical revelation), I was not trapping myself into the preoccupying preconception that only a traditional deal with a major record company could produce happiness and success."

How she was able to use a 'traditional' label and the music 'biz' to further her goals, she felt was instructive. "As fate would have it, and after six years of busking, touring, and self promotion, I did have an opportunity to work with a major label, but in a less than traditional arrangement whose terms were predicated on my ability, by that point, to produce and finance my recordings, deliver finished masters and finished artwork without borrowing from 'the bank of Warner.' (Ultimately, the difference between borrowing from the bank of the majors versus, say, the Bank of Montreal, is that with real banks, when you pay off the 'mortgage' on your recording, you own the masters.) My monetary investment and willingness to take on that risk afforded me the ability to incorporate certain very desirable features in my deal: a higher-than-usual royalty rate, creative autonomy and complete ownership of my masters and publishing. Lesson #3, then: learn the business by following the money. Get a good lawyer with a creative approach to problem solving; one who's not necessarily stuck in traditional formulas, and who can help ensure you are being looked after (by your manager, by your record company) and that you are looking after others (your band members, your co-writers). A common, often disastrous step occurs at the point when no one is making money and it doesn't seem worth the effort to concern oneself with legal structures and frameworks. In fact, the opposite is true."

And as fate would have it again, Loreena McKennitt discovered that 'the label' was not a bogey man, so long as you kept the lights on — or, to use, her metaphor, these emperors had no clothes, at least some of the time. "As time played itself out, any preconceptions that I had had about the industry began to soften. I learned that the full equation of success comprises more than just the creative component; it includes the formidable and costly tasks of marketing, promotion and distribution. As I found myself walking the corridors of the emperor's palace of the music industry, I found that, at times, these emperors really did have no clothes (and we won't get into that here) but at many levels, if not all, they were folks just like us. People who had chosen a career path and were slugging it out with real and challenging tasks which involve considerable resources of time, money and personnel, and whose efforts are often underappreciated by artists and managers. Lesson # 4? There is a lot more to the equation of success than meets the eye."

The fifth article of her indie philosophy recognized the all-important role of the audience. "In the mad scramble of everyone's quest for their personal piece of the music business pie, there is a very important question which is asked all too infrequently. Is the public getting the value and service it deserves, not only online but in the traditional retail environment and in the live concert arena? Of course artists and everyone else involved need to be properly compensated, but after all, the public ultimately are the people who give meaning to our work and provide us with a livelihood. As artists, we must take more responsibility for our own careers. We must not become complacent or completely self-serving, but must concern ourselves with the quality of the goods and services we are offering or which are being offered on our behalf. No matter how many people are between ourselves and our audience, it is always our reputations which are at stake if the public are badly served. Lesson # 5: the public's need and love of music should be paramount in our considerations. If we undermine their interest in incorporating music into their lives, we may find ourselves with an audience of one, and singing to our rubber ducks in the shower."

Lesson # 5 was the driving force behind the creation of THE VISIT, Loreena McKennitt's first offering to Warner and her first recording to go worldwide.

5

EPIPHANIES

While Loreena McKennitt claims that the Warner deal had no impact on the composition of THE VISIT, only on its subsequent promotion and marketing, including her first world tour, this album did mark a turning point in her career artistically as she added something more spiritual to the 'parallel' philosophy behind her arrangements of Celtic songs and dead poets' verse. Like Yeats, her quest now went beyond the revival of the 'old ways' in search of an aesthetic or mystical experience which she loosely articulated as a 'visit'. During the late 1980s while she was composing music for her fourth album, the 'visit' became a wonderfully flexible metaphor for her in describing the creative process and the affect she hoped her art would have on her audience . The idea of a 'visit' had been at work in her travels in Ireland in search of Celtic 'old ways' and again in the 'visit' mummers paid to their neighbors to re-enact these primitive rituals. The 'visit' also took on an added meaning related to the work of Blake and Yeats, the idea of an imaginative epiphany when a visionary or mystical state is realized through our imaginative perception of the world, something English poet William Wordsworth in *The Prelude* called a 'spot in time'.

During her interviews leading up to the release of THE VISIT, Loreena McKennitt was much more forthcoming in her discussion of her creative process. In *Innerviews*, she spoke of the challenge of continuing to work with traditional Celtic material. "I've been finding it more challenging to find traditional material as of late," she commented. "There's a lot of traditional material that's been very well mined. And it's hard to go out and do field recordings of music sessions in Ireland and Scotland to find music that hasn't already been found and recorded. The rest of the music, which is sort of original, comes to me in various ways. Its part of what the album title 'The Visit' is about. I maintain that the creative impulse is a kind of visit. There's a certain energy that your body becomes a vehicle through which something else happens. I think everybody experiences that in their respective work to some degree." When the interviewer for *Folk Harp Journal* pursued this idea of her music as a visit or "spiritual expression," Loreena elaborated. "I feel that when it happens, or when it's working, it's not a solo experience. . . . I'm a vehicle through which something greater happens . . . that it's an interaction and a shared interaction with people who are exposed to the music. And that becomes, I suppose, what one might call a spiritual experience. But again, I try not to make it, I don't really like talking about it. I think when it happens, everyone knows. It explains itself, or something. All I can do is set up the circumstances in which it is likely to happen . . . like a concert, and a good voice, and all the elements going smoothly, and so on. I call it 'The Visit,' you see." Still, McKennitt was somewhat shy to claim this effect for her music. When the interview questioned, "A spiritual visitation?" McKennitt replied, "Well, sort of. Without being kind of corny about it."

In the liner notes to the album and in subsequent press releases, Loreena has not been so shy about her notion of a visit as an act of creating and experiencing a work of art. "I have long considered the creative impulse to be a visit — a thing of grace, not commanded or owned, so much as awaited, prepared for. A thing, also, of mystery. 'Who is this, and what is here?' wonder Arthur's knights at the sight of the Lady of Shalott. This recording explores some of that mystery. It looks as well into the earlier eastern influences of the

Celts, the likelihood that they started from as far away as India before being driven to the western margins of Europe in the British Isles. With their musical influences came rituals around birth and death which treated the land as holy and haunted; this life itself as a visit. Afterwards, one's soul might move to another plane, or another form — perhaps a tree. The Celts knew then, as we are relearning now, a deep respect for all the life around them. This recording aspires to be nothing so much as a reflection into the weave of these things."

What McKennitt describes here as a 'visit' is, in the aesthetic terms, what could be called an epiphany, from the Greek *phainen* and *epi*, to show on, over, at, after. To cause light, to cause to appear. The word at the root of fantasy, phantom, phenomenon. The Greeks described the visits of gods and goddesses as epiphanies. Such visitations testified to their desire to experience the divine in the mundane. Such visits were at the core of everyday life in epic poems like *The Iliad* or tragic drama like *Electra*. By Shakespeare's time, gods and goddesses, like Ceres and Juno in *The Tempest*, appeared to man in masques. The term epiphany took on religious meaning, applied to miracles, the manifestation of the power of a divinity, not necessarily an appearance of the gods, like the Christian notion of the Holy Spirit or the Hindu notion of Ana vatar, God's agent sent to earth to manifest power and light.

During the Romantic Movement in European literature, music, and painting, the epiphany became the ultimate effect of art. Coleridge called this experience the effect of the poetic imagination. What William Wordsworth called 'spots in time' when our vision cleared and the world appeared whole, the mystical state he experienced while climbing Mount Blanc as a young man, was called by poets and novelists as diverse as Robert Browning, Gerard Manley Hopkins, Alfred Lord Tennyson, Walter Pater, Dante Gabriel Rossetti, Oscar Wilde, James Joyce, and Virginia Woolf the 'glimmer', the 'flash', the 'intense moment', the 'aesthetic moment', the 'good moment,' the 'infinite moment', the 'conscious moment', the 'epiphany', the 'hard-edged flame'. Rossetti described "the sonnet as a moment's monument." These aesthetic moments invested the commonplace with visionary significance.

To experience this world as a living force, we have to lift the veil and recover the dream to feel the magic fire burning within. Students of meditation try to see the divine in every moment, try to create meaning in every moment with the attitude of passionate intensity. Language tries to break free to suggest new meanings, tries to unite in each moment the greatest number of forces with their purest energy. The poets wanted to break through the thick wall of the personality to get beyond the limitations of the world, as if they had turned up the card 'the tower' in the Tarot deck which represents a walled up personality. In a scientific time, these poets and prose writers wanted a different kind of perception. Something to get beyond the limitations of the world. This is the Romantic quest.

Such effects were also sought by Romantic composers as the composer assumed a new role of an explorer of new modes of perception, no longer a servant of the old order, the aristocracy or the church. The liberation and secularization of music is the single greatest art achievement of the 19th century. Religious experience might be need to be preserved, but in new forms of musical expression. Music became a religious experience. Romantic music and poetry — seeking a fresh contact with nature, valuing the importance of dreams, the elevating the individual self — sounds remarkably New Age. Add to this a deep longing for the ritual values of the past and you have the substance and imagery of Loreena McKennitt's composition of Alfred Lord Tennyson's poem, *The Lady of Shalott*.

For Romantic and Victorian poets like Tennyson, historical settings liberated the imagination. The past became a realm to 'visit' in search of aesthetic moments. Poems like Tennyson's *Lady of Shallott* or *Idylls of the King* give an aesthetic distance that provides settings outside time. The exaggerated characters are a counterpoint to our history. The castle-like architecture perfectly accommodates those long ago inhabitants even as it encourages us to live decently and harmoniously. While our city is in decay, an impersonal society, with a decaying psychology, the destructive power of time and imaginative forces, we can always reach back to Camelot. No one denies the roughness or unpleasantness of the Middle Ages, the brutality of feudalism, but somehow art over-reaches these stressful realizations so that faraway Camelot or Shalott seem more secure than the present.

Tennyson was a mystic who claimed he went into trances. Poetry should lead us to a world of mystery, what he called a 'world-whisper'. His poems are rich with images of gleaming light, fresh breezes, lightning bolts, wizards. T.S. Eliot claimed Tennyson was "capable of illumination which he was incapable of understanding." But open-ended and ambiguous are good in a poet, and certainly influenced Eliot in *Four Quartets*.

Like his earlier poem *The Place of Art*, *The Lady of Shalott* presents the dilemma of the romantic artist living in an (ivory) tower who creates a world of art separate from the everyday. On an island in a river stand four gray walls and four gray towers. Within, the Lady of Shallot weaves a magic web with "colours gay." She never looks through the window, only seeing the shadow of the world in a mirror. But should she turn from the mirror to the window, from loom to life, she will invoke the curse of mortality. She has the power to kill the dreamer by destroying the dream. But she is not content. "I am half-sick of shadows." Sir Lancelot passes by. The Lady takes three steps from loom to window. The web floats away. The mirror cracks. The curse descends. Dressed in white, she floats, singing and dying, down the river to Camelot, to the world she will never know, floating past an indifferent Sir Lancelot.

"Who is this? And what is here?" Tennyson has the citizens of Camelot ask in this moment of time as the Lady of Shalott makes her visit. It is just this effect that Loreena McKennitt would seem to be trying to achieve in composing the poem as a song.

The Lady of Shalott

. . . And under tower and balcony,
By garden wall and gallery,
Dead-pale between the houses high,
Silent into Camelot.
Out upon the wharfs they came,
Knight and Burgher, Lord and Dame,
And round the prow they read her name,
The Lady of Shalott.

Whi is this? And what is Here?
And in the lighted palace near
Died the sound of royal cheer;
And they crossed themselves for fear,
The Knights at Camelot;

Lancelot mused a little space
He said, 'She has a lovely face:
God in his mercy lend her grace.'

Beneath narrative are the secondary processes of tone, the way the tune is sung and played, and an indescribable manner that can't be notated. To a secondary process (reason and logic) we have added a primary response (subconscious) that agitates the quality of sadness, loneliness, and melancholy. A luminous moment. Somehow the world takes on wider significance.

Loreena McKennitt's research into the Celtic tradition has been a quest for such historical visits. While summarizing her career upon the release of THE VISIT, she told KMTT in Seattle, "I began this part of my career in the Celtic 'pool', as it were, in the traditional repertoire. By about 1989 I started writing more of my own material and weaving it in with the traditional pieces. Still very much anchored in the Celtic culture, but as I prepared the material for my fourth recording, THE VISIT, I learned that the Celts were much more than this mad collection of anarchists from Scotland, Ireland and Wales. They were this vast collection of tribes that came from middle and Eastern Europe from as far back as 500 BC. And I used this whole pan-Celtic culture as a creative springboard for my music."

A visit, Loreena McKennitt told Anil Prasad at *Innerviews*, can be "a time of discovery, in which new places, people and ideas are uncovered. It also draws from Celtic beliefs and rituals which state that life itself is a visit." This is the notion of the visit she would develop through her explorations of 'pan-Celtic' culture. "THE VISIT has some overt Eastern influences that have a lineage stemming back to early Celtic culture," the interviewer for *Innerviews* commented. "I've been very interested in the early Eastern influences of the Celts," McKennitt added. "Now, when people talk about the Celts, they think of the people who come from Ireland, Scotland and Wales. But in actual fact, the Celts were an assemblage many, many tribes around Middle Eastern Europe. At the height of their art in 500 BC, they were influenced by peoples who came from the Russian Steppes — the area we now call Hungary — as well as peoples from North America. A lot of this can be traced through the burial rites. So, the title 'The Visit' has another meaning. It can refer to a visit to these earlier influences from the people we now call the Celts. So, given that, I wanted to weave — in an impressionistic kind of way — some of these Eastern influences and include the tamboura, sitar, udu drums, and balalaika."

McKennitt's personal epiphany that would set her on a quest across Europe and Asia to discover 'creative springboards" came in 1991 when she visited Venice to attend an exhibit of Celtic art and artifacts gathered from throughout the Western and Eastern world — Spain, Turkey, and beyond. McKennitt describes this pivotal event in the press release for THE VISIT. "Until I went to that exhibition, I thought that Celts were people who came from Ireland, Scotland, Wales, and Brittany. ... I felt exhilarated. It was like thinking that all there is to your family are your parents, brothers and sisters, and then you realize there's a whole stretch of history that is an extension of who you are." There she became, quite simply stated, a pilgrim. Here first pilgrimage would take her on the route of St John of the Cross to Santiago de

Compostella in Galacia, Spain, then into North Africa to Marrakesh. The artistic result would be THE MASK AND MIRROR. The second pilgrimage saw her venture to Instanbul in search of the Celtic presence in the splendors of the Byzantine world, then across the Caucasus and beyond the Russian Steppes on the Trans-Siberian Railway from Vladivostok to St Petersburg. THE BOOK OF SECRETS followed. In this international or 'world' phase of Loreena McKennitt's career, the 'pilgrimage' would replace the 'visit' as her preferred metaphor for her art.

PILGRIM'S PROGRESS

1
NO JOURNEY'S END

"I would like to say that I am a pilgrim like everyone else is a pilgrim," Loreena McKennitt states as her credo in the video *No Journey's End*, "in the sense that we use our tools, our skills to make our way through this life and try to make the sense of it the best that we can. When I am able to stand back and look what I am doing, I am definitely using my career and my talents as a vehicle of exploring, in one sense, many things and many subjects that are of interest to me and, I suppose, more than just a deep fascination. I wonder, How does the world go round? What makes us tick? It's wonderful to be able to use my music, my travel and research, to explore these questions. So when I take that back to my music ... my recordings become like a travelogue; they become a document of my path of exploration." While reflecting back on her career, dating from her first visit to Ireland, McKennitt recognizes that "a sense of journey, I suppose, has been a major part of what I do, but in different ways and at different times. When I got interested in Celtic music, my first major trip was to come to Ireland and to track it down in its various indigenous forms. But again, at that point it time, I was just following something that really fascinated me, but I wasn't really aware of myself on a quest, as it were. I had, through my research, discovered that the Celts were much more than just this mad collection of anarchists from Scotland and Ireland and so on. They were actually a motley collection of tribes that emanated from middle and eastern Europe as far back as 500 BC, and throughout the course of centuries — and with a good deal of encouragement from the Romans, you might say! — were thrust to the western margins of Europe."

Dating from her epiphany in Venice ten years later while attending the exhibit of Celtic artefacts, Loreena McKennitt has thrust herself, in quest of her Celtic roots, beyond the western margins of Europe to the eastern margins of Asia, first following the course of the Celts along the pilgrimage route to Santiago de Compostella in Spain, then researching Celtic archeology in Italy, Istanbul, and even Marrakesh, before setting out on her greatest adventure, across the Asian continent from Vladivostok to St Petersburg, looking for the Celtic shadow along the Russian Steppes, on the Trans-Siberian Railway. Following the release THE BOOK OF SECRETS, she took a break from touring the album to complete a two-week bicycle trip through China, which will, no doubt, become substance for her next album. Along the way she has explored the Christian mystic tradition of St John of the Cross, Dante's Hell and Heaven, and Sufi literature and philosophy, raising more questions about what make us tick and what makes the world go round than she could ever hope to answer. The great joy of listening to the music that has resulted from these physical and spiritual pilgrimages is the wonderful sense of curiosity we feel in the music, an opening of the soul into a wider world.

For the past decade, Loreena McKennitt has adopted the attitude towards life captured in the words of Lao Tzu, the celebrated Chinese poet, whom she cites in the epigraph to THE BOOK OF SECRETS: "A good traveler has no fixed plans and is not intent on arriving." "When I came across Lao Tzu's words," McKennitt confessed in an interview, "I felt I had found an encapsulation of not only the manner in which THE BOOK OF SECRETS and almost all of my recordings have unfolded, but of my life in general." Her career has unfolded in ways she never expected when she set out from Winnipeg in 1981. At times, this attitude has led McKennitt in directions she never imagined she would travel. "In casting your inspirational net as an artist, you become familiar with the humility that comes with watching your best-laid plans veer sideways, and recordings becoming something other than what you expected," she adds, with a great sense of pleasure in the unexpected. "So, you set out to travel to Rome . . . and end up in Istanbul. You set off for Japan . . . and you end up on a train across Siberia. The journey, not the destination, becomes a source of wonder." Loreena McKennitt has followed her muse, without charting a 'career' plan, and now finds herself a thoroughly 'well-traveled' artist, in the best sense of the term.

Indeed, her travels have become such an integral part of her creative process that she now refers to herself as a kind of 'travel' musician, working much like such celebrated travel writers as Bruce Chatwin, Paul Theroux, or Jan Morris. "I'm not going to put myself in the same category as travel writer," McKennitt told Nick Krewen in *Canadian Musician*, "but it is the kind of function where you're marrying historical detail with personal experience. By doing that, sometimes that kind of expression allows other people to latch on to the corners of history or cultural strata that they wouldn't have imagined." Again, she would tell Mark Keating in *Rhythm* magazine that in creating THE BOOK OF SECRETS "I have presented my travel journal as a musical document." During an interview for *Inside Borders*, she elaborated on this metaphor of a 'musical travelogue'. "Having a passion for Celtic music," McKennitt explained, "I've used that as a vehicle for learning more about history and acquainting myself with subjects and themes that I might not have engaged in otherwise. In a more specific sense, with this recording I wanted to look at the more eastern direction of the Celts, or at least begin there, but again as with anything, you set yourself off in a direction and you really have no idea where you'll end up. I look at the recording as a document of my path of exploration. It's a kind of musical travelogue, the process very similar to what professional travel writers go through: they land upon a theme, do a lot of research, read a lot of books, and then go to these places because there's a lot of essential information you can only pick up as a result of traveling to places — the light of the sky, the smell of the streets, the sounds of people." Elsewhere she refers to her work on THE MASK AND MIRROR and THE BOOK OF SECRETS as 'musical travel writing': "Given the many unexpected journeys that led to its creation, THE BOOK OF SECRETS could probably best be described as a kind of musical travel writing. It would be impossible to describe the varied and numerous events and personal exchanges that took place during its research and recording, but a look at THE BOOK OF SECRETS CD liner notes should give you hints of a number of its sources of inspiration, whether in the books and music I have discovered, or experiences I have had."

Driven by her intense cultural and spiritual curiosity, Loreena McKennitt has also taken to 'armchair' traveling, reading widely and diversely classic works of travel literature, especially where the quest of the author meets her own interests. Works cited in the liner notes to THE BOOK OF SECRETS include masterpieces of travel literature like John Ruskin's *The Stones of Venice* and Jan Morris' *Venice*, as well as William Dalrymple's *From the Holy Mountain*, a travel book within a travel book, which McKennitt describes as "the account of his journey following in the footsteps of two monks who set off for Byzantium from the monastery of Iviron on Mount Athos in 587 AD. One of these monks, John Moschos, wrote about his arduous travels in a book called *The Spiritual Meadow*. Dalrymple's book highlights striking similarities between archetypally Celtic illuminated manuscripts such as *The Book of Durrow* and *The Book of Kells*, and earlier Byzantine works, and suggests that these influences may have been transported via monastic migration from east to west in the early centuries after Christ." Among other titles cited are William Eamon's *Science and the Secrets of Nature*, "whose look at the history of science touches on how the mysteries of nature gradually became explainable;" Murat Yagan's autobiography *I Come from Behind Kaf Mountain*, "which touches on his initiation to the Sufi path via equestrian training" with a respect for horses shared by the Celts; and Dante's *The Divine Comedy*, which leads McKennitt to reflect, while reading this classic work of Western literature aboard the Trans-Siberian Railway, on how we share this "human condition . . . Are we helping or hurting each other?" The liner notes for THE BOOK OF SECRETS end with an invitation to contact Quinlan Road for "a bibliography of the texts used in researching this recording."

More so than most contemporary artists, McKennitt has revealed the sources of her inspiration and her process of composition, using the liner notes from her CDs. It is here in the liner notes to THE BOOK OF SECRETS where we see McKennitt suggesting that her passion for 'musical travel' is a distinctly Celtic trait of character, perhaps a state of being — or rather, becoming. "Over a number of years spent ruminating on the distinctive characteristics of the Celts," she explains, "I began to wonder if their legendarily nomadic ways arose from an inner need. An involuntary response, rather than a pragmatic one; a restlessness that had its roots in an insatiable curiosity. I suspect it was my growing awareness of my own wanderlust and curiosity that made me aware of the real sense of connection I felt to the Celtic lineage, as part of that New World extension of a people who ranged so astonishingly far and wide. And the more I learned of pan-Celtic culture and its unexpected turns and twists, the more I was drawn to learn about the Celts' contemporaries, which in turn set me off on tangents which might have little or no connection to the Celts themselves. . . . Sometimes that pan-Celtic springboard would project me into corners of history such as those hinted at in *Skellig*, where Dark Ages monasteries in Ireland helped to keep knowledge alive at a time when the Roman Empire was distancing. Or I might find myself on an excavation site in Tuscany, where digs revealed more of the Etruscans, contemporaries of the Celts whose arts and society influenced the Romans. *The Mummer's Dance* was the culmination of a line of encounters stretching from a puppet makers studio in Palermo to the traditional May Day celebrations in a remote corner of Cornwall. Sometimes, I was led to areas that had little or no connection at all to the Celts, as when I found myself on a winter train journey across Siberia, an experience later woven into *Dante's Prayer*."

McKennitt's aim as a 'travel musician' or 'musical traveler' thus becomes to communicate this same curiosity to her listeners, as she explained in an interview for *Pulse* magazine. "My challenge then becomes, how do I repaint all of these smells and colors and sounds through the texture of the instruments or the lyrics?" This is the challenge she faced in THE MASK AND MIRROR as she followed the pilgrimage route of the Medieval mystic poet and saint, St John of the Cross. The result is the creation of a distinct 'world' music that resonates further and deeper than her previous Celtic recordings.

2

THE ROAD TO SANTIAGO

"When I make a record," Loreena McKennitt declared while composing the songs for THE MASK AND MIRROR, "I'm not really interested in compiling eight or ten tracks of just my point of view. I really want to throw spotlights on certain aspects of history or culture or religion that bring about more questions than answers." For this album, the spotlight was focused geographically and historically on Spain, with a side glance at Morocco, as she promised in *Saturday Night* magazine, with a rush of enthusiasm. "This recording — I'm going to shine this flashlight I've got on Spain, I'm going to shine it on Morocco, I'm going to shine it on the Gnostic Gospels ... on the Knights Templar. We're going to talk about astronomy and mathematics." The points of view came from the works of Shakespeare (*Prospero's Speech*), W.B. Yeats (*The Two Trees*), St John of the Cross (*Dark Night of the Soul*), and Rumi (*The Mystic's Dream*), while the questions raised and the themes pursued include the Christian mystic quest for union with God and the philosophical images of the mask and mirror. On this album, Loreena McKennitt began to explore the 'big' questions of philosophy and religion, questions of ontology or Being, that she would pursue on *Skellig* from THE BOOK OF SECRETS, questions prompted by her journey to the monastery of Bobbio in Italy where she found traces of Celtic culture. "Here I'm shining a spotlight on a corner of history that is of value," she explained. "I am interested in the question of Who is God? What about sacrifice that enhances your understanding of God?" As she explains elsewhere, "I wanted to cast a spotlight on certain pre-conceived notions that people have on their own religion or spiritual embodiment. We are all an extension of each other's history. And if you know where you've come from, you can interpret much better where you are."

Her description of THE MASK AND MIRROR from the CD liner lines is especially telling about her concerns in this recording. "I looked back and forth through the window of 15th century Spain, through the hues of Judaism, Islam and Christianity, and was drawn in a fascinating world: history, religion, cross-cultural fertilization. . . . From the more familiar turf of the west coast of Ireland, through the troubadours of France, crossing over the Pyrenees and then to the west through Galicia, down through Andalusia and past Gibraltar to Morocco. . . . The crusades, the pilgrimage to Santiago, Cathars, the Knights Templar, the Sufis from Egypt, One Thousand and One Nights in Arabia, the Celtic sacred imagery of trees, the Gnostic Gospels . . . who was God? and what is religion, what spirituality? What was revealed and what was concealed . . . and what was the mask and what the mirror?" *On No Journey's End*, she further traced the connections between Celtic culture and Medieval Spain. "I learned that Spain, in those years, for example, heavily influenced the way our Western civilization developed in the areas of agriculture and architecture and literature. On the subject of literature, for example, it appears that the Arthurian legends may have been influenced by poetry that came from the north of Africa via Spain through the Moorish community. As I researched the material on this project, I discovered that people do reveal or conceal themselves to and with each other in different ways, and certainly in the area of religion and spirituality." How she met the challenge of transforming this curiosity into music we can share, McKennitt explains in an interview with Cindy McLynn. "I started studying Spanish history and quickly learned that prior to 1500 there we primarily three communities in Spain. The Judaic, the Moorish Islamic and the Christian. I was quite curious to see to what degree these religious communities were able to live together in this relatively small country, confronted all the time with a different interpretation of who God is. To me, it threw out the question, 'What is the difference between religion and spirituality?' I'm very preoccupied by this subject. It's woven in different ways through my music and through the recording's themes and ideas. I doesn't surprise me that people are drawn to my music, to some degree, intellectually. I also feel that when I sing, I really try to capture the feeling that one is a vehicle. My body or voice is an instrument — it's the spirit or soul that resonates. . . . The Sufis have an expression of personal refinement that is expressed as a tarnished mirror. As you try to perfect yourself, you polish the mirror of your soul. I think it's a lovely image. I would say I'm madly polishing this unbelievably tarnished mirror and hoping something shines forth and is of some value to people."

McKennitt's research spotlight came to rest on the city of Santiago de Compostella, where she found the inspiration for composing *Santiago*, the instrumental song recorded on THE MASK AND MIRROR. "The inspiration began in the north-west corner of Spain in Galicia," she explained during an interview on the BBC. "It is a very Celtic corner of the country, particularly in a city called Santiago de Compostella, which was a pilgrimage site for people in the Middle Ages. It was on a par with Jerusalem, for example. People came from various corners of Europe down through the south of France and over to this shrine, and they became like bees carrying the pollen of those influences as they went back to their homes elsewhere in Europe. So to highlight that point, I was drawn to a piece of music that actually comes from that period. We simply called it *Santiago*." The Chieftains recorded an album called SANTIAGO, which, no doubt, added further Celtic inspiration to McKennitt's arrangement.

In her journal entry for this song on THE MASK AND MIRROR, McKennitt describes her journeys to Santiago. "January, 1992 — Just performed in Santiago de Compostella in the Galacian area of Spain ... misty and lush as we arrived from more arid regions of the country; clearly Celtic territory in the language and the music, and a place I must visit again soon ... We arrived a day early; band et al went for a wonderful Sunday lunch and then wandered over to the cathedral to observe the wonderful faces on the Portico." She returned to Santiago a few months later. "May, 1992 — Santiago de Compostella (St James in the Field of the Star) ... had occasion to return to Galacia and Santiago sooner than I'd thought ... I learned the story behind the city. Supposedly the remains of St James arrived mysteriously in the village of Padron (which we visited ... lovely line of trees along the waterway lading to the place where the relics were found) and interred here in Santiago ... I picked up a CD collection of music emanating from the pilgrimage route to Santiago, as well as a CD by Spanish group Els Trobadors ... wonderful feeling to this music." Then a year later, she returned to her study of this pilgrimage site while arranging the song *Santiago*. "May, 1993 — Now studying liner notes, books and pieces of music, putting together a clearer picture if Santiago in the years 900 to 1500 when it rivalled Jerusalem and Rome as a pilgrimage destination, playing host to a motley tide of humanity pursuing both religious and more earthy goals. It was also the site of unprecedented cross-cultural fertilization between the Christian, Jewish, and Moorish communities. When I heard this piece, I was struck by its Semitic tone, and realised that, even in the area of music, the three communities were influencing each other."

In the image of Santiago de Compostella, Loreena McKennitt began her own meditation on the meaning of a pilgrimage and began to develop what could be called her 'art of the pilgrimage'. "There were pilgrimage routes which stretched from all corners of the world to this place," she learned from her research, "with monasteries, inns and resting places set up along the way. These routes, which were at their most active between 1000 and 1598, became tremendously influential in the cross-fertilization of the Judaic, Christian and Islamic cultures, including them fields of music, mathematics, and astronomy." The holy route to Santiago de Compostella is still well traveled by pilgrims today, conducted as an act of obedience to God in quest for a union with his divine being. Among the various pilgrimage cities in the Middle Ages, the most visited city was Santiago, Spain, the third largest city of the Christian world, after Rome and Jerusalem. While pilgrims to Jerusalem, known as 'Palmers' for the palm branches they brought home, traveled to the cite of Christ's crucifixion, and 'Romeros' made their pilgrimage to the cite of the founding of the Church by St Peter, pilgrims to Santiago went to see the silver reliquary of the apostle James. The pilgrimage had a powerful spiritual hold in the Middle Ages. A pilgrimage assured a blessing on one's soul, and pilgrims who traveled to all three shrines — Rome, Jerusalem, Santiago — could be considered exalted.

The legend of the shrine at Santiago is thus told. James and John were the first two disciples of Jesus and both were present at the Crucifixion. James, beheaded by Herod Agripa, was the first follower of Jesus to be martyred. Tradition claims James converted nine Iberians to Christianity before he returned to the Holy Land for his martyrdom. His decapitated body was returned to Spain in a ship of stone crewed by Knights Templars and buried in a field in northern Spain. Eight hundred years later, a shepherd or hermit reported a star, comet, or meteor hovering above a field. The body was excavated, mysteriously restored with head intact. In 844, James was seen riding a white horse, swinging a great sword, and battling the Moorish invaders of Spain. James Michener, in his travelogue *Iberia*, suggests the legend was less an article of faith and more a practical invention of generals who needed a rallying point to counteract the Moors belief that the preserved arm of the prophet Mohammed in Cordoba was a relic that would render them invincible. But relics still matter: in 1962, the mummified left arm of Saint Teresa was received in Madrid with an honor guard. In another related miracle, a bridegroom was drowned on the way to his wedding; his bride appealed to Santiago,

The Road to Santiago

and he arose from the sea covered in white cockleshells. This beautiful white shell became the mark of those who fought the Moors and made the pilgrimage.

Under the banner of James, Christianity conquered Spain, expelled the Moors, then conquered the Americas. St James became the patron saint of Spain, his burial place the most sacred spot, known as Santiago de Compostella. The word 'compostella' derived either from *Camp de las estella* — countryside where the star shone (in Latin *Campus Stellae*) — or from Latin *Compost Terra* — from *compstum*, burying ground. The name James is also known as the Latinate *Jacobus*, so the pilgrimage is sometimes called the Jacobean route. In Old Spanish, James is known as Iago, Jacome, Jaime, even Diego, and in France as Jacques.

The Santiago journey began in Paris, near Note Dame Cathedral, at the Tour St Jacques on the Right Bank. The pilgrims might be royalty, knights, clergy, criminals sentenced to the journey, criminals taking advantage of the opportunities, various merchants and artisans who used the trip as a marketplace, and spies who reported back to the king. All Santiago pilgrims wore a heavy cape, the eight-foot stave with drinking gourd, sturdy sandals, and a broad-rimmed felt hat turned up at front and decorated with three or four cockleshells. (A French dish of scallops in wine sauce served in a cockleshell is known as *coquille St Jacques*). Walking about 10 miles a day, the journey took three months. Tradition dictated that the first pilgrim on the road to see the towers of the church in Santiago would call out in French, '*Mon Joie*, I am King!' Many families with the surname King, Konig, Leroy, Rex obtained these names because an ancestor was first in line.

By the year 1130 more than half a million people made the pilgrimage. The first travel guide was published at the request of the French church praising the glories of France, but warning travelers in Spain to expect the dangers of contaminated water, thieves and murderers, bad food, poor accommodation, and miserable hospitals. One could argue that modern tourism began in Santiago, Spain, in the Middle Ages. The Hostal de los Reyes Catolicos became the foremost hospital in the world during the 16th century at the height of the pilgrimage 'craze' and is now one of the world's great luxury hotels.

Some two million pilgrims still arrive on July 25 to see the Dance of the Giants and fireworks over the Cathedral dedicated to St James. The immense cathedral has a gigantic plaza, which holds several thousands without crowding. The cathedral itself is a work of art, the highlight of which is the Portico de la Gloria, one wall of which is 60 feet high with some of the finest sculptures of

Romanesque art, one of the supreme artistic creations in the world, comparable to the Sistine Chapel at St Peter's Basilica. Pilgrims bow before the 25 magnificent arches across the front of the Palacio de Rajouz. The immense towers of the Church glisten like gold in the setting sun from the effects of a kind of lichen over the Plaza del Obradoro. On such a journey, the smallest detail becomes holy. To drink water from a public fountain. To find refuge for the night. A daily meal. To touch relics of the saints. And holiest of all, to see the silver reliquary of St James.

One carved pillar inside the cathedral shows the 'family' Tree of Jesse, from which Jesus sprang. Among the vines and leaves are indentations made by the artist, a perfect fit for the hand. Centuries of pilgrims and hundreds of millions of finger and palm prints later, the marble is deeply worn, a stone tree that still has life and gives energy. On the platform of the tree is the statue of Santiago, and above that angels, images of the evangelists, and a depiction of the passion surrounding a statue of Jesus in a semi-circle surrounded by the 24 elders of the Apocalypse. The images come from the first chapter in the *Book of Ezekial* and a passage from *Revelations* in which John beholds the throne of God. The elders form an orchestra, grouped two by two, playing various instruments: 14 zithers, four psalteries, two harps, two lutes, and a zanfona, or hurdy gurdy, which looks like a guitar with a crank, an instrument Loreena McKennitt used for her recordings on THE BOOK OF SECRETS. During solemn High Mass on July 25, a silver-plated iron censer some three feet high is filled with charcoal and incense and swung by men using a complicated series of ropes and pulleys in a gigantic arc of some 90 feet, whizzing above the heads of watchers, from one side of the cathedral to the other, spitting out sparks and trails of smoke, an extraordinary sight.

Sacred places, say the pilgrims, are where heaven and earth touch. Pilgrims want to experience the spiritual world while still alive in the material world. On a pilgrimage, travelers find all creation is interconnected. A true pilgrimage transforms. A pilgrim can be surprised by joy and bring to life the sacred. The pilgrimage also brings about acts of compassion, generosity, love, and faith. To walk into this world as a pilgrim is to know we are not alone. To undergo a pilgrimage is not to become a tourist but to enter into dialog with one's god. A pilgrimage helps us recognize we exist only to the extent that we participate in innumerable practices that collectively establish a living tradition. That is our heritage, given by the real presence of those who came before. In a world of spiritual diversity, the pilgrimage, or any travel that involves spiritual quest, is still important. On the Internet are 20,000 or more sites concerning pilgrimages.

Some of our greatest literature has been structured by the art of the pilgrimage — Geoffrey Chaucer's *The Canterbury Tales*, for example, an account of an actual pilgrimage to Canterbury in the form of a human comedy, or John Bunyan's *Pilgrim's Progress*, very much a spiritual pilgrimage through the Christian divine comedy of sin and salvation, heaven and hell, traveling through the slough of despair and the dark night of the soul toward the light of God's grace. This is the journey the mystic poet, St John of the Cross, traced in his poem *The Dark Night of the Soul*, which Loreena McKennitt arranged and recorded on THE MASK AND MIRROR.

3

MYSTICS AND SUFIS

"In the course of assembling the music for THE MASK AND MIRROR, which seemed to be focused on Spain and the 15th century," Loreena McKennitt stated in an interview with the BBC on *Women's Hour*, "I wanted to find poems from that period that examined some of the broader philosophical things about that period. St John of the Cross, being a mystic, was also influenced by another mystic called Teresa of Avila — he took a more direct approach to connecting with his God, which was very much discouraged within the Christian Church at that time. It's a beautiful metaphorical love poem and if one didn't really know the background you would interpret it as that." In the "exquisite" work of St John of the Cross, she found a "richly metaphorical love poem between himself and his god," McKennitt explains in her liner note to her recording of *The Dark Night of the Soul*. "His approach seems more akin to early Islamic of Judaic works in its more direct route to communication to his god ... I have gone over three different translations of the poem, and am struck by how much a translation can alter our interpretation. Am reminded that most holy scriptures come to us in translation, resulting in a diversity of views."

The verse and prose works of St John of the Cross are the most grandiose and the most melodious spiritual canticles of all the mystic writers. A web site on St John of the Cross notes, "his treatises — principally the *Ascent of Mount Carmel* and *The Dark Night of the Soul* — give the impression of a mastermind that has scaled the heights of mystical science, and from their summit looks down upon and dominates the plain below and the paths leading upwards. These treatises illustrate the theological truth that ennobles and dignifies nature, the agreement always found between the natural and the supernatural — between the principles of sound reason and the sublimest manifestations of

Divine grace." When Spain was a world power, exploring the New World for El Dorado, the art, music, and literature of Spain extended through all of Europe and the New World. St John of the Cross, Juan de la Cruz, joined the Carmelite monastic order, where he developed an interest in these arts. Then he met Teresa de Avila, La Madre, a radical reformer, and joined her monastic following, which advocated more ascetic practices than the Carmelites, contemplative prayer and lengthy fasting, stern dress and bare feet. When the order was persecuted, Juan was imprisoned in a small dark cell, fed scraps and sardines. Forced to kneel on a stone floor and whipped with a knotted rope, he suffered his dark night of the soul, feeling God had abandoned him to torment and pain. A crisis of being descends and threatens to annihilate him. Despair. Loneliness. Crushed and alone, he was suddenly filled with passion and desire in the realization that the soul must suffer on its way to God. In a dream vision, he has the sudden insight or epiphany that spirit and love, like a log and flame, cannot be extinguished. Neither prison, nor punishment, nor painful death could destroy his love for God and for mankind. With this insight, he began the writings now called a *Spiritual Canticle*. In many old mythologies, humans went through an initiation called the 'darkest night' which involved a journey into the underworld. In *The Magic Flute*, Mozart called it the "ordeal of fire and water." The only way to individual self-discovery leads through such suffering, a dark night of the soul.

This is the spiritual transformation and power of divine love Loreena McKennitt celebrates in arranging *The Dark Night of the Soul*, the epiphany of St John's spiritual pilgrimage.

The Dark Night Of The Soul

Upon a darkened night
the flame of love was burning in my breast
And by a lantern bright
I fled my house while all in quiet rest
Shrouded by the night
and by the secret stair I quickly fled
The veil concealed my eyes
while all within lay quiet as the dead

Oh night thou was my guide
oh night more loving than the rising sun
Oh night that joined the lover

to the beloved one
Transforming each of them into the other . . .

I lost myself to him
and laid my face upon my lover's breast
And care and grief grew dim
as in the morning's mist became the light
There they dimmed amongst the lilies fair
there they dimmed amongst the lilies fair
there they dimmed amongst the lilies fair

Three years after his death in 1591, at age 49, St John's 'undecayed' body was quartered. The monastery of Segovia got the torso and head, where it remains to this day in an ornate marble box above a great altar; an arm went to Madrid; the other arm and legs, plus a finger, went to Obidos.

The mystic experience in the Christian tradition has always been suspect, but in Eastern faiths, mysticism is at the core of religion. The mystic bypasses the clerical hierarchy, communing directly with god through a visionary experience or illumination, and thus threatens the order of the church and the state. Mystics find extreme joy in suffering. To fulfill God's love is to die; death is the bridge that leads to God. The dark night of the soul moves in two directions. Part of the struggle is to find a state of union with the divine. But mystics cannot stay long enough to become God intoxicated. Mystics can experience God, but cannot be God. They have to return to this realm, a pain comparable, say the texts, to lovers separating.

In an interview with Karen Bliss for swaymag.com, Loreena McKennitt connected the mystic tradition of St John with the desire of W.B. Yeats for a visionary experience of divinity. "As dissimilar as Yeats and St John of the Cross were, living in different times and different places," explains McKennitt, "both were concerned with the human need to be spiritually engaged, and how religion has often times not served that need but manipulated those needs to serves other interests, political and imperialistic." On THE MASK AND MIRROR, this mystic tradition of spiritual quest becomes McKennitt's preoccupation, not only in arranging *The Dark Night Of The Soul* but also in composing the lyrics and music for *Marrakesh Night Market* and *The Mystic's Dream*, perhaps her richest expression of her own mystic attitude, inspired by the Sufi poetry, philosophy, music, and dance of the 13th-century poet Rumi and his disciples.

In her journal entry for *The Mystic's Dream*, Loreena McKennitt writes:

"January 24, 1993 — Granada, Spain ... evening ... lights across the city embrace the body of the Alhambra ... Rambled around the Moorish section of the city; picked up a little gold mirror, an incense burner, a tiny bottle of perfume ... Reading Indries Shah's book 'The Sufis,' prefaced by Robert Graves ... a secret tradition behind all religious and philosophical systems, Sufis have significantly influenced the East and the West ... They believe not that theirs is a religion, but that it *is* religion .... The 'common sufi' may be as common in the East as in the West, and may come dressed as a merchant, a lawyer, a housewife, anything ... to be in the world, but not of it, free from ambition, greed, intellectual pride, blind obedience to custom, or awe of persons higher in rank.... It appears there may be an association with the Druidic order of the Celts." For November 26, 1993, her journal reads: "Indries Shah on Rumi: 'the union of the mind and intuition which brings about illumination, and the development which the Sufis seek, is based upon love ....' "

Between the Christian mysticism of St John of the Cross and the Islamic mysticism of the Sufis, Loreena McKennitt, no doubt, found many parallels, as she is wont to do. A mystic sect of Islam, Sufism began to develop in the 7th century (the first century of Islam) in Persia, in response to mystic interpretations of the teachings of Muhammad, influenced by Hindu and other Eastern religions. Originally an ascetic order given to wearing coarse woolen clothing, the Sufis gained their name from the Arabic term 'sufi' or 'man of wool'. Devotees to Sufism were referred to as dervishes from the Persian '*darvesh*' or 'beggar'. Some Sufis were wanderers, spreading their faith from Northern Africa to Northern India, like the Kalenderis or Calendars who vowed to travel perpetually. Others were monastic, living in tekkes or khanagahs, where they observed special rites of meditation, and still others were ordinary tradesmen who performed their mystic rites only on special occasions.

The Sufis developed a well-defined method for reaching a mystic knowledge of Allah, experienced in an ecstatic illumination. Often described as pilgrims on a journey, the Sufis follow a path to union with God involving seven stages — repentance, abstinence, renunciation, poverty, patience, trust, and acquiescence to the will of God — all guided by a growing love of Allah and loss of self. To initiate this meditation on the ways of love, some Sufi orders, like the Kadiris, developed a peculiar chant or drone and became known as the 'howling dervishes'. Once articulated in the theosophical (wisdom) writings of Suhrawardi and his 'School of Illumination' and in the gnostic works of Ibn 'Arabi in the 12th century, the Sufi faith became a vital religious force, especially in western Asia, and found sympathy among Christian mystics in Spain where the cultures met.

MYSTICS AND SUFIS

By the 13th century, hundreds of Sufi monastic communities, with several million adherents, had been established. Among the most influential of these orders was the Malaawiya or Mevlevi sect founded by the Persian poet Jalal al-Din Mohammad Rumi. Born in 1207 in what is now Afghanistan, Rumi moved to Konya in what is now Turkey, where he became a disciple of the Muslim mystic Shams al-Din, who mysteriously disappeared in 1247. Rumi composed over 30,000 verses in memory of his master, leading to his epic poem *Masnavi-ye Manavi* (Spiritual Couplets). Rumi soon attracted his own followers, Mevlevi Sufis known for their entrancing music and ecstatic dancing which has gained them the name "whirling dervishes." This powerful combination of poetry, music, and dance leading to a mystical spiritual experience has survived the intervening centuries and crossed over into the Christian world to the extent that today Rumi is the most widely-read poet in the United States of America. Much as Zen became the pop faith for the Beat Generation in the 1950s, fifty years later Sufi art has become the pop path to wisdom and enlightenment.

Contemporary seekers of wisdom and enlightenment not only look to Rumi's elliptical yet inspiration poetry but also to the Mevlevi music he inspired. In their desire to find a musical style that would lead the Sufi pilgrim on the journey to illumination, the Mevlevi sect adapted the ancient makam system of music, based on the mystical mathematical theories of Pythagoras and written by the Arabic musicologist Safi al Din. "This system, which uses units of four and five notes, known a tetrachords and pentachords, was extensively used by Pythagoras in his experiments into the true nature of the human psyche," an article on Mevlevi Music on the internet posted by the Saraswati Society claims. "Mevlevi music provides a link with pure human attitudes which exist naturally within the human psyche and assist realization of the true Self." For Mevlevi Sufis, this music is, in effect, "holy scripture in musical form, written by accomplished souls. It is not music for pleasure but for cleaning the mirror of the heart. By divine and artful weaving of normal and mystical intervals it assists the appreciation of the inner experience. Cymbals, the ney (flute) and drums are the traditional instruments. ... This music wakes the sleeping soul to God and tunes the inner being toward higher things."

This is the power of the Rumi-influenced lyrics and the Melevi-like music on *The Mystic's Dream*, where the love described takes on an allegorical meaning of spiritual or divine love on the pilgrimage to illumination, while the music wakes the sleeping soul.

A clouded dream on an earthly night
Hangs upon the crescent moon
A voiceless song in an ageless light
Sings at the coming of dawn
Birds in flight are calling there
Where the heart moves the stones
It's there that my heart is longing
All for the love of you . . .

On *Marrakesh Night Market* and *Full Circle*, the two songs clearly linked to *The Mystic's Dream* in time and tone on THE MASK AND MIRROR, the Sufi image of the soul as a mirror to be polished in the quest for the divine light merges with the image of the mask McKennitt explored in her Stratford Festival Theatre days, embodied on this album in *Prospero's Speech*.

According to her 'journal' entry for *Marrakesh Night Market*, Loreena McKennitt arrived in Marrakesh on March 16, 1993, less than two months after her entry for *The Mystic's Dream*. "It is Ramadan," she observes, "and there is heightened activity all around. I am struck by the hooded features of men as they pass through the lights and shadows: they look monk-like. Horses, carriages, cars, bicycles and thousands of people are embroiled in the activities of the night . . . a cacophony of sound . . . each involved in their own drama of music, storytelling, monkey's on men's shoulders, or cobras being coaxed to 'dance' on rugs; 'magic' concoctions of bone, seeds, stones and spices are sold . . . women veiled to a great degree . . . I am struck by the sense of intrigue the environment creates; as much is concealed as is revealed . . . ." Such is the substance and tone of *Marrakesh Night Market*.

They're gathered in circles
the lamps light their faces
The crescent moon rocks in the night sky
The poets of drumming
keep heartbeats suspended
The smoke swirls up them it dies

Would you like my mask?
Would you like my mirror?
Cries the man in the shadowing hood
You can look at yourself
you can look at each other
or you can look at the face of your god . . .

The image of the heart or the soul as an image that constantly needs polishing by piety is a complex image in Loreena McKennitt's work, part Western and part Eastern, part Christian and part Islamic in reference. Since Plato, mirrors and reflective surfaces have been the central metaphor of philosophy, art, and religion. In Plato's terms, works of art — indeed, everything we create — are themselves illusions, reflections of the absolute realm of ideas. The 'idea' of a table is purer than the actual thing we sit at. In the Christian tradition, the mirror represents the mind, heart, and soul, reflecting a divine image. In the Bible, the mirror image, representing the difference between our understanding of God in this life and our experience of Him in heaven, occurs in St Paul (*1 Corinthians*.13.12): "For now we see in a mirror dimly, but then face to face. Now I understand in part; then I shall understand fully, even as I have been fully understood." The ancient Christians spoke of the soul as a mirror receiving the image and form of God, so that God becomes present in it, though remaining there mostly unknown and hidden, while awaiting the moment of conversion or interior revelation.

Oriental religious practices, such as Zen and Taoism, also often use images of mirrors. The perfect mind is empty and still, as clear as water or a mirror. In Tibetan temples we find pots of water symbolizing this idea that the wisdom of penetrating insight is like a mirror. The mind of a sage, wrote one Taoist mystic, is empty, like a mirror, going after nothing, welcoming nothing, responding, but not storing. "The mind in stillness is the mirror of Heaven and Earth, the glass of ten thousand things." Such wisdom brings contentment so that the ten thousand things of worldly distraction present no problem, provided the mind or mirror is kept free of dust. "For while the mind and heart of the sage cannot tolerate the least particle of dust," Confucian scholar Wang Yang-ming (1472-1529) wrote, "and has naturally no need of polishing, the mind and heart of the average man ... resembles a spotted and dirty mirror, which needs thorough polishing, to have all its dust and dirt removed. Then will the tiniest streak of dust become visible, and only a light stroke will wipe it away, without anyone having to spend much energy." When the mirror of the soul is thoroughly polished, we are at one with the universe, Rumi believed.

For Loreena McKennitt, the mirror symbol holds a double meaning, as she explains in her Introduction to THE MASK AND MIRROR: "For some medieval minds the mirror 'was the door through which the soul frees itself by passing' ... for others the pursuit of personal refinement was likened to 'polishing the mirror of the soul'." Not surprisingly, she transforms this mirror image into a metaphor to describe her music, in this case, the instrument of her voice. "I've a belief that voice is the instrument of instruments in so as it is connected to the human being, and it has a great range of articulating and expressing ideas and feelings," Loreena McKennitt speculates in *No Journey's End*. "The Sufis have an expression of 'polishing the mirror of your soul', and perhaps my voice becomes that polishing aspect: that it is a vehicle of expressing things in a very primal and instinctive way, and I think that that is part of the strength of what I do. You try not to have any barriers. You've opened your soul; you've opened yourself up." There is no finer description of the power of voice in music than this.

One week after recording her impressions of the Marrakesh market in her journal, Loreena McKennitt left Marrakesh to the sound of "men chanting in the mosque, one of the most moving and primitive sounds I have ever heard. They are calling their God. I think, when have I heard this before?" In recalling her visits to the Benedectine monastery in St Benoit-du-lac, Quebec on November 1, 1988, she finds the resonance needed for composing the instrumental, *Full Circle*. "It was the first snowfall today," she wrote in her diary for November 21, 1988, "and the brothers were out walking along the long lane as I approached ... hooded figures slowly making their way to Mass as the snow fell like blessings.' Three days later, she continued this meditation. "I have wondered about who these men are who have made their way here, who they were before they came. How did each connect to God, and how did it differ from each other's journey, and from mine? ..." By casting a spotlight on 15th century Spain and the mystic faith of the Christian St John of the Cross and the Sufi Jalal al-Din Mohammad Rumi, Loreena McKennitt had come full circle from her studies of the Celtic history and musical meditations on the monastic life of Irish scholars and saints at Bobbio or on Skellig when she began asking the question, "Who is God? What about sacrifice that enhances your understanding of God?" Along the way, Loreena McKennitt, the pilgrim, had truly found her voice in the mirror of her soul and discovered a form of music for polishing that mirror.

4

NIGHT RIDES

Loreena McKennitt did not abandon her interest in the Sufi path to illumination when she completed her exploration of these themes and tones on THE MASK AND MIRROR. Sufism was one of the 'threads' she picked up when composing songs for THE BOOK OF SECRETS. "The whole process of assembling that alternate musical and thematic tapestry called THE

BOOK OF SECRETS," she told Nick Krewen in *Canadian Musician*, "took two and a half years. In the first year, I began with an unexplored thread that remained from the previous recording. I discovered that early Celtic tribes came from eastern Europe, near Czechoslovakia, and decided to anchor myself in Italy. I knew that the Etruscans were contemporaries of the Celts, a people that heavily influenced the Romans in their social structure. Water systems, artwork and even some burial rituals although their language is little known. I based myself out of Italy to follow a Celtic and Irish thread, to gather and weave to end up ultimately with the musical document I have." For this album McKennitt based herself in Venice, Italy, a cultural crossroads between West and East, not unlike Santiago, Spain, where she could venture into Greece and Turkey to the home of Rumi, pursue the route to the Orient taken by Marco Polo, explore the imaginative landscape of Dante's *The Divine Comedy*, and board the Trans-Siberian Railway in her effort to satisfy her archeological curiosity about the origins of the Celts, continuing her journey towards enlightenment, polishing the mirror of her soul. "Curiosity is probably a very casual word for the force that causes you to understand and to know certain things," she commented in *Pulse* magazine. "I feel that it's like asking a person why are they interested to learn riding a bicycle. Or I don't think you totally understand why, but there is a force like gravity that is pulling you toward it."

La Serenissima on THE BOOK OF SECRETS is Loreena McKennitt's tribute to the architectural splendor and imaginative riches of this capital of Renaissance culture where Celtic and Byzantine art cross-fertilized and the spice routes to India and China originated. Her inspiration for the song dates back to her first 'visit' to Venice: "November 3, 1991, Venice: For a thousand years, the 'most serene' and most glittering city of the Adriatic. This is a wonderfully quiet time of the year to explore the city. I walked down the narrow inner streets and canal edges, damp with mist; an unworldly blend of sight and sound." Several years later, while at home in Stratford, she picked up this thread, prompted by reading the travel literature of Jan Morris. "July 1995, Stratford: I have just come across an amazing account of Venice in Jan Morris' book of the same name. She describes, in delicious detail, the occasion of Henry II of France's visit to the city in 1574. Upon his arrival, he was dazzled by an extraordinary pageant arranged in his honour: barges decorated with triumphal arches; rafts peopled by glass-blowers who created figurines as they floated past; paintings commissioned from masters of the era." The song captures both this serene mood and sense of splendor.

While *Serenissima* picks up this thread from THE VISIT, *Prologue*, another instrumental on the album, returns to the themes of THE MASK AND MIRROR as McKennitt records her impressions of her travels through Greece and Turkey. The narrator of *The Travels of Marco Polo* also begins his account of Marco's adventures with a 'Prologue'. In Athens, she discovers, "during the course of interviews with local journalists, certain themes arise again and again: people's spiritual needs, and the time and space need to nurture that process." While in Turkey to play at the Istanbul Jazz Festival in 1996, the festival organizers remind her "that a certain section of the city can be traced back to Celtic roots ... In tracing the mosaic of history, I am eager to learn of the influences that come from this place." In the press release for THE BOOK OF SECRETS, McKennitt describes this song as having "been assembled like a mosaic, with disparate pieces collected from many places and fitted together one by one." While she cites William Dalrymple's *From the Holy Mountain*, with his account of the pilgrimage of John Moschos to Mount Athos, McKennitt must surely have recalled perhaps the most celebrated work by W.B. Yeats, *Sailing to Byzantium*, where his Celtic sensibility finds a parallel in Byzantine art.

McKennitt's cultural curiosity about the Celts — her archeological imagination — led her to explore the life of one of the first great world travelers and travel writers, Marco Polo. From Marco Polo she also gained the title for this album, as she explains in her journal entries for the song *Marco Polo*: "November 3, 1991, Venice: Threads of history reverberate around me, including the story of Marco Polo, the thirteenth century merchant-adventurer who claimed to have travelled all the way to China. Some historians now suggest that Polo's account, his 'book of secrets' about the East, may have been cobbled together from many sources, growing gradually in the telling over the centuries." McKennitt evokes this story through a Sufi melody. "March 1997, Real World Studios: At the beginning and middle of this piece, I have interwoven an authentic Sufi melody that I first heard performed by a group called Ensemble Oni Wytars." On the quinlanroad website, McKennitt elaborates on the origins of this song. "This piece was conceived with the exotic voyages of Marco Polo in mind. A thirteenth-century Venetian merchant, Polo's quest may have been for the rich rewards of silks and spices, but he brought back more than merchandise: his tales of the East fired the imaginations of his fellow Europeans for centuries to come. What wonders did he encounter on his journey? What new sights and sounds?" One such new sound may have been Sufi music. "He probably would have encountered some Sufi groups," McKennitt conjectures in an interview in *Pulse*, "and in terms of that, I wanted to weave in some thread of authenticity. And so the melody that is at the very beginning of *Marco Polo*, and which I'm singing in the middle, is an authentic Sufi melody." To create this authentic sound,

McKennitt used an Middle Eastern hurdy-gurdy, leading her to describe the song, playfully, as "an Indian song you can dance a jig to," in recognition of the eclectic blend of Celtic and Sufi melodic traditions and instruments used on *Marco Polo*.

During her time based in Italy, McKennitt began a serious study of Middle Eastern music which became the background to *Night Ride Across The Caucasus*. In her journal entry for October 1996 concerning this song, McKennitt quotes a number of Middle Eastern philosophers on the meaning and function of music. "Studying Middle Eastern music," she comments, "I come across these words from ninth-century philosopher Abu Sulaiman a-Davani: 'Music and singing do not produce in the heart that which is not.' Other near contemporaries suggested: 'Those who are affected by music can be divided into two classes: those who hear the spiritual meaning, and those who hear the material sound' . . . Listening causes me to find existence of truth behind the veil'." When her study of the spiritual role of music in revealing the truth coincided with her reading of William Eamon's *Science and the Secrets of Nature* and Murat Yagan's account of his "initiation into the Sufi path via equestrian training in the remote Caucasus," the result was the inspiration for *Night Ride Across The Caucasus*.

Night Ride Across The Caucasus

Ride On Through the Night Ride On
Ride On Through the Night Ride On . . .
There are visions, there are memories
There are echoes of thundering hooves
There are fire, there is laughter
There's the sound of a thousand doves . . .

Take me on this journey
Where the boundaries of time are now tossed
In cathedrals in the forest
In the words of tongues now lost

Find the answers, ask the questions
Find the roots of the ancient tree
Take me dancing, take me singing
I'll ride on till the moon meets the sea.

Loreena McKennitt's next night ride across Asia would not be via her research. Following an appearance with The Chieftains in Japan in December 1995, she chose to travel home via the Trans-Siberian Railway across the Mongolian and Russian Steppes from Vladivostok to Moscow and on to St Petersberg. Constructed in the late 19th and early 20th century under the rule of Czar Alexander III and his son Nicholas, the Trans-Siberian Railway is the longest rail line in the world, nearly 6,000 miles long, covering one-third of the circumference of the earth. From the Pacific Ocean harbor of Vladivostok, the train passes through Khabarovsk, Irkutsk on Lake Baikal, Ekaterinburg in the Ural Mountains, and Yaroslavl on the Volga River, before reaching Moscow, with connections to St Petersburg on the Baltic Sea. Trans-Siberian travelers speak of this 7-day journey as a mystical experience, with little human contact other than the faces seen while passing through the stations. In her journal entry for December 17, 1995, Loreena McKennitt reports: "It is now Day 5 on this train journey across wintry Siberia. . . . I saw some men on the platform today and one resembled my father. He had reddish hair and a long, very Celtic-looking face I would have expected to see in Ireland, not Russia . . . I am reminded again of the Celtic exhibition in Venice and the suggestion that the Celts may have originated in the Russian steppes. Perhaps the love of horses which began there is the very same that can be seen in County Kildare today." Traveling across the Russian Steppes, seeing images of her father in the passing faces, Loreena McKennitt, no doubt, was left reflecting on where this whole pilgrimage had begun, on the prairies of Manitoba.

While she meditated on the pan-Celtic presence in Russia, McKennitt read Dante's *The Divine Comedy*. "Although my initial intention was to find a solitude which would allow me to work on the themes and ideas for this recording," McKennitt explains her motive in taking this Trans-Siberian journey in her press release for THE BOOK OF SECRETS, "I was drawn in and distracted by the moving tableau of humanity which passed by my window. At the same time, I had begun to make my way through Dante's *The Divine Comedy*. When I returned to it, something about all those souls I had met and seen seemed to haunt me; seemed connected, somehow, to Dante's words." In a *Pulse* interview, she elaborated: "There seemed to be a very strong resonance of the human condition that Dante was describing in these books to what I was witnessing outside the window of this train. A country which had its strength in it own dignity and pride, but now which is barely, barely hanging on."

There may have been other subliminal reasons she found Dante's work so meaningful. Yeats had suggested that Dante may have been inspired by the pilgrimage of St Patrick to write *The Divine Comedy*, the greatest work in the history of Christian literature. Dante's Christian epic also has affinities with the mystic literature of the Sufis. As noted in the *Dictionary of the History of Ideas*, some of the ideas of the great Sufi philosopher Ibn 'Arabi, "such as the correspondence between the heavens and the inner state of being and certain cosmological symbols, are particularly discernible in Dante.... The 'gnostics' among Christian mystics such as Master Eckhardt, Angelus Silesius, and Dante himself in fact reveal certain similarities to Ibn 'Arabi and his School of Illumination, often due more to similarity in spiritual types than to historical influences, which in this order must of necessity remain at the level of providing a means of expression or a particular language of symbolism, rather than the vision itself from which flows the truths expressed by these mystics." Like the Sufis, Dante believed that the path to the visionary experience of divinity was paved by love. Just as the Sufis were often referred to as *fidele d'amore* or servants of love, so were the followers of Dante.

Born in the same era as Rumi in Florence, Italy, Dante Alighieri wrote two great works of literature in his lifetime, *La vita nuova* (The New Life) and *La divina commedia* (The Divine Comedy). Composed of lyrics woven together with prose commentary, *La vita nuova* tells the story of Dante's love for Beatrice, singing praise for a woman he met in his youth but who died soon after. Influenced in tone by the love poetry of the Provencal troubadours, the work takes on mystic overtones as Dante elevates Beatrice to a spiritual or divine realm. His love for this ideal becomes a love of God, his desire for reunion with her becomes his desire for union with God. Dante's method of writing on several levels of meaning is articulated in his famous letter to Can Grande Della Scalle, where he discusses the 'allegory of theologians' and the 'allegory of poets', arguing that his work can be interpreted allegorically on four levels of meaning: literal, moral, mythological, and mystical.

In *The Divine Comedy*, Dante chronicles an allegorical journey through hell (Inferno), Purgatory (Purgatorio), and heaven (Paradiso), guided by the poet Virgil, a symbol of reason, through hell and purgatory, then by Beatrice, symbol of divine love, through heaven. A magnificent dramatization of Catholic theology, a profound encyclopedia of Western mythology, and a compendium of medieval science and philosophy, *The Divine Comedy* can also be understood on the mystical level as a Dante's quest for illumination and purification through the agency of reason and love, another servant of divine love polishing the mirror of his soul.

Before he begins his journey, the descent into hell and the ascent to heaven, the poet finds himself in a dark wood of despair, one of the most famous passages in all world literature:

Canto I

In the middle of the journey of our life
  I came to my senses in a dark forest,
    for I had lost the straight path.
Oh, how hard it is to tell
  what a dense, wild, and tangled wood it was,
  and the thought of which renews my fear! . . .

The poem ends after the poet has ascended the mountain to Paradise and, with Beatrice (love) as his guide, he receives a beatific vision of the divine Trinity of God, The Son, and The Holy Spirit, though he cannot find the words to describe this ineffable experience.

Canto XXXIII

. . . I wanted to see
  how the human images was conformed
  to the divine circle and has a place in it,
But my own wings were not enough for that —
  except that my mind was illumined by a flash
  of Grace through which its wish was realized
For the great imagination her power failed;
  but already my desire and will in harmony
  were turning like a wheel moved evenly
By the Love which turns the sun and the other stars.

Loreena McKennitt begins her most accomplished lyrics on *Dante's Prayer* in that same dark wood and discovers a love no less powerful for climbing the 'Mountain' that lies 'Beyond the ice and the fire' — allusions, perhaps, to Dante's Inferno (fire) and Purgatorio (ice).

Dante's Prayer

When the Dark wood fell before me
And all the paths were overgrown
When the priests of pride say there is no other way
I tilled the sorrows of stone

I did not believe because I could not see
Though you came to me in the night
When the dawn seemed forever lost
You showed me your love in the light of the stars
Cast your eyes on the ocean
Cast your soul on the sea
When the dark night seems endless
Please remember me

Then the Mountain rose before me
By the deep well of desire
From the Fountain of forgiveness
Beyond the ice and the fire . . .

Though we share this humble path, alone
How fragile is the heart
Oh give these feet wings to fly
To touch the face of the stars . . .

Breathe life into this feeble heart
Lift this mortal veil of fear
Take these crumbled hopes, etched with tears
We'll rise above these earthly cares

Remarkably encompassed in the lyrics of *Dante's Prayer* is a Divine Comedy accentuated by brilliant turns of phrase such as "I tilled the sorrows of stone," which Loreena McKennitt cites as the most powerful line she has written as a lyricist. "It's of great concern to me that I'm able to address the theme or subject, and its language," she told Nick Krewen in *Canadian Musician* while discussing this song. "I'm not the best person as a lyricist, because more often than not I feel I've fallen short from what I wanted to say. I would say that *Dante's Prayer* on this recording came the closest to the wordsmithing that I liked. You're really causing words to resonate in culmination with a phrase, 'I tilled the sorrows of stone'. I like 'the sorrows of stone'. It makes sorrow resonate in a different way, having sung it."

Dante's Prayer, with lyrics inspired by a classic of world literature, is enriched by an eclectic world music arrangement. The inspiration for the music came by chance. McKennitt heard a BBC broadcast of the St Petersburg Chamber Choir singing *Alleluia, Behold the Bridegroom*, and when she learned that the choir was performing in Zurich, Switzerland in March 1997, she attended the concert and asked the choir for permission to use an excerpt from the song on THE BOOK OF SECRETS, which she was then recording at Peter Gabriel's Real World studio in England. *Dante's Prayer* is given greater musical and thematic resonance by the choir from the city at the western terminus of the Trans-Siberian Railway where her journey ended. The final song on THE BOOK OF SECRETS, *Dante's Prayer* is the culmination of Loreena McKennitt's pilgrimage — her research into Celtic history and exploration of the pan-Celtic world, her inward spiritual journey and longing for mystical experience — her Celtic quest.

5
REAL WORLD MUSIC

Serendipity also came to play in Loreena McKennitt's traditional folk arrangement of Alfred Noyes' poem *The Highwayman* on THE BOOK OF SECRETS. As she tells the story of recording this popular poem in her journal entry for July 1993, "Some friends have offered the suggestions that I set Alfred Noyes' poem *The Highwayman* to music. This dramatic, tragic narrative, rich with the imagery of 18th-century rural England, could be fun to work at Real World, where the surrounding landscape seems to exude that very atmosphere." Three years later, while recording at Real World, she writes: "I come across a local tourist map that confirms that there was indeed a highwayman in the area a mere two hundred years ago! It's easy to imagine the sound of horses galloping down a moonlit lane, or on the ridge visible from the studio." Then in the press releases for the album, McKennitt reflected on her sense of accomplishment in arranging this song. "Of the various disappointments I encountered on this project was that I wasn't able to find the literary material I had hoped to. When it comes down to it, even when you find material that resonates in the right phonetic way, it sometimes doesn't scan well, or fit the meter of the music. *The Highwayman* on this project was my personal

Mount Everest. I had no idea that it was going to be so, so difficult. And I'm still not convinced that it's as successful as the poem can be. But it wasn't until we started working on it that I encountered the various challenges within the metric structure of the poem, and at various times I was ready to just ditch the piece. Then it became a personal challenge of mine, and at the end of the day I decided that this rendering might be strong enough to find its place on the recording." The song has in fact become one of McKennitt's most popular recordings.

Real World Studios has provided Loreena McKennitt with more than the setting for *The Highwayman:* the 'Credits and Thanks' notes for the book of secrets lists no less than 32 musicians who contributed to the recording, playing instruments as diverse as the mandola, bodhran, hurdy gurdy, serangi, rebec, lira da braccio, bouzouki, viola da gamba, tabla, timba, tin whistle, esraj, shawm, and oud, as well as acoustic, classical, electric, and Victorian guitar, cello, acoustic bass, violin, viola, various percussion instruments — all accompanying Loreena McKennitt's piano, keyboards, harp, kanoun, accordion, and vocals. Add in the St Petersburg Chamber Choir, assembled vocal drones, and string arrangements and you have a virtual catalog of traditional Western, Middle Eastern, and Celtic instruments playing traditional English folk arrangements, Sufi melodies, Celtic jigs — an eclectic mix of world music. Perhaps more so than any other artist, Loreena McKennitt has combined a wide variety of 'like-sounding' world music to create what she prefers to call 'Eclectic Celtic'. Without access to the musical resources of Real World Studios, this achievement may not have been possible.

In October 1986, Peter Gabriel, formerly lead singer of the band Genesis, needed a practice space for a world tour. He decided to invest in a state-of-the-art audio-video studio, in the village of Box, just outside Bath, in southern England. The site features an attractive set of Victorian buildings, including a manor house, barns, and a moat. Gabriel planned the studio along the lines of a theme park, a combination holiday camp, art gallery, and university for looking at music in the broader cultural context, and like Disneyland, he planned to call it Gabrieland, though the studio was eventually christened 'Real World'. Real World was to have a public café, residential retreats for visiting musicians, and a research and development center. Using the cellular model, each studio would be linked to another by computer. Plans also included flight simulators, virtual reality games, supermarkets, and the world's longest, and narrowest swimming pool, 250 meters long, but three meters wide to keep everybody moving, as well as the world's longest bar, outstripping the 2,500 foot-long bar at Lulu's Roadhouse, now demolished, in Kitchener, Ontario,

Canada, just down the Highway 7 from Stratford. Gabriel saw computers not only as a way to organize information but also as an opportunity to discover the soul. In l987, he toured the Media Lab at MIT and the high tech sites in California's Silicon Valley, including Sun and Apple computers (the Macintosh II was launched with Gabriels' song *Red Rain*). George Lucas' Industrial Light and Magic inspired Gabriel to set up a post production company to work on videos, concert films, and ambitious stadium effects using giant screens and smaller screens with a montage of images. (U2 would do that on the Zoo tour.) He found backing in Richard Branson's Virgin Group, to invest 30 million pounds for his Real World theme park in Sydney, Australia.

At the same time, Gabriel became the leading proponent of world music, setting out to find and promote musicians from many countries and cultures, sponsoring recordings and recording what became known as 'world music' himself. He helped with the plans for the WOMAD festivals, the first time anyone had flown in artists from Africa, Indonesia, and China to perform alongside British and European musicians. Gabriel's fourth solo album featured Ethiopian pipes, surdo drums and Ghanian drums, and Brazilian rhythms. In 1989, he created *Passion*, the global music-inspired soundtrack for Martin Scorcese's *The Last Temptation of Christ*. Gabriel's global rhythms, Paul Simon's collaboration with South African musicians on *Graceland*, and the undying popularity of Jamaican reggae, ska, and dub met the revival of Celtic music in the late 1980s head-on to merge in what has become world music, with its own recording companies like Putumayo World Music, Billboard charts, and stars, among the brightest, Loreena McKennitt.

Loreena McKennitt has generously acknowledged her debt to Real World Studios and its founder, Peter Gabriel, where she recorded and mixed several songs from THE MASK AND MIRROR before becoming a 'campus' resident to record THE BOOK OF SECRETS. "The actual process of recording THE BOOK OF SECRETS," she explained while touring the album, "took place over a year or so at Real World Studios in England. Real World is Peter Gabriel's wonderful rural residential recording facility, a place which feels, at times, like a cross between a commune and a kibbutz. What made this arrangement particularly attractive to me aside from the fact that it is located in a stunningly beautiful part of the world, was that I knew that as the recording evolved I would probably want to have access to a rather eclectic assembly of instruments and players, over and above my regular crew of 'idling porsches', many of whom will be familiar to you from both past tours and tonight's performance. As Real World is only an hour and a half away from London, which is a Mecca for old and strange instruments and players alike (no offense meant), I knew it would afford me the opportunity to work spontaneously. The main control room, where we primarily worked, has a glorious front window looking onto a pond with ducks and swans. Some of my most favorite moments came when the room was filled to the rafters, with as many as 13 people working at once, playing together and working creatively off each other: my regular colleague on fiddle, Hugh Marsh, jamming with the Egyptian fiddler Osama, or the faces of Martin Brown and Martin Jenkins when we called them back for the tenth time for the sixth version of *The Highwayman*, or the bemused patience of Nick Haley when engineering assistant Jacque Turner and I began covering our faces with purple dots, for no reason other than to test his sense of humor."

Counted among Loreena McKennitt's 'idling porches' are Canadian musicians Brian Hughes (guitars), Hugh Marsh (fiddle), Donald Quan (keyboards and programmer) and Rick Lazar (percussion). "I think they are all very curious people," McKennitt told *Canadian Musician*, "and they have an appreciation for things eclectic. They know already that I'm looking for eclectic combinations, and they're game to try the different ways to really get into the non-linear kind. Just having that curiosity, that attitude and that openness is fantastic. As very accomplished players, they bring lots of chops to the table. There's quite a wide range of talent. Donald is quite proficient on the computer and editing, and Brian is an assistant to me. His area of responsibility for the most part on THE BOOK OF SECRETS was coordinating the schedules of the musicians and studio and engineer — logistics and timing. It was an immense responsibility, because there were 28 people who came and went. . . . But when it comes done to the whole area of choosing music, the whole creative area is mine entirely. I'm there all the time when the tracking is going down, and it has to satisfy me — but he is the person who has been with me the longest and who . . . would know how I want it done." In bringing her 'idling porches' together with the Real World menagerie of musicians, McKennitt took on a role she is especially proud of: "for me, to be this musical social Madam was a great thrill." The process proved to be highly stimulating, as she told *Rhythm Magazine* while explaining her studio work. "I have the melody identified; I have the lyrics more-or-less sorted out; I have developed the personality or the characteristic or the cultural sound that I would like the piece to have. But after that, I try to leave the process open to spontaneous combustion — for spontaneity between myself and the musicians."

McKennitt's enthusiasm for exotic instruments from other cultures seems unbounded but is grounded in her quest for music with spiritual resonance. As she told Ian Menzies in *Canadian Musician*, "I was really thrilled to find this hurdy-gurdy player when we were at Real World. The fellow's name is Nigel

Eaton from a band called Blozabella. A real young guy — all hip in black — and he plays this medieval instrument. You have to listen very carefully on the song *Santiago*: there's a drone and this rhythmic sound both produced by it. . . . Over the past few years, I've learned that the structure of ancient music was really built on three elements and they include drones and rhythm. The drone philosophically represents the universality of all things, so the instrument has associations much larger than its musical function, both spiritual and sacred." Mevlevi Sufi musicians would agree.

Loreena's long-time collaborator Brian Hughes brings more light to bear on McKennitt's eclectic method of recording. For THE MASK AND MIRROR, he told Ian Menzies, they worked with the oudh and esraj. "The oudh is an example of an instrument I've been using lately. It's a fretless 10-string lute from East India with the middle four strings doubled. I used it on *The Mystic's Dream*." Other exotic instruments were brought to the table by George Kohler, Hughes explains. "The instrument playing the melody at the beginning of *Full Circle* is an esraj. George has always been into exotic things . . . so we thought we'd try it out. It's about the size of a viola but it looks like a sitar. You play it with a bow like a cello, sitting on the floor." To record the haunting sound at the end of *Prospero's Speech*, nothing so exotic was used, but nothing less creative: Loreena simply blew into the pipe of a church organ. On tour, the band cannot transport this exotic collection of instruments and musicians, though. For THE MASK AND MIRROR tour, Hughes explains, "I went into the studio and sampled all the weird instruments and sounds off the multi-track and all the percussion that Rick had played. Onstage, he triggers all of it with a KAT pad and foot pedals. He's still got his full array of acoustic drums, but it enables him to play things like talking drum fills without having to physically pick one up and strap it on, which would be impossible to do. Regrettably, we can't take ten people out on the road, so we tried to make it sound the best it could." And Loreena McKennitt's tours have recently been truly 'world' tours, taking her on the road to Spain, Italy, and Turkey besides the regular North American and British circuit. 'The Book of Secrets Tour 1998' included shows in "Roman, Firenze, Torino, Genova, Bologna, Milano, Mestre, Trieste, Frankfurt, Berlin, Dresden, Stuttgart, Munster, Dusseldorf, Hamburg, Nurnberg, Munchen, Amsterdam, Utrecht, Brussels, Zaragoza, Malaga, Murcia, Barcelona, Paris, Toronto, Montreal, New York, Chicago, Los Angeles, San Francisco, Seattle, and Vancouver" — as listed in the LIVE IN PARIS AND TORONTO CD liner notes.

There is a double danger in the eclectic method Loreena McKennitt employs. The result could end up being just a novelty — or a noisy appropriation of other voices and cultures. In an interview on the BBC, McKennitt addressed these dangers when she answered the question, "How do you combine the Celtic, the North African, the Middle Eastern, the Indian — how does it all fit together musically?" by explaining, "For me it's like a musical chemistry where I do research either by reading, listening to documentaries, certainly traveling to places, talking to people, getting impressions of the configuration of the culture. And then I use that as a creative springboard so that the pieces become more like impressionistic paintings. I am interested in weaving the similarities of various kinds of music — for example, in Indian music you have a drone that would come from a tambour, so I would then go into the Celtic tradition to see what functions of the drum may go to the highland pipes — there is a drone in the pipes. So I might replace the pipes with the tambour or vice versa. Or trying to blend the dumbeg rhythms of the Middle East with the patterns of Celtic. Sometimes they blend better than at other times. . . . You can take some of the Irish music and find glimmers of similarities to, say, Indian music. The tabla kind of rhythmic patterns are very similar to the kind of rhythmic patterns you can get from the Bodhran in jigs and reels or *Sean nos* singing." Forestalling the charge that she is turning indigenous music into Western 'white bread', McKennitt argued in *Rhythm Music*, "there are those that might say that I've reduced the indigenous music into a white-bread form. For *Marco Polo*, I brought in Egyptian players in addition to my regular troops. I do a lot of soul searching, and I feel I don't have to apologize." There is one other charge McKennitt has been challenged to answer — that she is no longer 'true' to her traditional Celtic roots, to which she replied in *Rhythm Music*, "I didn't buy into the conventional formula. I didn't want to be trapped re-articulating a genre that had been already thoroughly mined." Loreena McKennitt chose instead to expand her music beyond the traditional Celtic songs she discovered on her first pilgrimage to Ireland into the pan-Celtic world she explored in Spain, Italy, Turkey, and the Russian Steppes. She has from time to time called her music 'eclectic Celtic'.

When asked how she would define her music by Maireid Sullivan during an interview for *Celtic Women in Music*, Loreena replied, "frequently, I call it eclectic Celtic, but in many respects it is more an expression of a hybrid form of world music. A lot of people associate world music with primarily African music, and, obviously, it's not African music. . . . The musicians and myself come from such a broad spectrum of musical styles there are bound to be these influences woven into the framework of my music. For example, I come from a classical and folk background. Brian Hughes, my guitarist, comes from a rock and jazz background. Rick Lazar, our percussionist, and Donald Quan come from a Latin and world music background, Hugh Marsh, my violinist, comes from a very experimental and imaginative musical background. At the essence of my music, there is a Celtic or Irish resonance. But it is embroidered with Eastern and Middle Eastern influences. Since world music has impacted mainstream music so strongly, it is not unusual to find my albums nestled in the pop section of record stores."

"I think categorization is an unfortunate reality," McKennitt commented in *Rhythm Music*. "The music comes from a personal place, so even if I only sold a hundred copies, I'd still do it that way." On *No Journey's End*, she lays to rest this question of categorization by going back to her own Canadian roots for the answer. "I've had a very difficult time coming up with the answer to the question of how to categorize my music. I think it's largely because the influences are quite diverse. People ask me how it is that I got involved with Celtic music, coming from Canada, and my response is that in Canada we live in a very multi-cultural society now. It's a country that has a lot of immigrants from all over the world. So in that sense, I suppose one could call my music ... 'world music'! Born into a multicultural society, Loreena McKennitt has become a leading exponent of world music, not just in the culturally eclectic music she composes but also in the magnanimous attitude she exudes. "In the end," she reflects on THE BOOK OF SECRETS, "I wonder if one of the most important steps on our journey is the one in which we throw away the map. In jettisoning the grids and brambles of our own preconceptions, perhaps we are better able to find the real secrets of each place; to remember that we are all extensions of our collective history. ... From all journeys, be they imaginative or geographic, the most important souvenirs to be collected are the reminders that people's lives are fortified by family and friends; by our ability to create our lives like creating a work of art; and by our efforts to reconcile our material needs with the importance of our connections with each other."

This is the sentiment she expresses in *No Journey's End* when reflecting back on her career and summarizing her achievement to date. Loreena McKennitt does not count the records sold, money earned, or awards won during her career, but rather the knowledge gained, the imagination opened, and the faith inspired by her Celtic quest. "I feel extraordinarily lucky to be able to marry the vehicle of my talents with the fuel of my curiosity and imagination. This process has allowed me to explore the greater depths of our humanity and the human condition in a way that is tangible and full of meaning. It has taught me that indeed we are a culmination of our collective histories and that at the end of the day, not only are we and have been more or less the same, but also there is probably more to bind us together than tear us apart. It is a force of faith I must believe in." These articles of faith would be sorely tested soon after the release of THE BOOK OF SECRETS when Loreena McKennitt's fiancé drowned at sea.

6
BIOGRAPHY

"The musical career of Loreena McKennitt came to a tragic end when her fiancé, Ronald Rees, died while on a sailing trip with his brother and a family friend in Georgian Bay in July 1998," the *All Music Guide* biography of Loreena McKennitt reads on the internet. "Although she was one of contemporary folk music's most successful artists, having sold more than four million copies of her 1998 album, THE BOOK OF SECRETS, she claimed her hiatus from music was permanent. As she told one interviewer, her songs remained tied to memories of her loss. ... At the time of her fiancé's death, McKennitt was mixing a new album, LIVE IN PARIS AND TORONTO, at Peter Gabriel's Real World studios. Recorded in Salle Pleyel in Paris and Massey Hall in Toronto during the Spring of 1998, the album was released in 1999. All profits from the album have gone to the Cook-Rees Memorial Fund, which McKennitt set up to finance water safety and recovery equipment for the Ontario Provincial police."

While one instinctive response Loreena McKennitt may have had to the death of Ronald Rees while he was sailing with his brother and a colleague on Georgian Bay would have been to compose traditional Irish complaints about lovers lost at sea, a common theme — or even to hope that all was a test of her fidelity, like the fair maiden Betsy in Banks of Claudy who "flew into despair / By the wringing of her milk white hands / and the tearing of her hair" in the mistaken belief that her 'Johnny' was drowned — she did not turn to her music for solace. She chose rather to suspend her recording and touring career while grieving. Perhaps she felt like resigning to the furies, those ironic agents of fate who may have heard human pride, not human compassion, when she sang the lines "Cast your eyes on the ocean / Cast your soul on the sea / When the dark night seems endless / please remember me" from *Dante's Prayer*. While she did return to the community of her friends in Stratford for solace, she soon looked to find a way to turn this tragedy into something of benefit for the 'human condition'. "You have a lot of emotional energy that comes after such an event," she reflected in the *National Post* during a December 2000 interview. "It would have been a travesty to just surrender to grief. You have to engage yourself in some meaningful response." That

PILGRIM'S PROGRESS

response took the form of establishing the Cook-Rees Memorial Fund to promote water safety and search and rescue efforts. Proceeds from the LIVE IN PARIS AND TORONTO album ($10.00 per CD) were directed to the fund, while McKennitt reluctantly returned to the media spotlight to encourage other donations. During her press conference announcing the fund, as reported in the *Toronto Star*, she stated, "I feel a responsibility ... If this campaign can help save just one life, then it will be more than worth the effort, and the loss of my friends' lives will seem less senseless." By the end of 2000, over three million dollars had been raised.

Despite her hiatus from recording and touring, Loreena McKennitt's music could be heard almost everywhere. *The Mummers' Dance* re-mix single crossed over into the *Billboard* pop charts, rising into the Top 20 list. THE BOOK OF SECRETS album rose to the top of the *Billboard* World Music chart, selling over four million copies worldwide while becoming the most successful world music 'crossover' album in history. The album also topped the national album charts in Greece and Turkey, while appearing in the Top 10 in Germany, Italy, New Zealand, and Canada, with Top 20 rankings in Spain and Italy. U.S.A. figuring skating champion Michelle Kwan skated to *Dante's Prayer* during one of her routines. Loreena McKennitt was also briefly in the public eye when the NASA space shuttle *Discovery* was launched in May 1999 carrying a copy of THE BOOK OF SECRETS which Canadian astronaut Julie Payette had chosen to play in space. During a pre-launch press conference, Payette discussed the personal 'patch' she wore, featuring a cat, a flower, a moon, and a musical note. "The musical note," she explained, "reminds us that we are human, distinguished by our creativity, our sensitivity and our adaptability." McKennitt responded enthusiastically to an invitation to watch the launch at Cape Kennedy. "One of the astronauts in May's launch of the shuttle was Canadian," she told the story during an interview, "and she is a big fan of my music. The first we knew of all this was that there had been a request from the Canadian Space Agency — whatever that is — saying they wanted a copy of the album. It was signed and sent up to space and brought back. They also invited me to attend the launch. I thought, you can't attend a launch on your own; there really should be kids there. So I rounded up as many kids as I could find on short notice, rented a tour bus, and brought this bus of kids and their parents down to Florida, and we watched the launch. It was great."

McKennitt's music was also being heard down on earth in first-runs and re-runs of such films as *Jade*, *The Peacekeepers*, *Holy Man*, *Soldiers*, *Roar*, *Ever After*, and *Highlander III* as well as the television shows and documentaries *Northern Exposure*, *Due South*, *EZ Streets*, *Roar*, *Margie Gillis*, *Legacy*,

Providence, Seasons of the Eider, Island of Shadows, Boston Public, and *Strange Luck*, among others. Loreena McKennitt, to her surprise, I'm sure, had become mainstream, compared to New Age diva Enya, reviewed in *Entertainment Weekly*, featured in *Flare*, nominated for Juno awards, interviewed on network television night shows, built into dozens of internet sites — in a word, she had become a celebrity, or a 'commodity', as she complained in a chat on the Barnes and Noble internet bookstore site. "I find it odd that people are talking about me, rather than my work," she observed, "but I see that as a by-product of living in a time and a culture where there's a lot of effort and money put into cultivating the cult of the celebrity. All of a sudden, who you are as a person becomes of intense interest to other people, and I find the whole exercise quite uncomfortable. My own natural tendencies are much more private."

Recently, Loreena has broken the silence of her grief. She granted an extensive interview to Michael Hunter of *dB Magazine* in Australia (reprinted in *Fiddlestix: The Magazine of the Australian Friends of Fairport*) where she casts more light on her private life than she has at any other time. She seems less guarded, more personal, willing to let us know where exactly she stands and what she plans. Discussing the duration of her hiatus from recording and touring following the death of her fiancé, she comments, "It's for the foreseeable future because essentially it just takes a long time to recover from these kinds of things, and setting the accident aside, I had completed my deal with Warner and I was looking to sort of 'emphasize' my life in a different way. That meant spending less time with my career and profession — which I love very very much — and just put more time on my personal life. You know, having friends over, going out to movies, that kind of thing. Because I wear so many hats, including managing my career — as anybody who owns their own business can tell you, you're very much strapped to the mast, your responsibilities are really ongoing all the time — I needed to stop my career-oriented things and allow more space for me just personally. This will take all you have to give it and then some. I just have to consider myself extraordinarily lucky that everything has turned out so well and I've been very successful at what I've done. And when you feel there's more to be squeezed out of the toothpaste tube, the temptation is to go for it. But on the other hand, life goes by. For myself, I've tried to remind myself about the importance of attempting to be kind of a normal balanced person. I think anybody who devotes all day every day to work, you're probably not as balanced as you could be."

Despite her personal loss, the experience of touring in support of LIVE IN PARIS AND TORONTO , and thus the Cook-Rees Memorial Fund, proved to be rewarding, largely because of the camaraderie she felt among the musicians.

"The tour itself was really the highlight of my touring career," she confided, "insofar as that I was able to afford to bring along with me an absolutely top shelf group of people, musicians as well as crew and caterers and a massage person. The caliber of skill and expertise that everyone brought to their responsibilities was very high, so that makes things go much more smoothly, and you can really enjoy your time. It is a lot of work and there is a lot demanded of yourself when you're constantly traveling and having to adapt to a new environment every day, but the camaraderie was fabulous, of the whole touring party. It becomes your surrogate family on the road. I miss it terribly — when we finish up it's really quite heartbreaking. ... They are just such a high caliber of musicians that getting on stage each night was a real joy. People were constantly trying new things and we were never satisfied at just simply rolling out the same performance that we'd given the night before. ... It's good you don't try and sound the same each night, or the same as the CD. That's the sign of good music, that it can withstand different arrangements, different treatments ..."

And for one of the first times on record, McKennitt tried to account for the popularity of her music. "When I'm asked by people, 'What is it that I think people are attracted to in my music?' I think part of it is the Celtic sound. I think there's also the eclecticism of the arrangement, and then there's a texture to my voice and maybe a kind of vulnerability that I'm able to achieve in singing. To take me out of the Celtic music and my arrangements, I don't think my voice is that exceptional. I don't think I'd do a lot of other repertoire a whole lot of good. I think this particular formula or blend of things is what works and not any one of them singularly of themselves. ... I think that once it leaves my hands, if people want to put it on while they're vacuuming or while they're reading a book, or just to sit and listen to the music and consider the liner notes or whatever — it's really up to them. Through a lot of the mail that we receive, we see that people do use it in many different circumstances."

But the international success of the Cook-Rees Memorial Fund truly warmed her heart as the message has spread from the Canadian Coast Guard to the Royal Lifesaving Society in the United Kingdom, even to Brittany in France — essentially, wherever her music travels. "The primary information I'm interested in imparting these days," she announces, "is in regard to the recording and its tie-in to the fund or a water safety message. There are a few principles that apply the world over. The first is wearing your life jacket. The second is insuring that you submit a sail plan to somebody who is responsible so if you don't come back in an hour or two after you said you were ...

they've got to call the authorities. The third thing is taking a full inventory of your safety equipment and making sure it's in full working order. And the fourth thing is making sure you're acquainted with the weather conditions for the location you're going out in. So that's my message of the day."

With this memorial to her love for Ronald Rees and concern for all adventurers established, Loreena McKennitt has again begun to dream of composing music. She is considering returning to Venice, the site of her 'pan-Celtic' epiphany, to produce a televised concert, a project she had planned before the death of her fiancé. Her fond memories of Venice will come to play at the Stratford Festival Theatre during the 2001 season where she has been contracted to score the music for a production of *The Merchant of Venice*, scheduled to open in late April. Her Stratford friends, including Festival artistic director Richard Monette, have rallied around her to encourage the resumption of her career. "I think Richard Monette has been interested in my music, but I don't know, I wonder if he has been doing his part in thinking 'I'm going to get her back to doing music'," she speculated during her 'coming-out' profile in the *National Post*. She trusts her work on *The Merchant of Venice* score will inspire her to compose original music. "In the creative process, there might be ideas that won't work for the play, but that I can save and park in the parking lot for the next recording." Perhaps we can look forward to Loreena McKennitt composing music to Lorenzo's grand song for Jessica from *The Merchant of Venice*:

> *How sweet the moonlight sleeps upon this bank!*
> *Here will we sit, and let the sounds of music*
> *Creep in our ears. Soft stillness and the night*
> *Become the touches of sweet harmony.*
> *Sit Jessica. Look how the floor of heaven*
> *Is thick inlaid with patens of bright gold.*
> *There's not the smallest orb which thou behold'st*
> *But in this motion like an angel sings,*
> *Still quiring to the young-ey'd cherubins;*
> *Such harmony is in immortal souls,*
> *But whilst this muddy vesture of decay*
> *Doth grossly close it in, we cannot hear it.*

And perhaps as the dawn breaks after her personal dark night of the soul, the gods of comedy will restore the harmony of the spheres in her mortal soul and bless Loreena McKennitt with great happiness.

LOREENA MCKENNITT
ELEMENTAL

To Drive the Cold Winter Away
Loreena McKennitt

LOREENA MCKENNITT
PARALLEL DREAMS

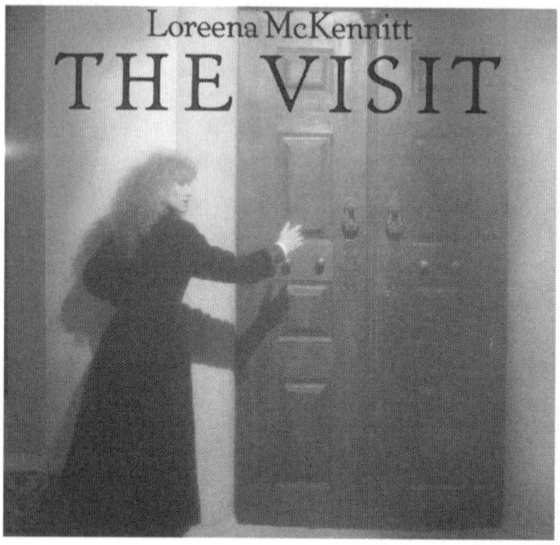
Loreena McKennitt
THE VISIT

Discography

ALBUMS

ELEMENTAL
1985 Quinlan Road Limited
(QRCD 101)

1. *Blacksmith* (3:20)
2. *She Moved Through The Fair* (4:05)
3. *Stolen Child* (5:05)
4. *The Lark In The Clear Air* (2:06)
5. *Carrighfergus* (3:24)
6. *Kellswater* (5:19)
7. *Banks Of Claudy* (5:37)
8. *Come By The Hills* (3:05)
9. *Lullaby* (4:26)

TO DRIVE THE COLD
WINTER AWAY
1987 Quinlan Road Limited
(QRCD 102)

1. *In Praise Of Christmas* (6:06)
2. *The Seasons* (4:55)
3. *The King* (2:04)
4. *Banquet Hall* (3:53)
5. *Snow* (5:35)
6. *Balulalow* (3:09)
7. *Let Us The Infant Greet* (3:46)
8. *The Wexford Carol* (6:07)
9. *The Stockford Carol* (3:02)
10. *Let All That Are To Mirth Inclined* (6:52)

PARALLEL DREAMS
1989 Quinlan Road Limited
(QRCD 103)

1. *Samain Night* (4:27)
2. *Moon Cradle* (4:29)
3. *Huron 'Beltane' Fire Dance* (4:20)
4. *Annachie Gordon* (8:22)
5. *Standing Stones* (6:56)
6. *Dickens' Dublin (The Palace)* (4:40)
7. *Breaking The Silence* (6:23)
8. *Ancient Pines* (3:35)

THE VISIT
1991 Quinlan Road/Warner Bros/WEA
(CD 75151)

1. *All Souls Night* (5:04)
2. *Bonny Portmore* (3:57)
3. *Between The Shadows* (4:03)
4. *The Lady Of Shalott* (11:05)
5. *Greensleeves* (4:15)
6. *Tango To Evora* (4:03)
7. *Courtyard Lullaby* (4:50)
8. *The Old Ways* (5:50)
9. *Cymbeline* (4:48)

Released in the United States in 1992 with different cover artwork and a re-mixed version of *The Old Ways*. The collector's edition from Quinlan Road features a promotional interview CD with extensive liner notes.

THE MASK AND MIRROR
1994 Quinlan Road Limited /Warner Bros/WEA (CD 95296)

1. *The Mystic's Dream* (7:40)
2. *The Bonny Swans* (7:18)
3. *The Dark Night Of The Soul* (6:44)
4. *Marrakesh Night Market* (6:30)
5. *Full Circle* (5:57)
6. *Santiago* (5:58)

Discography

7. *Cé Hé Mise Le Ulaingt?/The Two Trees* (9:06)
8. *Prospero's Speech* (3:23)

The Australasian tour limited edition of THE MASK AND MIRROR, to commemorate Loreena McKennitt's tour of Australia and New Zealand, includes the 6 track EP, LIVE IN SAN FRANCISCO.

A WINTER GARDEN: FIVE SONGS FOR THE SEASON
1995 Quinlan Road Limited/Warner Bros/WEA (CD 12290)

1. *Coventry Carol* (2:20)
2. *God Rest Ye Merry, Gentlemen* (6:49)
3. *Good King Wenceslas* (3:17)
4. *Snow* (5:02)
5. *Seeds Of Love* (4:54)

LIVE IN SAN FRANCISCO AT THE PALACE OF FINE ARTS
1995 Quinlan Road Limited (QRCD 105SF)

1. *The Mystic's Dream* (7:26)
2. *Santiago* (5:25)
3. *She Moved Through The Fair* (5:33)
4. *Between The Shadows* (4:17)
5. *The Lady Of Shalott* (8:50)
6. *The Bonny Swans* (6:55)

Originally released as a 10 song promotional CD. Available exclusively from Quinlan Road Limited.

THE BOOK OF SECRETS
1997 Quinlan Road Limited /Warner Bros/WEA (CD 19404)

1. *Prologue* (4:22)
2. *The Mummers' Dance* (6:07)
3. *Skellig* (6:07)
4. *Marco Polo* (5:15)
5. *The Highwayman* (10:19)
6. *La Serenissima* (5:09)
7. *Night Ride Across The Caucasus* (8:30)
8. *Dante's Prayer* (7:11)

The collector's edition of THE BOOK OF SECRETS includes the *Words and Music* promotional CD.

LIVE IN PARIS AND TORONTO
1999 Quinlan Road Limited (QRCD 108)

Disc One
1. *Prologue* (5:00)
2. *The Mummers' Dance* (3:54)
3. *Skellig* (5:24)
4. *Marco Polo* (4:35)
5. *The Highwayman* (9:19)
6. *La Serenissima* (5:55)
7. *Night Ride Across The Caucasus* (6:22)
8. *Dante's Prayer* (5:25)

Disc Two
9. *The Mystic's Dream* (6:29)
10. *Santiago* (5:32)
11. *Bonny Portmore* (3:50)
12. *Between The Shadows* (4:18)
13. *The Lady Of Shalott* (9:05)
14. *The Bonny Swans* (6:33)
15. *The Old Ways* (5:03)
16. *All Souls Night* (4:13)
17. *Cymbeline* (6:27)

First released by Quinlan Road for mail order purchase only, then distributed by Warner Bros/WEA. All proceeds from sales donated to The Cook-Rees Memorial Fund for Water Search and Safety.

DISCOGRAPHY

Discography

SINGLES

ALL SOULS NIGHT (1991)

1. *All Souls Night* (Edit)
2. *Bonny Portmore*
3. *Huron 'Beltane' Fire Dance*

THE BONNY SWANS (1994)

1. *The Bonny Swans* (Edit) (4.57)
2. *The Lady Of Shalott* (11.33)
3. *Prospero's Speech* (3.23)
4. *The Bonny Swans* (Album Version) (7.18)

THE MUMMERS' DANCE (U.S.A. 1997)

1. *The Mummers' Dance* (Single Version) (4.00)
2. *The Mummers' Dance* (Album Version) (6.07)
3. *The Mystic's Dream* (7.40)

THE MUMMERS' DANCE (Europe 1997)

1. *The Mummers' Dance* (Edit) (3.29)
2. *The Mummers' Dance* (Album Version) (6.07)
3. *Between The Shadows* (Live) (6.44)
4. *The Stolen Child* (Live) (6.20)

Tracks three and four from LIVE IN SAN FRANCISCO; track 4 omits spoken introduction.

THE MUMMERS' DANCE (Europe 1997)

1. *The Mummers' Dance* (Edit) (3.29)
2. *The Mummers' Dance* (Album Version) (6.07)
3. *Marrakesh Night Market* (Live) (6.44)
4. *The Dark Night Of The Soul* (Live) (6.20)

MARCO POLO (1998)

1. *Marco Polo* (Edit) (4.01)
2. *Marco Polo* (Album Version) (5.15)
3. *God Rest Ye Merry, Gentlemen* (Abdelli Version) (7.20)

Track three is an extended version from THE WINTER'S GARDEN.

THE MYSTIC'S DREAM (1995)

Released in conjunction with the motion picture *Jade*.

BOOTLEG RECORDINGS

The following is a listing for some Loreena McKennitt performances illegally recorded.

MILANO '95 BOOTLEG (Cassette)
Date: March 6, 1995
Venue: Teatro Nazionale

SPILIMBERGO '96 BOOTLEG (Cassette)
Date: July 26, 1996
Venue: Italy Folkfest '96

FIRENZE '98 BOOTLEG (Cassette)
Date: March 20, 1998
Venue: Teatro Verdi

GENOVA '98 BOOTLEG (Cassette & CD)
(also incorrectly named Geneva)
Date: March 23, 1998
Venue: Teatro Politeama

MUNICH '98 BOOTLEG (Cassette & CD)
Date: April 8, 1998
Venue: Philharmonie im Gasteig

DISCOGRAPHY

VIDEO DOCUMENTARY

NO JOURNEY'S END (1996)

This video contains interview footage and imagery, with Loreena McKennitt performing *The Lady of Shalott*, and the *Bonny Swans* music video is excerpted.

CD INTERVIEW

WORDS AND MUSIC (1997)

1. *Segment One* (22:10)
2. *Segment Two* (31:53)

FILM SOUNDTRACKS

BAYO (1984)
Carrighferghus

HEAVEN ON EARTH (1986)

TO A SAFER PLACE (1987)

A WAKE FOR MILTON (1988)

ADAM'S WORLD (1989)

BRIDGING THE RIVER OF SILENCE (1991)

MOTHER EARTH (1989)

THE GODDESS REMEMBERED (1989)
Ancient Pines

THE BURNING TIMES (1990)

LÉOLO (1992)
Lady of Shalott

FULL CIRCLE (1993)
Full Circle

THE DIVINERS
Pique's Song (vocals)

HIGHLANDER 3 (1994)
Bonny Portmore
The Two Trees

THE SANTA CLAUSE (1994)
The Bells of Christmas (non-album track)

JADE (1995)
The Mystic's Dream

MARGIE GILLIS: WILD HEARTS IN STRANGE TIMES (1997)
Stolen Child

SOLDIER (1998)
Night Ride Across The Caucasus

THE HOLY MAN (1998)
Prologue

THE PEACEKEEPERS
Full Circle

ROAR
Cymbeline
The Mystic's Dream

EVER AFTER (1998)
The Mummers' Dance

LEGACY (1998)
The Mummers' Dance

PROVIDENCE (1999)
Dante's Prayer

SEASON OF THE EIDER (2000)

ISLAND OF SHADOWS: D'ARCY ISLAND LEPER COLONY, 1891-1924 (2000)
The Mystic's Dream

DISCOGRAPHY

TELEVISION SOUNDTRACKS

NORTHERN EXPOSURE
Tango To Evora

DUE SOUTH
Prospero's Speech
Full Circle

STRANGE LUCK
The Mystic's Dream
Full Circle

EZ STREET
The Old Ways

The Mystic's Dream
Bonny Portmore
Full Circle
Prospero's Speech
Santiago
Huron 'Beltane' Fire Dance
Cymbeline
The Seeds of Love
Let All That Are To Mirth Inclined
Ancient Pines
Snow
Courtyard Lullaby

Bibliography

The books, articles, and web sites listed below have all proved useful, for consultation, quotation, background, or inspiration. This list represents a selection of essentials and some favorites. For a comprehensive list of articles and interviews, see the 'Old Ways' web site (www.ualberta.ca/~lslater/oldwaysfaq).

Abrams, M.H. *The Mirror and the Lamp: Romantic Theory and the Critical Tradition.* London and New York: Oxford University Press, 1953.

Alaton, Salem. "Loreena McKennitt: Velvet Gown, Iron Soul." *Chatelaine*, March, 1995.

Alexander, Dick and Pat. "Famine Ship: A Potent Peace Symbol." *Toronto Star*, August 7, 1999.

Alighieri, Dante. *The Divine Comedy.* Trans. H.R. Huse. New York: Holt, Rinehart and Winston, 1954.

alt.music.lor-mckennitt.

Angus, Charles. "No One's Fiddling as Canada Burns." *The Globe & Mail*, March 1, 1992.

Anonymous. "An Interview with Loreena on Tour." KMTT 103.7 FM (Seattle), December 12, 1994. http://student.uq.edu.au/~s307963/loreena/.

———. Biography: http://ubl.artistdirect.com

———. "Bonny Portmore: The Song that Wouldn't Die." www.7parabians.com/Portmore/bportmore.

———. "On Harp History." wwww.silcom.com/~vikman/isles/scriptorium/harps/harps.

———. "The Loreena McKennitt Links and Photo Page." http://historyoftheworld.com/music/loreena/loreena.htm.

———. "Loreena McKennitt's Musical Travelogue." *Inside Borders*, November, 1997. http://student.uq.edu.au/~s307963/loreena/

———. "Loreena McKennitt: The 1994 Honour Roll." *Maclean's*, Vol. 107, No. 52.

———. "Mevlevi Music." http:/www.binternet.com.

———. "Modern Writers Blowing Cobwebs from an Old Idea." *The Globe*, April 17, 1965.

———. "Rumi, Jalal al-Din Mohammad." http:/encarta.msn.com.

———. "Russia's Trans-Siberian Railway." http:/www.interknowledge.com/russia/trasib01/htm.

———. "A Seasoned Soul." *The Irish Times* (Online), January 22, 2000.

Arciniegas, Germain. *America in Europe: A History of the New World in Reverse.* New York: Harcourt, Brace, Javonovitch, 1975.

Band, Ira. "Loreena McKennitt Casts Her Celtic Spell." *Toronto Star*, May 4, 1998.

Berman, Marshall. *All That Is Solid Melts Into Air: The Experience of Modernity.* New York: Simon and Schuster, 1982.

Billigheimer, Rachel V. "Symbolic Birds in Yeats's Cyclic Vision of History," *Yeats-Eliot Review*, Winter, 1994.

Blake, William. *The Writings of William Blake.* Geoffrey Keynes, ed. London: Oxford Univ. Press, 1957.

Bliss, Karen. "An Interview [with Loreena McKennitt]."
www. swaymag.com.

Bouw, Brenda. "McKennitt Re-emerges." *National Post*, December 11, 2000.

Bowra, C.M. *The Romantic Imagination.* London and New York: Oxford University Press, 1961.

Boyle, Sean. *The Irish Song Tradition.* Dublin: Gilbert Dalton, 1976.

Bright, Spencer. *Peter Gabriel: An Authorized Biography.* London: Sidgewick & Jackson, 1988.

Brody, Alan. *The English Mummers and Their Plays: Traces of Ancient Mystery.* Philadelphia: University of Pennsylvania Press, 1969.

Brown, Dee. *Bury My Heart at Wounded Knee: An Indian History of the American West.* New York: Holt, Rinehart, & Winston, 1971.

Brook, Peter. *The Open Door: Thoughts on Acting and Theatre.* New York: Pantheon Books, 1993.

Bumstead, J.M. *The Winnipeg Strike of 1919: An Illustrated History.* Winnipeg: Watson & Dougan, 1994.

Carmody, Denise Lardner. *Mythological Woman: Contemporary Reflections of Ancient Religious Stories.* New York: Cross Road, 1992.

Carr-Gom, Philip. *The Elements of the Druid Tradition.* New York: Element Books, 1991.

Christ, Carol, *The Finer Optic: The Aesthetic of Particularity in Victorian Poetry.* New Haven: Yale Univ. Press, 1975.

Cobb, Noel, *Archetypal Imagination: Glimpses of the Gods in Life and Art.* Dublin: Lindisfarne Press, 1992.

Conover, Kirsten A. "Loreena McKennitt: Melding Faraway Times and Places into Song." *The Christian Science Monitor*, October 1, 1997.

Costner, Kevin, Michael Blake, Jim Wilson, Diane Landau, ed. *Dances with Wolves: The Illustrated Story of the Epic Film.* New York: Newmarket Press, 1990.

Curtis, P.J. 'Tommy Peoples: The Musician's Favorite." *Ireland of the Welcomes*, Vol. 48, No. 2, March-April, 1999, 22-27.

De Graff, Coos. "Bush and Briars Fan Site."
http://home.conceptsfa.nl/~coos78/bandb/main

Delaney, Frank. *The Celts*. London: BBC Publications, 1986.

Densdort, Robin, *When the Music's Over: The Story of Political Pop*. London: Faber & Faber, 1989.

Dickason, Olive Patricia. *Canada's First Nations: A History of the Founding Peoples from Earliest Times*. Toronto: Oxford University Press, 1997.

Diliberto, John. "Samarkand of Wonderful." *Tower Pulse*, No. 165, November 1997.
http://student.uq.edu.au/~s307963/loreena/

Douridas, Chris. "A Christmas Interview," Broadcast on *Morning Becomes Eclectic*, KCRW-FM, December 20, 1994,

Durcholtz, Daniel. "An Interview [with Loreena McKennitt]." www. cdnow.com.

Ehrlich, Dimitri, *Inside the Music: Conversations with Contemporary Musicians about Spirituality, Creativity, and Consciousness*. London: Shambala, 1997.

Ewers, John C. *The Horse in Blackfoot Indian Culture*. Washington: Smithsonian Institution Press, 1955.

Feniak, Peter. "Irish Soul." *Saturday Night*, February 1994.
http://student.uq.edu.au/~s307963/loreena/

Folk Roots Magazine.
www.froots.demon.co.uk/features/world-music-history/minutes

Foster-MacLeod, Lauren. "An Interview [with Loreena McKennitt]." *Folk Harp Journal*, Spring 1991.
http://student.uq.edu.au/~s307963/loreena/

Furlong Nicholas. "And for the Green Again." *Ireland of the Welcomes*, Vol. 14, No.1, January-February, 1998.

Gatti, Robert, "Music for the soul (and light bodies)."
www.mybestlilfe.com/music/loreena.htm.

Godard, John. "To Help Save Just One Life." *Ottawa Citizen*, May 1999.
http://student.uq.edu.au/~s307963/loreena/

Griffin, Fiana. "Why Do the Irish Speak English?" *Ireland of the Welcomes*, Vol. 47, No. 6, November-December 1998.

Harrison, Dick, *Unnamed Country: The Struggle for a Canadian Prairie Fiction*. Edmonton: Univ. of Alberta Press, 1977.

Hayden, Tom, ed. *Irish Hunger: Personal Reflections on the Legacy of the Famine*. Dublin: Roberts Reinhard Publishers, 1998.

Henjes, J. Loreena McKennitt Musical Artistry.
http://www.mindspring.com/~jhenjes/loreena2.htm; or
www.geocities.com/Area51/4585/loreena2.htm

Hunter, Michael. "Loreena McKennitt: An Interview." *dB Magazine*; *Fiddlestix: The Magazine of the Australian Friends of Fairport*, No. 55, Summer/Autumn.
www.greenmanreview.com

Keating, Mark. "Loreena McKennitt: Eclectic Celtic." *Rhythm Music Magazine*,

Bibliography

November, 1998. http://thor.prohosting.com/~noriega/index.html

Kenner, Hugh. *Dublin's Joyce*. Boston: Beacon Press, 1956.

Kenner, Hugh. "At the Well of the Universe." *Yeats-Eliot Review*, Winter, 1994.

Krewen, Nick. "Loreena McKennitt: The Book of Secrets Revealed." *Canadian Musician*, November 1997.

Knowles, Richard. 'The Legacy of the Stratford Stage.' *Canadian Theatre Review*, Winter, 1988.

Lewis, Thomas, P., ed. *The Pro/Am Book of Music and Mythology*. New York: Pro/Am Music Resources, Inc., 1992.

Laubin, Reginald and Gladys. *Indian Dances of North America*. Oklahoma City: Univ. of Oklahoma Press, 1977.

Laxton, Edward. *The Famine Ships: The Irish Exodus to America, 1846-51*. London: Bloomsbury, 1997.

Lings, Martin, *What Is Sufism?* London: George Allen Unwin, 1975.

Lippard, Lucy R. *Overlay: Contemporary Art and the Art of Prehistory*. New York: Pantheon, 1983.

Mathews, John, ed. *Choirs of the Gods: Revisioning Masculinity*. New York: Mandala/HarperCollins, 1991.

McGlynn, Cindy. "Loreena McKennitt: The Spirit that Sends Her." *Network*, April/May, 1994.

MacKay, Donald. *Flight from Famine: The Coming of the Irish to Canada*. Toronto: McClelland & Stewart, 1990.

Malcomson, Anne, ed. *William Blake: An Introduction*. New York: Harcourt, Brace & World, 1967.

McKennitt, Loreena. 'Eight Million Albums Later, Canada's Most Successful Independent Artist Urges Her Contemporaries: Take Control of Your Own Destiny." *Canadian Country Musicians Association Newsletter*. www.ccma.org/newsletter-eightmil/

———. Home Page. www.quinlanroad.com.

———. "No Journey's End" booklet from the video *No Journey's End*,

———. "Press Release: The Book of Secrets.' Warner Brothers www.wbr.com/mckennitt.

Melhuish, Martin, *Celtic Tides: Traditional Music in a New Age*. Kingston: Quarry Music Books, 1998.

Mellors, Wilfrid. *Angels of the Night: Popular Female Singers of Our Time*. London: Basil Blackwell, 1986.

Menzies, Ian. "Loreena McKennitt: Canada's Celtic Maven." *Canadian Musician*, Vol. 16, No. 3, June, 1994.

McGregor, Gaile. *The Wacousta Syndrome: Explorations in the Canadian Langscape*. Toronto: Univ. of Toronto Press, 1985.

Murphy, Eliot Russel. "Byzantium as the Centre of History: Yeats and the Quest for Cosmopolis." *Yeats-Eliot Review*, Winter, 1994.

BIBLIOGRAPHY

Nichols, Ashton. *The Poetics of Epiphany*. London and New York: Oxford University Press, 1991.

Noreiga, James. "Where the Moon Meets the Sea." http://thor.prohosting.com/~noriega/index.html

O'Connor, Donal. "Loreena McKennitt Explains How She Keeps Firm Control of Her Career." *Stratford Beacon-Herald*, September 24, 1999.

———. "Fan Payette Rakes McKennitt's CD into Space." *Stratford Beacon-Herald*, June 8, 1999.

O'Donnell, Mary. "Rough Hands and a Sick Culture: The Irish Writer and Cultural Tourism." *Irish University Review*, Winter, 1995.

O'Pratt, Samuel. *More Affairs of the Harp*. Dublin: Saro Publishing, 1977.

Parisi, Paula. *Titanic and the Making of James Cameron*. New York: Newmarket Press, 1998.

Polo, Marco. *The Travels of Marco Polo*. Trans. Ronald Latham. Harmondsworth: Penguin Books Ltd., 1958.

Powell, Betsy. "Loreena McKennitt's Life Changed When Fiance Died in Summer Boating Tragedy." *Toronto Star*.

Prammaggiore, Maria, ed. *Jouvert: Special Issue: Ireland 2000*, Vol. 4, Issue 1, Fall, 1999, College of Humanities and Social Sciences, North Carolina State University. http://social.chass.ncsu.edu/jouvert

Prasad, Anil. "Loreena McKennitt: Canada's Celtic Catalyst." *Dirty Linen*, April/May 1992.

———. "Loreena McKennitt: Times of Discovery." innerviews. org. September 1991.

Redgrove, Peter. *The Black Goddess and the Sixth Sense*. London: Paladin, 1989.

Rodnitzky, Jerome L. *Minstrels of the Dawn: The Folk-Protest Singer as a Cultural Hero*. London: Nelson-Hall, 1976.

Rosenberg, David. *The Book of J*. Trans. Harold Bloom. New York: Grove Weidenfeld, 1990.

Shakespeare, William. *The Riverside Shakespeare*. G. Blakemore Evans, ed. Boston: Houghton Mifflin, 1974.

Sikka, Shalini. "Yeats and the Upanishads: An Introductory Note." *Yeats-Eliot Review*, Fall, 1993.

Sikka, Shalini. "Yeats's 'Unity of Being' in the Perspective of Upanisadic States of Turiya and Sushupti." *Yeats-Eliot Review*, Winter, 1994.

Schafer, Murray. "Limits of Nationalism in Music." *Tamarack Review*, No. 18, 1961.

Schiff, Marvin. "A Blaring Bandwagon Rolls towards Obscurity.' *The Globe*, April 25, 1964.

Skura, Meredith Anne. "The Case of Colonialism in The Tempest." In *Caliban*, Harold Bloom, ed. New York: Chelsea House Publishers, 1992.

Slater, Linda. "The Old Ways FAQ." www.ualberta.ca/~lslater/oldwaysfaq.html.

Sleet, Chris. "Of Straws and Bonfires." http://student.uq.edu.au/~s307963/loreena/

Bibliography

Steel, Bruce. 'Taking the Music to the Folks." *The Globe and Mail*, June 15, 1985.

Stevenson, Jane. "Loreena McKennitt's Top Secrets." *Toronto Sun*, October 31, 1997.

Stevenson, Jane. "Loreena Tells the World Her Secrets." *Toronto Sun*, May 2, 1998.

St John of the Cross. Excerpts from His Works. www.ccel.org/john_of_the_cross/dark_night.htm

Standford, Derek. *Poets of the '90s: A Biographical Anthology*. London: John Baker Publishers, 1965.

Stone, Merlin. *When God Was a Woman*. New York: Harcourt, Brace, Javonovitch, 1976.

Stock, A.B. *W.B. Yeats: His Poetry and Thought*. Cambridge: Cambridge Univ. Press, 1961.

Sullivan, Maireid. "Loreena McKennitt." *In Celtic Women in Music: A Celebration of Beauty and Sovereignty*. Kingston: Quarry Music Books, 1999.

Trager, Oliver. *The American Book of the Dead: The Definitive Grateful Dead Encyclopedia*. New York: Fireside Books, 1997.

Tucker, Jenny. "An Interview [with Loreena McKennitt]." Woman's Hour, BBC Radio Radio 4, September, 30, 1996. http://student.uq.edu.au/~s307963/loreena/.

Turner, Victor, *From Ritual to Theatre: The Human Seriousness of Play*. New York: Performing Arts Journal Publication, 1982.

Walker, Lynn. "Kaleidoscope Interview [with Loreena McKennitt]." BBC Radio 4, December, 1996. http://student.uq.edu.au/~s307963/loreena/

Weiner, Philip F., ed. *Dictionary of the History of Ideas: Studies of Selected Pivotal Ideas*. New York: Charles Scribner's Sons, 1973.

White, Timothy, *Catch a Fire: The Life of Bob Marley*. New York: Holt, Rinehart and Winston, 1983.

William, H.A. William. *'Twas Only an Irishman's Dream': The image of Ireland and the Irish in the American Popular Song Lyrics, 1800-1920*. Chicago: University of Illinois Press, 1996.

Wilson, Tim. "Loreena McKennitt: The Voice of Celtic Secrets." *Renaissance Magazine*, No. 19, 2000.

Yeats, W.B. *The Collected Poems of W.B. Yeats*. New York: Macmillan Publishing Company, 1956.

ACKNOWLEDGEMENTS

The greatest contribution to this project has come from my life partner, Gay Allison, whose aesthetic imagination and passionate devotion to the cultivation of soul has been the greatest experience of my life.

Other influences who may not be so apparent are the musicians who led me decades ago to explore deeper into the meaning of music: Mahavishnu John McLaughlin, Carlos Santana, Gato Barbieri, Jimmy Smith, Randy Weston, Charles Mingus, and Carla Bley.

For friendship, the repertoire of the Hammond organ, the art of the cinema, blues harmonica, and stimulating conversation: Randy Menard, Bob Newland, Chris Campbell, and Dean Dougherty who stood by me as I struggled to free my own imagination and limited perspectives. Another shaping influence has been that of James Hillman, Robert Bly, and Michael Meade, through a study of their writings, lectures, and brief, but deep personal contact has continued to point me towards the active, invisible life of the creative imagination. Jane Kirkpatrick and her valuable staff at the Stratford Public Library are a reminder that books need not be secrets and ongoing support of the public library system is a necessity in a free society.

I would like to sincerely thank the editorial and design team at Quarry Press Music Books, especially Bob Hilderley and Susan Hannah, who lent me constant support when the heartbeat of the book was barely discernable through the grainy ultrasound of my intention.

And Loreena McKennitt whose gifts are divinely inspired and whose passionate devotion to the living roots of culture should be an example to us all. For consultation I used the Tarot of Ceremonial Magick.

CREDITS

LYRICS

Kellswater
Traditional arranged and adapted by Loreena McKennitt.

Banks Of Claudy
Traditional arranged and adapted by Loreena McKennitt.

Lullaby
Lyrics by William Blake, music by Loreena McKennitt.

In Praise Of Christmas
Traditional arranged and adapted by Loreena McKennitt.

Let All That Are To Mirth Inclined
Traditional arranged and adapted by Loreena McKennitt.

The Seasons
Traditional arranged and adapted by Loreena McKennitt.

Snow
Lyrics by Archibald Lampman, music by Loreena McKennitt.

Samain Night
Music and lyrics by Loreena McKennitt.

Standing Stones
Lyrics traditional, music by Loreena McKennitt.

Dicken's Dublin (The Palace)
Lyrics and music by Loreena McKennitt.

Breaking the Silence
Lyrics and music by Loreena McKennitt.

All Soul's Night
Lyrics and music by Loreena McKennitt.

Bonny Portmore
Lyrics and music traditional.

The Lady Of Shalott
Lyrics by Alfred Lord Tennyson, music by Loreena McKennitt.

Greensleeves
Lyrics by King Henry VIII, music traditional.

Courtyard Lullaby
Lyrics and music by Loreena McKennitt.

CREDITS

The Old Ways
Lyrics and music by Loreena McKennitt.

Cymbeline
Lyrics by William Shakespeare, music by Loreena McKennitt.

The Mystic's Dream
Lyrics and music by Loreena McKennitt.

The Bonny Swans
Traditional lyrics adapted by Loreena McKennitt, music by Loreena McKennitt.

The Dark Night Of The Soul
Lyrics by St John of the Cross, arranged and adapted by Loreena McKennitt, music by Loreena McKennitt.

Marrakesh Night Market
Lyrics and music by Loreena McKennitt.

The Two Trees
Lyrics by William Butler Yeats, arranged and adapted by Loreena McKennitt, music by Loreena McKennitt.

Prospero's Speech
Lyrics by William Shakespeare, arranged and adapted by Loreena McKennitt, music by Loreena McKennitt.

The Mummers' Dance
Lyrics and music by Loreena McKennitt.

Skellig
Lyrics and music by Loreena McKennitt.

The Highwayman
Lyrics by Alfred Noyes, abridged by Loreena McKennitt, music by Loreena McKennitt.

Night Ride Across The Caucasus
Lyrics and music by Loreena McKennitt.

Dante's Prayer
Lyrics and music by Loreena McKennitt.

All lyrics and music by Loreena McKennitt copyright by Quinlan Road Music Ltd (SOCAN/BMI for the world, excluding Europe, South America, and Southeast Asia, where copyright by Quinlan Road Music Ltd./BMG Music Publishing International.

PHOTOGRAPHS

Cover: Richard Haughton

p. 2: Elisabeth Feryn, courtesy of Warner Music Canada.

p. 7: Ann Elliott Cutting, courtesy of Warner Music Canada

p.105 – 108, 110: courtesy of Sun Media Corp.

p. 109, 111 – 112: courtesy of the Edmonton Journal